GLOBAL ELECTRONIC COMMERCE

CATHERINE L. MANN
SUE E. ECKERT
SARAH CLEELAND KNIGHT

GLOBAL ELECTRONIC COMMERCE
A Policy Primer

INSTITUTE FOR INTERNATIONAL ECONOMICS
Washington, DC
July 2000

Catherine L. Mann, senior fellow, held several posts at the Federal Reserve Board of Governors, (1984-87 and 1989-97), including assistant director and special assistant to the staff director, International Finance Division (1994-97). She was a senior economist on the staff of the President's Council of Economic Advisors (1991-92), the principal staff member for the chief economist of the World Bank (1988-89), and a Ford Foundation fellow at the National Bureau of Economic Research (1987). She is an adjunct professor at the Owen School of Management at Vanderbilt University and has also taught at the University of Chicago, Princeton University, University of Maryland, Georgetown, Boston College, and MIT. She has written numerous articles on international trade and finance, publishing in the *American Economic Review, Journal of International Money and Finance, Brookings Papers on Economic Activity,* and *International Economy,* among other journals and volumes. She is author of *Is the US Trade Deficit Sustainable?* and coauthor and coeditor of *Evaluating Policy Regimes.*

Sue Eckert, visiting fellow, is senior fellow at the Thomas J. Watson Jr. Institute for International Studies at Brown University. From 1993 to 1997, she was assistant secretary of commerce for export administration, where her responsibilities included US export control, nonproliferation, technology transfer policies, economic sanctions, and defense trade and industrial base programs. Previously she was a member of the professional staff of the Foreign Affairs Committee of the House of Representatives, specializing in international trade issues. Her current research focuses on multilateral sanctions, barriers to US exports and issues affecting high-tech industries.

Sarah Cleeland Knight is vice president of HomeTies.net, an Internet startup. Previously, she researched electronic commerce issues at the Institute for International Economics and worked with USDA's export promotion program and the international trade office of the Seattle Chamber of Commerce. She has performed several in-country assessments of electronic commerce readiness, including in Morocco as part of the Presidential Initiative on Internet for Economic Development.

INSTITUTE FOR INTERNATIONAL ECONOMICS
11 Dupont Circle, NW
Washington, DC 20036-1207
(202) 328-9000   FAX: (202) 328-5432
http://www.iie.com

C. Fred Bergsten, *Director*
Brigitte Coulton, *Director of Publications and Web Development*
Brett Kitchen, *Marketing Director*

Typesetting and printing by Automated Graphic Systems

Printed in the United States of America
02 01 00   5 4 3 2 1

Library of Congress Cataloging-in-Publication Data

Mann, Catherine L.
    Global electronic commerce : a policy primer / Catherine L. Mann, Sue E. Eckert, Sarah Cleeland Knight.
    p. cm.
Includes bibliographical references and index.
1. Electronic commerce. 2. Electronic commerce—Government policy.
3. Electronic commerce—Law and legislation. I. Eckert, Sue E. II. Knight, Sarah Cleeland. III. Title.
HF5548.32 .M36 2000
383'.3—dc21   00-044898

ISBN 0-88132-274-1

Contents

Boxes

Preface

This Institute study addresses a relatively new topic of increasing importance—how the Internet and electronic commerce are affected by, and will affect, policymaking around the world. We believe it is the first analysis to focus squarely on the global pressures that policymakers face and need to address in these areas. Its insights should also be relevant for globally oriented businesses that should be aware of the policy pitfalls they may encounter abroad.

What are the key issues that policymakers face with the Internet marketplace and how should they respond? The study concludes that:[1]

1. Because synergistic infrastructures and policies are required to reap the potential gains, policymakers need to address reforms in a comprehensive way. Part of this approach is to appoint national "ministers-without-portfolio" who can keep the forward momentum going.
2. Because of the pace of technology, government intervention to support social objectives (such as adequate privacy on the Internet) must preserve the private incentives to find technologically appropriate solutions. Policymakers should thus voice objectives rather than mandate technological solutions or outcomes.
3. Because of network effects and global reach, national jurisdictions increasingly overlap and put a premium on policies that will work in the international context. National laws and standards, protection of privacy and consumers as well as tax and tariff regimes all increasingly dovetail with regimes in other countries. For example, the pressures of the international marketplace suggest a reconsideration of current tax regimes with a focus on larger targets (income rather than transactions) and core value-added (labor rather than firms).

4. Because the uptake of the Internet and electronic commerce remains uneven, policymakers need to emphasize public-private partnerships in order to focus on specific groups that are most at risk. The new study concludes that the learning, skills, flexibility, and spirit of entrepreneurship need to be fostered and bolstered for everyone.

The new study concludes that the potential gains from effective new policies are large, not only for the technological leaders but in the developing world as well. The long-run increase in the level of US GDP could be $400 billion. For the industrial world as a whole, the level of GDP could rise by about 5 percent. Significant changes in the policy and economic environment could yield GDP increases of $100 billion for developing countries in Asia, $45 billion in Latin America and a similar amount for Africa.

The Institute for International Economics is a private nonprofit institution for the study and discussion of international economic policy. Its purpose is to analyze important issues in that area and develop and communicate practical new approaches for dealing with them. The Institute is completely nonpartisan.

The Institute is funded largely by philanthropic foundations. Major institutional grants are now being received from the William M. Keck, Jr. Foundation and the Starr Foundation. A number of other foundations and private corporations contribute to the highly diversified financial resources of the Institute. About 26 percent of the Institute's resources in our latest fiscal year were provided by contributors outside the United States, including about 11 percent from Japan. The AT&T Foundation provided generous financial support to this project.

The Board of Directors bears overall responsibility for the Institute and gives general guidance and approval to its research program—including the identification of topics that are likely to become important over the medium run (one to three years), and which should be addressed by the Institute. The Director, working closely with the staff and outside Advisory Committee, is responsible for the development of particular projects and makes the final decision to publish an individual study.

The Institute hopes that the readers of this primer will find it an informative and thought-provoking exposition of how the Internet and electronic commerce affect policymaking and business, and how best to harness the new technologies to benefit people around the world. We hope that this study, like our other research results and activities, will contribute to building a stronger foundation for international economic policy around the world. We invite readers of these publications to let us know how they think we can best accomplish this objective.

C. Fred Bergsten
Director
July 2000

Acknowledgments

This book was written in "Internet time"—that is, very rapidly. But it started out more slowly in 1998, when, during several consulting assignments, it became clear that policymakers around the world were struggling with common issues brought on by these dynamic technologies in the global environment. Daniel Rosen, a former colleague at the Institute, and now a Senior Policy Advisor for International Economic Policy at the National Economic Council, played a central role in thinking about these issues at this very early stage. My coauthors and I conducted further fieldwork during 1999 and 2000, contacting both business and government representatives in China, El Salvador, Taiwan, and Thailand, as well as in Bulgaria, Morocco, and Sri Lanka, the latter as independent consultants to ARD, Inc. Randy Hartnett, my husband and Internet entrepreneur, encouraged me to write a book.

It was clear from the outset that this topic needed input from both policymakers and business. I would like to particularly thank Bob Kirkwood of Hewlett Packard Company for helping to convene a small study session at the very early stage of the project.

To move the book from concept to completion so rapidly, my coauthors and I would particularly like to thank C. Fred Bergsten and several outside readers including Everett M. Ehrlich, Rhett Dawson, Bruno Lanvin, Robert Kirkwood, Andrew Wyckoff, and John Wilson. Several people read all or part of the manuscript in its early stages and discussed it actively at the study group, including Claude Barfield, Dan Burton, Steve Clemons, Jane Coffin, Elizabeth Echols, Orit Frankel, Mark Goombridge, Shane Ham, Gary Hufbauer, Kent Hughes, Daniela Ivanescu, Robin King, Dana Marshall, Keith Maskus, Robert Miller, Jeff Schott, Elliot Schwartz, Tim Sheehy, and John Williamson. Our publications staff—Brigitte Coulton, Marla Banov, Kara Davis, and Madona Devasahayam—did an amazing job under exceptionally tight deadlines. All this assistance implies that I alone am responsible for what is left unsaid or undone.

Catherine L. Mann

Acronyms

APEC	Asia-Pacific Economic Cooperation
B2B	business to business
B2C	business to consumer
CA	certification authorities
CBBB	Council of Better Business Bureaus
CDMA	code division multiple access
COPPA	Children's Online Privacy Protection Act
EDI	electronic data interchange
EU	European Union
FTAA	Free Trade Area of the Americas
FTC	Federal Trade Commission
GATS	General Agreement on Trade in Services
GATT	General Agreement on Tariffs and Trade
GBDe	Global Business Dialogue on Electronic Commerce
GDP	gross domestic product
GPA	Agreement on Government Procurement
GSM	global system for mobile communications
GST	goods and services taxes
GUIDEC	General Usage for International Digitally Ensured Commerce
HTML	hypertext markup language
ICC	International Chamber of Commerce
ICANN	Internet Corporation for Assignment of Names and Numbers
IETF	Internet Engineering Task Force

ILPF	International Law and Policy Forum
ICC	International Chamber of Commerce
ISO	International Organization for Standardization
ISPs	Internet service providers
IT	information technology
ITA	Information Technology Agreement
ITU	International Telecommunications Union
NGO	nongovernmental organization
NIST	National Institute for Standards and Technology
OECD	Organization for Economic Cooperation and Development
P3P	Platform for Privacy Practices
PICS	Platform for Internet Content Selection
PTO	public telecommunications offices
PSTN	public switched telephone network
RTGS	real-time gross settlement
SDMI	Secure Digital Music Initiative
SIDSnet	Small Islands Developing States Network
SMEs	small and medium enterprises
TACD	Transatlantic Consumer Dialogue
TCP/IP	Transport Control Protocol/ Internet Protocol
TDMA	time division multiple access
TRIMs	Trade-Related Investment Measures
TRIPs	Trade Related Intellectual Property
TTP	trusted third parties
UCITA	Uniform Computer Information Transaction Act
UDRP	Uniform Dispute Resolution Policy
UETA	Uniform Electronic Transactions Act
UNCITRAL	UN Commission on International Trade Law
UNCTAD	United Nations Conference on Trade and Development
UNESCO	United Nations Educational, Scientific, and Cultural Organization
USAID	US Agency for International Development
USPTO	US Patent Office
VAT	value-added tax
W3C	World Wide Web Consortium
WCT	WIPO Copyright Treaty
WIPO	World Intellectual Property Organization
WPPT	WIPO Performances and Phonograms Treaty
WTO	World Trade Organization
WWW	World Wide Web

Introduction

The dramatic growth of the Internet and electronic commerce over the last few years has been matched and fueled by the hype. Certainly—as stock markets and investors indicate—the Internet can generate immense wealth, as entrepreneurs create new markets and established companies innovate production, marketing, and sales strategies. Certainly—as sociologists and futurists point out—the Internet and electronic commerce have already changed, and more fundamentally, will change the way billions of people work, learn, and live. Certainly—even though we can only imperfectly see the potential of the information revolution—it is likely to exceed the wildest projections.

Yet very little has been said about how the Internet and electronic commerce affect government and policymaking. Policymaking today must take place in a changed environment where technological innovation and diffusion are taking place at a dizzying pace; networks and information demand effective and synergistic infrastructures; governmental jurisdictions and policy issues overlap; and the need for human skills and flexibility has never been greater.

In other words, government policymaking is central to nearly all aspects of the Internet and electronic commerce. It influences how extensively citizens and businesses participate in and benefit from the new Internet marketplace.

This book will help policymakers understand the key new aspects of economic interactions in the Internet marketplace, how the Internet and electronic commerce influence and are influenced by government policy, and whether the methods and approaches taken by other policymakers might be appropriate for them.[1]

Policymaking is influenced by economic incentives. How much does the Internet change those incentives? (See chapter 2.) Traditional principles of economics—supply and demand—still ring true, but the Internet and electronic commerce increase efficiency, releasing resources that can support faster economic growth. Network effects and reduced economic frictions allow firms to better tailor products and services for new markets to satisfy unique needs and expand opportunities for new businesses. They also allow firms to delink the value-added chain of production to locations around the world to better employ each country's unique resources. They also allow poorer countries, small businesses, and diverse interests to tap into the large, global community. The Internet and electronic commerce thus increase marketplace diversity and support faster growth and greater economic well-being. Policymakers must understand both traditional economics and the new economics of the Internet and electronic commerce if they are to seize the benefits of the changing environment for their citizens.

Policymaking in turn influences access to and use of the Internet and electronic commerce. Particularly important are policies regarding service-sector infrastructures, including communications, finance and payment systems, and distribution and delivery (see chapters 3, 4, and 5). Communications policies directly affect Internet costs and usage by businesses and individuals. For example, competition among telecommunications providers can significantly lower the price of a local telephone call, thus encouraging the exploration of new information, products, and business opportunities online.

The performance of financial intermediaries influences the benefits and global linkages offered by electronic commerce. For example, a financial sector that swiftly and securely processes online transactions will significantly enhance the global reach of local firms.

Transport and distribution channels also influence the security and ease with which buyers and sellers meet and transact business over the Internet. For example, a multimodal and competitive transport sector may enable production facilities in rural areas to participate in the global value chain of production and distribution.

Infrastructure policies shape the material benefits of the Internet and electronic commerce that accrue to the individuals, private sector and government. Synergy among these policies is key for electronic commerce: It is not enough to liberalize only one sector—they operate together to generate gains from the Internet and electronic commerce.

---

1. See also OECD (1999b), UNCTAD (2000), and ITU (1999).

The government should not only understand the changing environment but also proactively embrace it. Just as private firms are changing how they do business, the Internet and electronic commerce should change how government performs core functions (see chapter 6). In some respects, a government is like a business that must raise and redistribute revenues and provide services to the public. Electronic commerce can reduce the costs of tax administration but also will strain existing tax-raising regimes. The Internet can also improve communication between agencies and citizens, enhancing the delivery of public services.

Government policies influence how consumers and businesses interact on the Internet and in electronic commerce (see chapter 7). For electronic commerce to thrive, there must be a trusted environment, underpinned by a clear and predictable legal framework, for the purchase and sale of products and services online. For example, the treatment of electronic contracts and verification and assurance of information privacy and consumer protection affect how much economic activity and information exchange take place over the Internet.

Policymakers face a difficult challenge as they consider how best to balance the benefits of the Internet and electronic commerce against concerns that the global marketplace will undermine national regulations and standards in areas ranging from protection of personal identity to professional licensing and intellectual property.

Given an enabling legal environment, the private sector should be free to innovate and lead the way in developing the Internet and electronic commerce. In this fast-paced, technology-intensive environment, the number and nimbleness of private sector firms are a great advantage. Technology is dynamic; government policy tends to be static. Consequently, while government can and should set objectives, private initiative and innovation, whenever possible, should be allowed to achieve society's objectives. Cross-border transmission of ideas and practices, as fertilized by international capital and management expertise, are integral to meeting such objectives and achieving the benefits of electronic commerce. Moreover, interoperability of solutions across national boundaries will ensure that the network benefits of the global marketplace will accrue.

A critical aspect of the policymaking challenge is that the Internet and electronic commerce change the relationships among the governments, businesses, and citizens of different countries. Increasingly, as the economic marketplace becomes global, national jurisdictions will overlap. The benefits of network effects and more global and efficient markets will be undermined by conflicting national approaches. At the same time, it is unrealistic to hope that all countries will agree on a single policy strategy.

A first step is to work through regional and multilateral organizations to present, discuss, and draft common principles to underpin policy approaches (see chapter 8). Only with give-and-take and common understandings can policymakers preside over an environment in which all businesses and consumers interact securely and to which all jurisdictions respond constructively.

The uptake of the Internet, however, has so far not been uniform among countries nor within countries (see chapter 9). To what extent have existing policies created the digital divides, and to what extent can proactive policies and partnerships close them? In a global and innovative electronic marketplace, governments increasingly need to create incentives for the private sector (both domestic and foreign) to broaden access to and encourage use of the Internet to bridge the digital divides. Policies that create incentives for private-sector leadership allow policymakers to target most explicitly those areas where government intervention is still needed— education in general and specific groups most at risk of being left behind.

So how can policymakers develop their service-sector infrastructures, enable an environment of certainty and trust, and support a virtuous cycle of technology and human development to get maximum benefit from the Internet and electronic commerce? Policymakers play a key role in establishing the general parameters in which businesses, consumers, and the government all interact, purchase, and offer goods and services online. But if government exercises too heavy a hand with respect to the technologies and processes that make electronic commerce possible, it runs the risk of stymieing their growth and development. As a result, four imperatives should guide policymaking:

- The private sector should be free to innovate, leading whenever possible.

- Internationally interoperable laws and standards must support and enhance network benefits while also creating an environment of certainty and trust.

- Policymakers should set out objectives rather than mandate approaches or outcomes.

- Skills, flexibility, and entrepreneurship are key to ensuring that all groups have access to and benefit from the Internet and electronic commerce.

First, *the private sector should be free to innovate and lead* in developing both the marketplace and the technical and process standards for the Internet and electronic commerce. It should work with government to build domestic and international policy frameworks and be a partner in resolving disputes or bridging differences, particularly across borders. The technologies that make the Internet and electronic commerce possible are evolving too quickly for government to get involved in specific technological implementation.

Second, *without internationally interoperable laws and standards*, electronic commerce cannot reach fruition. The Internet cannot lower barriers of distance and time to give small buyers and sellers global reach, build relationships between buyers and sellers, and hope to engage the private sector in bridging the digital divides unless the frameworks work together. Interoperable need not imply homogeneous policies, but ones where differences can be bridged so that all participants can benefit from interacting within a global network.

Third, *policymakers should set out objectives rather than mandate approaches or outcomes*. Governments lack both the agility and the foresight to mandate technological approaches or outcomes with regard to the Internet and electronic commerce. The point is not that policymakers have no objectives or influence: they must and they do. But government policy should create incentives for private-sector firms to achieve society's objectives in the most cost-efficient and technologically up-to-date way. This holds true whether governments are working with domestic or international companies. Because of both their newness and the speed at which they are developing, it is critical that policies toward the Internet and electronic commerce be flexible and forward-looking.

Finally, *skills, flexibility, and entrepreneurship are key*. Policymakers have a special responsibility to ensure that their constituents have the human capital necessary to thrive in the global information economy. Governments in many countries play a significant role in education, particularly at the primary and secondary levels. Internet technology itself may improve access to education and help in human capital development. The private sector has much to offer and much to gain by partnering with government to ensure that there are online users and technology-savvy workers who will participate in and increase the value of the Internet for everyone.

This book is relevant for policymakers whose decisions affect electronic commerce and for companies involved in global business. It speaks in particular to policymakers in emerging markets who must formulate and refine policies that affect the Internet and electronic commerce in areas ranging from communications and finance to international trade and domestic distribution to taxation and privacy. These policymakers may lack the personnel to formulate a comprehensive policy framework, yet their countries are likely to experience the greatest growth in Internet usage and in electronic commerce over the next 5 to 10 years. As well, companies considering doing business globally will find it useful to be aware of the problems policymakers face, the different policy approaches they choose, and the market opportunities that arise as more economies around the world embrace electronic commerce.

Given that the Internet and electronic commerce are still nascent phenomena with unforeseen potential to revolutionize the marketplace, this book will not attempt to offer readers one "correct" policy framework, to be equally applied in countries at different stages of development and with varying cultural preferences. Rather, it seeks to highlight relevant policy areas, present the current debate, and assess the most appropriate direction.

In certain areas, such as the service-sector infrastructures, existing empirical work allows for more precise recommendations. Indeed, it is here that the hype about future gains from the Internet and electronic commerce faces the sobering reality; there is still much to be done in unwinding traditional policy interventions that have hindered the growth and maturation of these infrastructures.

For other issues such as the protection of personal data, however, the evidence is less clear as to what combination of legislation and private sector action will maximize well-being. Shared experiences and critical assessments of how different countries are approaching these issues will help policymakers find the most appropriate approach for their countries. Just as governmental jurisdictions increasingly overlap in the global marketplace, policy approaches on one issue increasingly affect policy choices on others.

In sum, the Internet and electronic commerce change the environment in which policymakers operate. They change how policymakers interact with each other, with consumers, and with businesses, both within and across jurisdictional boundaries. In order to maximize the benefits of the global, information-rich network, policymakers need to align polices to take advantage of the new environment. Yet we acknowledge that nations and individuals are different. Policies must be interoperable yet reflect that heterogeneity.

OVERVIEW AND ECONOMICS OF ELECTRONIC COMMERCE

Overview

What Is Electronic Commerce?

Electronic commerce is a shorthand term that encompasses a complex of technologies, infrastructures, processes, and products. It brings together whole industries and narrow applications, producers and users, information exchange, and economic activity into a global marketplace called the Internet.

There is no universal definition of electronic commerce because the Internet marketplace and its participants are so numerous and their intricate relationships are evolving so rapidly.[1] (See box 1.1 for how electronic commerce over the Internet differs from electronic data interchange (EDI), a more traditional form of electronic commerce.) Nonetheless, the best way to understand electronic commerce is to consider the elements of its infrastructure, how it affects the traditional marketplace, and the continuum of ways in which electronic commerce is manifested.

Prerequisites in the Services Sectors

As it has evolved today, electronic commerce relies on a variety of computer and telecommunications technologies, the development of which is proceeding at breakneck speed. The arteries (or "backbone") for infor-

---

1. For a more elaborate discussion of definitions, see http://www.oecd.org/dsti/sti/it/ec/act/sacher.htm/ and OECD (1999, 28-9, box 1) and UNCTAD (2000, 9-23).

mation traffic increasingly thread through every country and girdle the globe, and include telecommunications wires, coaxial and fiber-optic cable, and satellites. Internet service providers (ISPs) collect and connect businesses and individuals to this backbone. End-user devices such as personal computers (PCs), televisions (TVs), and mobile telephones complete the delivery of the Internet to the individual user.

Electronic commerce also requires the technological and processing capability to make on-line payments and to deliver goods and services to consumers both physically and over the Internet. Credit, debit, and smart cards and digital cash link the Internet with the financial marketplace and speed the transaction process. Rapid and multimodal distribution and delivery bring those products purchased online to the business and consumer and interweave the Internet and physical marketplaces.

Electronic commerce needs standards, regulations, and laws to create an environment of certainty, trust, and security for the purchase and sale of products online, as well as for the conveyance and use of information provided online. Examples include technical communications standards; the legality of electronic signatures and certification; encryption and inter-connectivity standards; and disclosure, privacy, and content regulations.

Process and Product Changes in the Traditional Marketplace

Electronic commerce simplifies, makes more efficient, reduces the cost of, or otherwise alters, the process by which a transaction takes place. For example, when Cisco Systems replaced its phone and fax ordering process with on-line ordering, the company saved more than half a billion dollars and reduced error rates from 25 percent to 2 percent (OECD 1999b, 60-1). As Marketplace by Marriott (the $5 billion procurement division for Marriott International's 2,000 hotel properties around the world) moves its ordering system online, it expects each hotel to save 20 to 30 percent on items like bed frames, mattresses, shampoo, towels, and light bulbs. And when IBM moved its procurement of $13 billion in goods and services online in 1999, the company eliminated five million pieces of paper, saving an estimated $270 million (*Business Week Online,* 3 April 2000).

Electronic commerce also creates or facilitates new products and new industries not previously available. Internet appliances tailored to a specific need (such as e-mail-only devices) are now available in retail stores in both the United States and China. The MP3 online medium for music allows artists to record music onto a computer; consumers can then download it onto a CD-ROM or a mobile player, thus creating a new medium to produce, market, and distribute music. Companies like WebMD repackage health information in an easy-to-use online format, offer opportunities for people with similar health concerns to "chat," and provide real-time answers to health questions. Personal digital assistants like Palm Pilots and high-functionality cellular phones allow consumers to surf the Internet (or compare prices while in the aisle of the store) and buy products online using the mobile connection. How products and industries made available over the Internet, particularly those using high-speed broadband or cable delivery will evolve, is still unknown.

Facilitation of New Markets and Marketplaces

Electronic commerce creates new markets in time, space, and information where previously transaction and coordination costs were prohibitively high. The Brazilian bank, Banco 1, offers 24-hour online banking services. PeopleLink advertises globally via the Internet on behalf of artisans in remote parts of Latin America and Africa. Auctions through Priceline tell businesses exactly what prices buyers are willing to pay for products ranging from groceries to gasoline. And eSteel.com aggregates steel producers and purchasers from around the world into a single online marketplace.

The key forces that create this Internet marketplace and affect its participants are: synergies among services sectors, new processes of supply and demand, information richness and global reach.

How Fast Are Growth and Diffusion?

The Internet and electronic commerce are growing so fast that forecasters regularly underestimate how many users will be online and how much

Box 1.2 Measuring the Internet marketplace

Many researchers disagree on how to measure Internet access and electronic commerce revenue. This box highlights where the debate stands between the differing methodologies.

Internet access can be measured as either the number of computers connected to the Internet ("host computers"), or the number of individuals accessing the Internet through those computers. Some researchers count only those individuals accessing the Internet at least once a week, or distinguish between those who surf the Internet and those who dial up only to check electronic mail. Measuring any of these data is problematic, since it is difficult to ascertain in which country a host computer is located, or how many individuals are using any given computer and for what purpose.

Methodologies to measure *e-commerce revenues* are similarly varied. Most measurements include both business-to-business (B2B) transactions and business-to-consumer (B2C) transactions. Others distinguish between goods and services purchased over the Internet and delivered physically to the buyer, and those delivered digitally, such as music downloaded onto a CD-ROM. The US Department of Commerce's quarterly data of retail sales, for example, omits online travel and financial brokerage revenues, two of the largest areas of B2C electronic commerce.[1] And it remains highly controversial how to value nontransaction services like bid posting and customer service.[2]

These differing methodologies clash particularly when researchers try to calculate the economic impact of the Internet and electronic commerce. Particularly difficult is separating out this impact from the broader influence of the information technology sector, which also includes computer hardware and software. The US Bureau of Economic Analysis, for example, is working to improve its IT-sector data, including improving price indexes and real output measures, developing new estimates of software investment, and improving measures of electronic commerce retail and B2B sales. Assisting these efforts is a program by the University of Texas, commissioned by Cisco Systems, to calculate revenue and growth of the US "Internet Economy," a measure including infrastructure, applications, intermediaries, and electronic commerce.[3]

---

1. See http://www.census.gov/epcd/www/ebusiness.htm.

2. Haltiwanger John, and Ron Jarmin. 1999. ''Measuring the Digital Economy,'' paper prepared for the US Department of Commerce's conference ''Understanding the Digital Economy: Data, Tools, and Research,'' (25 May): 4.

3. See http://www.Internetindicators.com.

---

revenue will be generated by electronic commerce (see box 1.2). While growth has been fastest and activity remains greatest for the early adopter—the United States—as electronic commerce diffuses, growth rates (though not necessarily the amount of activity) are expected to be higher in other parts of the globe soon. The Internet and electronic commerce will no longer represent only a part of a domestic business strategy or an alternative way for people to communicate. It will be integral to the economic and social fabric of countries and commerce.

Figure 1.1   Exponential growth of the Internet

Compound annual growth rate 1990 (percent)

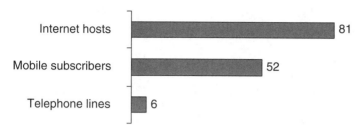

Years to reach 50 million users

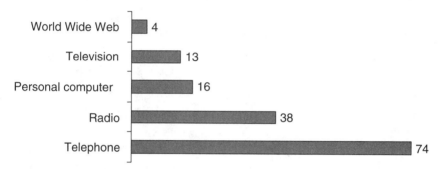

Source: International Telecommunications Union (ITU), *Challenges to the Network: Internet for Development,* Geneva: ITU, 1999.

Internet Growth and Diffusion

As recently as 1990, the Internet was essentially a tool for the military and academics. Today it is globally pervasive and highly commercial. The Internet has attracted more users in more countries in a shorter period of time than any other communications tool in history: it took only four years for the Internet to reach 50 million users, compared to 74 years for the telephone and 13 years for TV (ITU 1999, 2). (See figure 1.1.) As of January 2000, there were over 72 million computers from more than 220 countries connected to the Internet (also known as Internet "hosts"), with each computer giving access to one or more users (see figure 1.2). E-mail is a common form of communication not only in the United States but around the world.

Three factors have contributed to the breathtaking growth of the Internet:

- The steep decline in the prices of information technology (IT) products, such as computers and software;

Figure 1.2   Growing Internet connections, 1993-2000

number of internet hosts, January 2000 (millions)

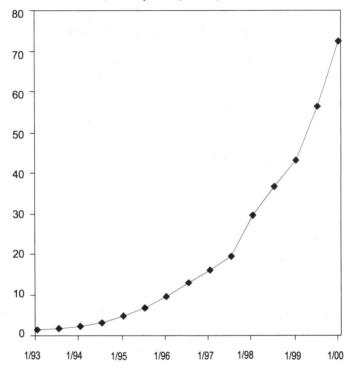

Source: Internet Software Consortium, *Internet Domain Survey*, http://www.isc.org, January 2000.

■ The development of interoperable platforms like TCP/IP, and the mass distribution of Internet browsers like Netscape, which on the one hand provide a relatively easy way for firms to develop user-friendly inter-faces such as Web sites and on the other enable individuals to receive and send electronic documents and surf the World Wide Web.

■ The commercialization of the Web itself with media-rich content and electronic commerce.

Currently, Internet use is concentrated in the United States, with Japan and Western Europe catching up fast (see figure 1.3), but most growth over the next three to five years is expected to take place in Asia and Latin America. The share of weekly Internet users in those areas could increase from 23 percent in 1999 to 35 percent in 2002.[2] In India, for

2. October 1999 statistic from http://www.emarketer.com.

Figure 1.3 Internet users by region (percent)

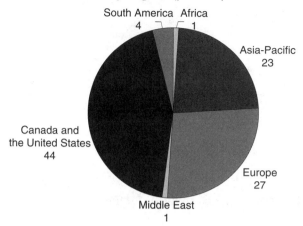

South America
4

Africa
1

Asia-Pacific
23

Canada and
the United States
44

Europe
27

Middle East
1

Source: Nua Internet Surveys, http://www.nua.ie/surveys/how-many-online/index.html.

example, the number of Internet users nearly doubled in 1999 to 270,000 and could rise to over 2 million by the end of 2000, a ten-fold increase in one year.[3] In Latin America, Internet usage rose nearly eight-fold between 1995 and 1997 (ITU 1999, 47). While Internet access growth has been slower for much of Africa, all countries on that continent save for Eritrea are now connected to the Internet.[4]

As the Internet diffuses around the globe, companies are racing to satisfy an increasingly diverse customer base. Although by far most Web sites are in English and based in the United States, sites in other languages are taking off as firms respond to demand. These sites tailor on-line content and products to firms and individuals in different countries and often to communities within those countries.

For example, one of the fastest growing languages on the Internet is Spanish, as Telefonica's Terra Networks takes off. ZonaFinanciera offers information in English, Portuguese, and Spanish about loans, certificates of deposit, insurance, and regional stock exchanges in Latin America.

Chinese is growing rapidly too. China.com, an online portal for users in China, offers a wide range of general, financial, and cultural news in English and Chinese. AfricaOnline tailors its content and language to users in the Ivory Coast, Ghana, Kenya, Swaziland, Tanzania, Uganda, and Zimbabwe.

---

3. See http://www.emarketer.com/estats/102599india.html.

4. Mike Jensen follows Internet access trends in all the African countries. His reports and data are available at http://www3.sn.apc.org/africa/.

Figure 1.4 E-commerce spending in Latin America

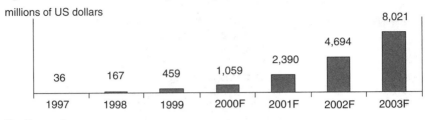

millions of US dollars

	1997	1998	1999	2000F	2001F	2002F	2003F
	36	167	459	1,059	2,390	4,694	8,021

F = Forecast

Source: Latin Trade, March 2000, 38, using data from IDC.

Electronic Commerce Growth and Diffusion

Growth in electronic commerce is similarly explosive. It is now projected that by 2005, electronic commerce in the United States alone could surpass the $6 trillion mark (Jupiter Communications, 27 June 2000). This figure is far larger than any of the forecasts for these same years published in an Organization for Economic Cooperation and Development (OECD) study in 1997; these ranged from $10 billion to $1.5 trillion (OECD 1999b, 27). Ninety percent of businesses in the United States say that electronic commerce soon will affect how they do business. Since these companies source from firms overseas and sell to buyers overseas, this implies that the tide of electronic commerce will not stop at the US border.

Indeed, though close to 85 percent of electronic commerce is concentrated in the United States—other parts of the world, especially Western Europe and Japan, followed by the rest of Asia, Latin America, and then Africa—are expected to see even faster growth. In China, for example, e-commerce revenues are expected to grow from $11.7 million in 1998 to $1.9 billion in 2002 (ITU 1999, 47). In Latin America, revenues could grow from $167 million in 1998 to $8 billion in 2003 (*Latin Trade*, March 2000). (See figure 1.4.) And in South Africa, electronic commerce was forecast to generate $1.1 billion in 1999.[5]

Perhaps because US businesses are the first to adopt electronic commerce, and because many US companies produce globally, electronic commerce by countries outside the United States tends to be more export-oriented. In the United States, the share of export sales in total electronic commerce revenues is only 10 percent, but in Canada it is 83 percent, in Latin America it averages 79 percent, and in Asia/Pacific, 38 percent (ITU 1999, 45, figure 3.2). The nature of the production process (comprising both manufacturing and services) is becoming increasingly fragmented

---

5. See http://www.nua.ie/surveys/.

and globalized.[6] Firms communicate, get price quotes, submit bids, transfer data, produce product designs, and basically *do business* in an international arena. Countries that do not have an environment conducive to Internet usage and electronic commerce will be marginalized from the globalized production process and global economy, at increasingly greater cost to their citizens.

Diffusion and Income

Diffusion and usage of the Internet and electronic commerce—both within individual countries and between developed and developing countries—is a function of a number of factors, including age, income, and education. Research shows a positive relationship, for example, between per capita GDP and the density of Internet hosts (which is one measure of access) (see UNCTAD 2000, 75, figure 12). Similarly, higher income per capita is associated with a higher share of those using the Internet. (See figure 1.5.) Finally, broader measures of development like the Human Development Index show that as human development indicators increase, Internet penetration increases even faster, suggesting important synergies among education, life expectancy, income, and Internet activity (ITU 2000, 22, figure 2.2).

Looking at this issue more narrowly within a country and over time, it is clear that even as access increases for a country as a whole, Internet usage does not increase proportionately for all groups. This is apparent in the United States, which has had relatively cheap and widespread Internet availability for some time. While the relationship between individual income and education is key in raising the likelihood of getting connected to and enjoying the benefits of the Internet, clearly this is not the only issue (US Department of Commerce 1999, 5). As important is the need to have information, products, and entertainment of value to the potential users.

For both rich and poor countries, policies directed at creating a facilitating infrastructure and basic development needs, particularly education, are key to reaping the benefits of the Internet and electronic commerce, for both countries and individual citizens. Similarly, transforming the disinterested or disenfranchised into new entrepreneurs to serve their communities is a key aspect of bringing the Internet to everyone. The last section of the book examines more closely these international and national digital divides, and considers how to use the technology itself to start a virtuous cycle of technology, human development, and economic growth.

---

6. For a discussion of the fragmentation and globalization of production in the context of US trade, see Mann (1999, 39-40).

Figure 1.5   Income and Internet penetration

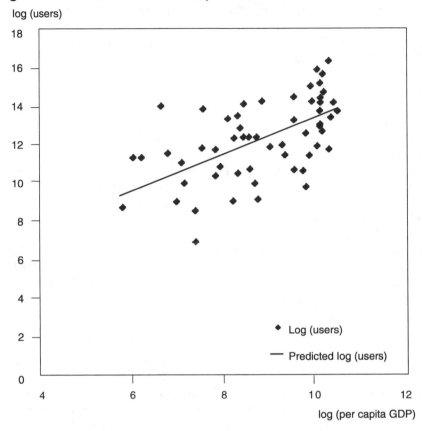

Note: Per Capita GDP in US dollars. Sample excludes Africa.

Source: United Nations Statistics Division and UNCTAD Trade and Development Commission on Enterprise, Business Facilitation and Development, Geneva, November 1998.

One point is clear: There is no conflict between policies directed toward development generally and policies that specifically enhance Internet access and usage.

Final Remarks

Some have said that the Internet is as important to the marketplace as the printing press or electric power. Others say it increases efficiency and extends market reach but is not revolutionary.

An analogy might be appropriate here: Everyone now agrees that the invention of electricity was revolutionary. But at the time, people spoke of electricity in terms relevant to the era: horsepower for kinetic energy or candlepower for lighting energy. We still use the word horsepower, but clearly 1,000 horses or one million candles can deliver very different services from those resulting from 10 horses or 100 candles. Electricity revolutionized economic activity by powering new markets that could not initially be imagined. Moreover, the vastly greater capability of electricity had tremendous impact on human geography and society, the educational system, and the workplace. It not only restructured existing economic activities, but also revolutionized human interaction with the environment. The Internet and electronic commerce will have a similar impact.

Looking forward, the *growth of Internet usage probably will slow* in the medium-to-long term, given that saturation will inevitably take place, especially in the United States, Western Europe, and Japan. No doubt there will always be some people in every country who, even without additional obstacles, will not want to connect to the Internet. But this should not be because it is too expensive; they feel insecure, or they find little available in their language or meeting their interests.

Once the infrastructures are in place, it is in the private sector's interest to ensure that the percentage of unconnected users continues to decline by creating content and electronic commerce offerings that attract their interest. *Electronic commerce will therefore continue to grow rapidly.* America Online's (AOL) recent media campaign targeted toward senior citizens in the United States is a good example of an existing Internet company broadening its consumer base. Other companies are being created solely for underserved audiences. For example, Everymail.com generates a "virtual keyboard" in a dozen languages so that a bilingual immigrant can write e-mail back home to parents who do not speak English, and penpals can learn the languages of their global friends (Kornblum, *USA Today*, 19 November 1999).

There are countless examples of these opportunities; the frontier of electronic commerce is moving the marketplace beyond our current understanding. Most of the future opportunities will be created by companies in the developing countries, or will be targeted to audiences there. Consequently, policymakers should and can take steps to prepare a facilitating environment, unleash incentives for the private sector, and start the virtuous cycle between technology and human development, so as to encourage the growth of the Internet and electronic commerce, and, in particular, to aid its pervasive diffusion across individuals of different income and education levels.

2

Internet Economics and the Economics of the Internet

The Internet and electronic commerce change the traditional marketplace in two ways: (1) process and product innovations, and (2) new markets in time, information, and geography. These changes, along with their supporting technologies, appear to have important macroeconomic implications for economic growth and inflation. Indeed, they are the forces behind the "new economy" in the United States. They therefore have important implications for the scope and type of policy intervention into the marketplace. In particular, policymakers should want to do everything they can to enable these technologies that deliver so much in terms of economic well-being.

Macroeconomic Implications of Information Technologies

US Experience

Most available data include the Internet and electronic commerce with the broader IT sector, which also includes computers and software. These data show that information technologies hold many benefits for a nation's economic performance, including faster growth with low inflation, which is made possible by higher productivity and sharply lower prices for computers and other IT hardware.

In the United States, the IT sector has played a growing role in the economy and its continuing expansion with low inflation. Information

Table 2.1 Contributions to labor productivity growth in the nonfarm business sector in the United States, 1974-99

	1974-90	1991-95	1996-99
Growth rate of labor productivity	1.43	1.61	2.66
Contributions from:			
Capital deepening	.81	.60	1.09
Information technology capital	.45	.48	.94
Hardware	.26	.22	.58
Software	.10	.21	.26
Communications equipment	.09	.05	.10
Other capital	.36	.12	.16
Labor quality	.22	.44	.31
Multifactor productivity	.40	.57	1.25

Source: Oliner and Sichel (2000).

technologies, and in particular the production of computers, account for two-thirds of the one percentage point step-up in productivity growth in the United States between the first and second halves of the 1990s (Oliner and Sichel 2000). (See table 2.1.) The US Department of Commerce calculates that between 1995-99 (the last year for which the data were available), IT-producing industries contributed on average more than one-third of US real economic growth. The IT-producing industries' share of the US economy is building, from 6 percent in 1993 to an estimated 10 percent in 1999 (US Department of Commerce 2000, 16; Economic Report of the President 2000, 103-5)).

There is increasing demand for employment in IT industries. The US Bureau of Labor Statistics estimates that by 2006, employment in IT-producing industries will reach almost 6 million US workers. IT workers in the United States also earn far more than their private sector counterparts: an average of $53,000 annually, compared to $30,000 (US Department of Commerce 1999, 38-9).

Focus on Business-to-Business Electronic Commerce

Studies that separate out electronic commerce from the rest of the IT sector illustrate that, while still a very small percentage of total revenue, this new method of buying and selling goods and services is growing quickly, with a beneficial effect on macroeconomic performance. Particularly important for efficiency gains are Internet business-to-business transactions (B2B).

B2B transactions, whether trade in inputs or in finished products, overwhelmingly dominate electronic commerce, accounting for nearly 80 percent of electronic commerce revenue. Goldman Sachs projects that worldwide B2B electronic commerce could grow from $39 billion in 1998 to over $1,500 billion in 2004 (Brookes and Wahhaj 2000). The dominance of B2B is already about 6 times the value of business-to-consumer electronic commerce (B2C), and could well grow to 12 times the B2C value.[1] Although there clearly are more consumers in the world, because production strategies increasingly fragment and recombine value-added into the final product for sale, there are a lot more B2B transactions associated with final consumption.

Examples of B2B electronic commerce include online trading of commodities like steel, plastics, chemicals, and Internet bandwidth; alliances between automobile, aerospace, and even retail companies to purchase inputs online; and production relationships between computer companies like Toshiba and package delivery companies like Federal Express to speed the delivery of made-to-order computers. Soon the online marketplace will offer bulk prices for services like pest control, insurance, and even electricity to big business, small business, and individual consumers.

The cost savings of B2B electronic commerce are substantial and pervasive across manufacturing, industrial supplies, and services; they could eventually translate into a lower rate of overall inflation. Martin Brookes and Zaki Wahhaj (2000) of Goldman Sachs estimate cost savings ranging from 10 percent in sectors like aerospace, paper and steel, and communications bandwidth and media advertising to more than 20 percent in electronic components and machining, forest products, and freight transport (see table 2.2).

Cost savings of this magnitude could affect about one-third of US GDP. Brookes and Wahhaj, applying their estimates of sectoral cost reductions to input-output matrixes of five large industrial economies (the United States, UK, Japan, Germany, and France), project that the index of GDP prices for each country could be lowered by about 3 to 5 percent as a consequence of B2B electronic commerce.

Modeling the Implications of Electronic Commerce for GDP Growth

Beyond cost reductions, however, electronic commerce increases the efficiency of resource utilization, which translates into faster productivity growth, which supports higher sustained GDP. Very different methods of modeling the implications of such cost reductions and efficiency gains show remarkably consistent results: electronic commerce undertaken by a country will bring significant increases in its GDP. These results hold for developing as well as industrial countries (see table 2.3).

Brookes and Wahhaj used a model (Multimod, used at the International Monetary Fund) that organizes time-series of data on many countries into

---

1. Initial estimate from Deloitte Consulting, as cited in *Business Week* (20 January 2000, 36). A similar initial estimate and projection is in ITU (1999).

Table 2.2 Business-to-business cost savings by industry (percent)

Industry	Cost savings
Aerospace machinings	11
Chemicals	10
Coal	2
Communications/bandwidth	5-15
Computing	11-20
Electronic components	29-39
Food ingredients	3-5
Forest products	15-25
Freight transport	15-20
Healthcare	5
Life science	12-19
Machinings (metals)	22
Media and advertising	10-15
Oil and gas	5-15
Paper	10
Steel	11

Source: Brookes and Wahhaj (2000).

Table 2.3 The macroeconomic impact of electronic commerce

		Impact on GDP		
	Size of shock (percent)	Long-run (percent)	Growth rate per year next decade (percent)	Long-run (billions of US dollars)
Brookes and Wahhaj				
United States	3.4	4.4	0.22	392
Japan	3.5	5.8	0.27	256
Germany	3.7	5.1	0.32	110
United Kingdom	4.0	5.3	0.27	67
France	4.0	5.3	0.27	78
5-cty average	3.6	4.9	0.25	903
UNCTAD (adjusted * 3.5)				
Industrial countries	3.5	4.9	n.a.	1067
Asia	1.05	1.2	n.a.	30
Latin America	1.05	1.0	n.a.	15

Source: Brookes and Wahhaj, (2000); "Shock" from Table 2; Growth change from Table 3. Authors' calculations for column 4; UNCTAD, (2000); all data from table 3, multiplied by 3.5 to normalize shock to size of B&W; assumes linearity of the model results.

complex models of the individual macro economies as well as their global interrelationships. To examine the potential impact of electronic commerce, Brookes and Wahhaj simulated how electronic commerce, which they estimated as two-thirds improved resource utilization and one-third simple reductions in costs, will affect real GDP in the five countries. Their simulations suggest that GDP in these countries would be almost 5 percent higher after 10 years, and the annual growth rate of GDP during this period would be about 0.25 percentage points higher. For the United States, GDP would be higher by about $400 billion.

The United Nations Conference on Trade and Development (UNCTAD, 2000) investigated the same question, looking at both developed and developing countries. Its researchers used a different type of model (the GTAP model) that focuses on the long-run effect that electronic commerce might have on GDP for regions of the world.[2] In one of the simulations, they assumed the potential impact of electronic commerce was a 1 percent improvement in resource utilization by industrial countries and a 0.3 percent improvement in developing countries. They note, "These percentages do not intend to reflect the actual differences in access to the Network . . . but simply represent a working assumption."

If we re-parameterize the electronic commerce benefits in developed countries to the size that Brookes and Wahhaj estimate using data for the five industrial countries, the UNCTAD "shocks" should be 3.5 times as large. Adjusting the UNCTAD simulations this way yields the result that GDP in the developed countries in the long run would be about 4.9 percent greater (about $1 trillion)—about the same magnitude as B&W. Under the UNCTAD assumption that the benefits from electronic commerce yield only one-third the gains in the developing counties, GDP would be 1.2 percent ($30 billion) higher in Asia and 1 percent higher in Latin America ($15 billion).

Suppose, however, that developing countries reform the services sectors (as will be discussed in Part Two) to create a facilitating environment for IT to take hold, and put in place frameworks that help create an environment of certainty and trust. In this case, the developing world would enjoy benefits of resource utilization as large as those estimated for the industrial countries—and their increased GDP would be multiples larger than those shown.

In one of their other situations, the UNCTAD study shows the consequences of inefficient services sectors. Without an efficient services sector, gains from the resource efficiencies of electronic commerce are less than half shown. Electronic commerce and the Internet can help in the reform process to liberalize the key service-sector infrastructures. Consequently,

---

2. GTAP was developed at Purdue University in conjunction with a number of international organizations, including UNCTAD. See UNCTAD (2000, 28-30) for more discussion of the model results.

the potential gains for the developing world could be much greater than suggested by the UNCTAD study.

The gains to resource utilization and the GDP growth stimulated by efficient services sectors, IT, and electronic commerce are dramatic. This is clear from data on the behavior of the US economy in recent years; it is projected to hold true in the future, both for other industrial countries and developing countries. One reason for this global gain is discussed more fully in the next section: A key source of the benefits from the Internet and electronic commerce is the existence of network effects. The more numerous the countries that put into place a facilitating environment, the greater the benefits to one and all.

A "New Economics"?

Consumer activity, business strategy, and government activities and policymaking all respond to fundamental economic forces as filtered through the general business and policy environment. The Internet changes the environment in which these activities are undertaken, but does it change the principles that underpin the decisions? Or does the Internet only modestly change the incentives that affect how economic actors react to traditional economic forces? From the standpoint of policymaking, is learning the basics in Economics 101 enough, or must policymakers understand a "new economics" of the Internet in order to fashion policies?[3]

Basic economics still rings true, in that supply and demand are still the forces underpinning prices and choices. But the Internet does change how these forces manifest themselves: More rapid technological change and innovation increase the speed of transactions and the creation of new marketplaces. Information is a key component of all products and services, as well as the production processes. Networks—a fundamental structure and pervasive force—have unique economic attributes.

These factors have important implications for how the Internet marketplace develops and operates. To an even greater extent than with traditional economic activity, service-sector infrastructures and an environment of certainty and trust are prerequisites for economic growth and market development. Products increasingly embody information content, are created from inputs from around the globe, and tailored to specific demands. Technology, innovation, and speed put a premium on flexible markets and human capital.

Both the forces of the Internet and their implications in the marketplace should affect government activities as well as policies. As is clear from

---

3. Two excellent books that include substantive discussions on the *economics* of the Internet (rather than just business strategies to exploit it) are: Choi, Stahl, and Whinston (1997) and Shapiro and Varian (1999).

the econometric models, policymakers should want to harness the power of the global network, yet networks and the Internet can be uncompetitive: For example, information content is key to the creation of new products that yield great benefits, yet there may be market imperfections in the use and collection of information; government policy can sometimes lead to a better functioning of the marketplace. Finally, because this marketplace depends on well-educated, skilled, and flexible workers and seeks to create products and services to satisfy those workers, policymakers should consider how they can best use the technology and the marketplace to help develop those citizens and workers.

Information and Network Effects

Information technologies, and increasingly the information itself, are key drivers of the Internet and electronic commerce. On the one hand, information technologies (computers, hardware, and software) have been used to process numbers, create databases, and enhance corporate operations for quite some time. Information about prices, preferences, inventories, and inputs has also been collected, processed, and stored in databases. But most of this information has been kept internal to a firm, generally inaccessible to other firms, consumers, or governments.

The revolution of the Internet builds on and extends IT to give global reach, interoperability, and accessibility to these systems and to the underlying information. The information that these technologies can access and process, once fragmented, can now be combined and recombined to create a much richer web of information flows and uses. The coming together of technologies and information from many sources and their accessibility to many new users around the world are what create the Internet marketplace and make it both unique and substantial. This new global marketplace is where businesses, consumers, and governments can communicate and find new sources of supply, new products to meet their demands, new information to help them make decisions, and new ways to assist in economic development.

The information technologies and the information that flows over them are characterized by "network effects." What are network effects? In simple terms, the whole is greater than the sum of the parts. That is, the more participants that use a network, the greater its value to all who use it.

Robert Metcalfe (Xerox, Palo Alto Research Center) considered this concept using the simple notion of access points to a network. Metcalfe's law says that the value or power of a network increases in proportion to the square of the number of access points to the network. For example, five PCs connected to a network would yield a value of 5^2 (25); add one more PC and the network's value becomes 6^2 (36); one more access point yields a value of 49 and so on. Thus, the value of a network increases much faster than the number of access points. It is the compounding or square-factor that is the key to network effects. Metcalfe's law can be extended to broader network issues, such as the interoperability of ways to access a network, the information on a network, and even the language used.

Consider the interoperability of hardware and software systems to access a network. More people using one particular type of hardware or software system yields the first round of network benefits. But if several types of hardware and software systems are interoperable with each other, the overall network instantly becomes much more valuable to each participant. For example, suppose my hardware and system allows me to send electronic documents to a mobile phone as well as a PC. This additional capability is not very valuable if the person I wish to contact can receive electronic documents only via a PC. However, if many users have the joint capability, we can communicate and work using the phone as well as the PC. This increases the usefulness and value of electronic document handling, as well as of the phone and the PC. The value of the network is one force that creates pressure among firms producing different standards of equipment and software to make them technically interoperable (see chapter 3).

Information itself exhibits network effects. Consider a Web site that brings together different types of visitors—say, truckers with empty trucks and consignors with products to move. A few visitors to this kind of Web site do not generate much value to the participants, but many visitors of both types increases the likelihood that deals can be consummated and information about future opportunities transferred. The more visitors, the greater the likelihood that truckers and consignors will meet on the Internet to negotiate deals, improving their use of time, money, and trucks. Such a virtual meeting place can be of particular value for independent truckers and small businesses.

The two elements of the Internet—IT and information itself—work together to enhance network effects. IT makes it easier and cheaper to collect and process information, and the network connectivity makes it cheaper to access information that has already been collected.

For example, Cybertrader[4] in Sri Lanka is an electronic mall (e-mall) for both traditional and nontraditional exports. The creators of Cybertrader hope to broaden the base of Sri Lankan exports beyond tea, clothing, and gems to include more products, particularly those from small businesses. To attract a global audience, Cybertrader needs to have a wide range of products and information about the products and producers. To have a wide range of products, Cybertrader is making it cheap for small businesses to join the e-mall by setting up a state-of-the-art computer

---

4. See http://www.tradenetsl.lk.

facility, complete with customer support, Web site design, and individual e-mail accounts for each business. The more products on the site, the more likely that a buyer will find something to buy. More buyers increase the value of the mall to Sri Lankan producers, so they are more likely to display their wares on Cybertrader. Cybertrader makes a commission on transactions. Network effects from both the IT and the information on the Web site build the virtuous cycle of benefits.

A third extension of Metcalfe's law is language. English has become the language of the Internet in part because the Internet has its greatest dispersion in the United States. The Internet is not accessible to people who do not speak English or who cannot read. Not only is this detrimental to their well-being, it also reduces the value of the entire network to everyone who can currently access it. Looking forward, the Internet will be of greatest value to those in developing countries if there is content in their own language as well as *language interoperability*—the ability to translate content into the language of the user.[5] One example of language interoperability that builds on the interoperability of network technologies is a device being developed by Telecom Indonesia called Rural Voice-rich Information Community. This device translates text into voice, using the key pad on a common phone to allow illiterate farm workers in rural communities to "download" information on pests and health as well as "upload" questions that can then be answered by local officials (McBeth 1999, 51).

Economic Frictions and the Global Internet Marketplace

Economic frictions help define where businesses locate and the scope of their operations as well as what consumers buy and where. Aluminum plants tend to locate near bauxite deposits because the material is hard to move. McDonald's franchises follow a set recipe for french fries so as to maintain brand-level flavor regardless of where the product is cooked. Ford's River Rouge automobile plant in Michigan was so completely integrated that steel went in one end and a finished vehicle came out the other. Parts producers had to congregate around the facility to reduce the risk of interrupting the straight line of the production facility. Similarly, before road and rail, consumers went to the market once a year to trade farm and household output for the items that they could not produce at home—to go more frequently was a waste of time and money.

Technology changes all this. Aluminum can be reclaimed at smaller recycling facilities close to the users, often at less cost than smelting

---

5. A related issue is Internet accessibility for people with disabilities of sight or keyboarding skills, and so on. Private businesses have been working on Internet translation programs for language as well as other aspects of access.

new aluminum. Ford's River Rouge plant was shut down as just-in-time methods of outsourcing increased the productivity of a narrower scope of operation within a single factory. Ford is now leading the way to complete integration of workers, parts suppliers, and customers in an e-commerce platform. Consumers of products like electronics can now buy directly from the manufacturer, which sources inputs (both tangible and intangible) from the United States and abroad.

The structure and capabilities of the Internet further reduce frictions in the marketplace in the three dimensions of time, distance, and information. The Internet marketplace fosters global production of products and services, which, thanks to more easily accessed information, are tailored exactly to what a buyer needs and are available exactly when the buyer wants it. Moreover, because access to the full power of the network is relatively easy and cheap, small businesses have the same opportunity as large businesses—as both buyers and sellers of online goods and services—to meet market demand.

The Internet allows the full 24 hours of the day to be exploited for production, customer service, information-gathering, design, and development. For example, combining Internet telephony with a global database of questions and details on orders allows English-speaking customers to be serviced from India, Ireland, or countries in the Eastern Caribbean, depending on the time zone of the caller. Spanish or Mandarin-speaking customers can be served in their own language from telecenters in their home country, even when they are calling from abroad.

Geography and size also present fewer barriers to participation. Businesses can tender designs and procurement details and find suppliers in other countries. Small businesses can reach a global marketplace with a Web site or just one or two mouse clicks. General Electric (GE), which posts procurement orders for office supplies on its Web site, gets responses and fulfillment from countries as far away as Africa. Without the Internet, these firms would not know about the GE tender. BTG, Inc., a small systems integrator, can on the Internet design details, post that fabrication shops in Taiwan can download, determine if they can build it, and then bid on the contract.

Greater access to niches in time and space does not reduce their value but increases the possibilities for how they can be used. Using the greater access to information about buyer preferences and needs, businesses can tailor goods and services to exactly what the buyer wants. The Internet marketplace increasingly will offer product "bundles," priced uniquely by time, location, and what was called the *final* good or service. Airlines have used this strategy for pricing seats for some time, as have package delivery services, such as FedEx, which has separate prices for overnight delivery of packages early in the morning, versus mid-day, and so on.

The Internet allows such bundling to become much more prevalent. Some Bloomberg clients pay for real-time stock prices; they can get the information free but lagged 20 minutes if their time preference is less urgent. Some women buy clothing from landsend.com, some from the L.L. Bean catalog, and some at Nordstrom in the shopping mall, not only because the clothing is different but also because preferences for shopping by time of day, location, and other factors, such as entertainment, matter; the clothes are just one part of the product bundle. Even for intermediate goods like industrial supplies, the Internet enhances this ability to bundle and use time, geography, and information more effectively.

The lower frictions to using time and space combine with the information and network characteristics of the Internet marketplace to allow more ways for businesses to create value. Firms can focus on which part of the value-added chain they do best and outsource other parts to subsidiaries or strategic allies anywhere on the globe. Moreover, more stages of production can be digitized (software production, for example) where assembly and the delivery of value is via the network.

Since buyers have different needs, firms following different strategies can coexist in the same marketplace. For example, more than one company builds computers to order because there is more than one type of customer. Dell Computer builds computers to order from online requests. Parts, software, assembly, and packing, come from distinct locations—some by plane and some electronically—before being bundled together in response to a specific customer request. Gateway Computer, seeing a market opportunity in a different segment of the marketplace, offers a different bundle. Gateway assembles computers from delivered tangible inputs and digitally downloaded software, just like Dell. But they sell the bundle in a Gateway Country Store to the person who wants more customer service when she buys a computer, or simply wants to try it out first, or perhaps wants to lease a computer (rather than buy one) so as to reduce the initial costs and enable a trade-up to a more powerful model when her needs change.

Between bundling and fragmentation, it is increasingly difficult to determine exactly where (in a geographical sense) or when (in terms of the stage of a production process) value is created. Product bundles can be offered through firms that can locate anywhere, whose locations can change quickly, and whose ultimate residence may be hard to track down. Even tangible merchandise, purchased at a point in time and at a particular location, may only be identified by the delivery destination of record, not the ultimate user. With a bundle characterized by a digitized and downloaded transaction, neither the origin point nor the ultimate user may be determinable. These issues have important implications for governments, whose jurisdictions are bounded by political or geographic rather than economic lines.

Policy Implications of Internet Economics

The elements of network effects and frictionless markets create two forces: Network effects push toward a homogeneous approach in hardware and software systems to developing the Internet and electronic commerce. Yet lower economic frictions allow greater heterogeneity in what is offered over the Internet and how production takes place. These two forces, rather than being in opposition, in fact are complementary. On the one hand, the desire to gain the benefits of network externalities suggests that key infrastructures and policy frameworks at home must be interoperable with the direction being taken abroad by the technological leaders. On the other hand, the ability of the Internet to reduce frictions to entry and to create unique product bundles means that heterogeneous tastes of global and local consumers and businesses can be satisfied. What are the broad policy implications of these two aspects of Internet economics?

The ingredients of the Internet marketplace—network benefits, frictionless markets, bundling and fragmentation, and global reach—have another feature of particular relevance for policymakers. These markets may be prone to certain kinds of imperfections, particularly when the reality of human and institutional pace is factored in. For example, competition in the marketplace for network access may be slowed by institutional inertia and vested interests. There may be an asymmetry in power between firms and users over the collection and use of the vast trove of information. These are two areas where government intervention by mandate may be considered, although the market may also be allowed to generate solutions. What motivates some governments to choose one approach or degree of intervention over another? What difficulties can arise when some governments choose intervention by mandate while other governments encourage market-oriented solutions?

Government Intervention and the Economics of Network Effects

Network effects underpin the success of the Internet and the uptake of electronic commerce. But does a country maximize its benefits and minimize its costs simply by joining *any* network? Internet policy and the economics of network effects need to be addressed at the individual level as well as the level of society (the policymaker's level).

For an individual, the decision is simple: if a network exists, join it. The economic benefits of joining a network will be immediate and large, and the costs of joining, relatively small. The individual does not bear the costs of setting up the network, just the costs to link to it. Nor does the individual have to wait until other participants join the network to reap benefits, because some already have—the network is already operating. It makes sense to "draft" in behind the leaders that incurred the costs for developing the network; the benefits are greater than the costs.

But what if the network is not a perfect fit for the individual, or the country? For example, an Internet infrastructure based on access via a PC will have greatest value to an individual who has a PC and to a country where PC penetration is relatively high. The third-generation wireless standard that delivers Internet capability to mobile phones may be a better network to favor if mobile phones are common. Does a government have to choose? Should it? Or should the private sector point the way and shoulder the burden?

Two phrases should drive any government intervention: (1) policy interoperability and (2) preserving private-sector incentives to augment and innovate existing network capabilities (whether domestic or foreign). Any policy that impedes network interoperability or commerce will undermine the benefits.

How is interoperability best achieved? To rely on a centrally-directed approach to guide the development of a local network rather than on the decisions of buyers and sellers presumes (1) that the policymaker knows what constituents really want and what technological capabilities might be offered now and in the future, and (2) that the private sector (domestic or foreign) does not. Some policymakers see such benefits to electronic commerce and joining global networks that they want to start right away, rather than wait for their private sector to get organized, try, and fail, and only then slowly succeed. Government pilot projects can show the private sector the possibilities and help the private sector sort out alternative approaches (see chapter 9). But the more important role for government is to create the facilitating environment in which local and foreign entrepreneurs can thrive, in part by applying what is on the Web to the tastes of the domestic marketplace. Too much government intervention removes any incentive for the private sector to learn how to meet market demand.

Some policymakers may be concerned that low teledensity and PC penetration doom their countries to be laggards in uptake of the Internet. But the evidence (presented in chapter 9) shows that the private sector (domestic or foreign, or increasingly likely, in partnership) rises to the task. Network effects are so valuable that firms do everything they can to ensure the widest Internet audience for its activities and information.

While there are advantages to being the first to create a network, there are even greater advantages to convergence on interoperable approaches. For example, the technology to access the Internet is cheap relative to the benefits to be gained by having subscribers, so innovation in ways to deliver the Internet to a variety of devices is very rapid. Private-sector entrepreneurs and firms direct their attention to ways to deliver the Internet to whatever device the user has available. For example, rental cell phones licensed under Grameenphone in Bangladesh may soon enable Internet access in remote areas of one of the poorest countries on earth. A private firm (WebTV) has recognized that there are about twice as many televisions in the world than telephones (about four times as many in developing countries), and so is developing technology for Internet access via TV. Microsoft, too, is pursuing this technology in China among other places.

Nevertheless, the legacy of telecommunications regulations can play a role in what technology ends up being favored—not by the government, but by the private sector. In Japan, the price of Internet access over traditional phone lines is among the highest in the world, and PC penetration is lower than would be expected based on per capita income. Internet usage as measured by access via phone and over PC thus has been slow to catch on there. However, deregulation of the cellular phone market yielded an explosion of hand-held devices, and DoCoMo is delivering the Internet (via I-Mode) to cell phones. Because the cell phone market is global, a consortium of hardware vendors (including Motorola, Nokia, and Ericsson) is working on interoperable standards so that the Internet can be delivered to any mobile device. In the end, network effects rule private-sector behavior and push for interoperability even if technologies do not converge.

Are there failures of the global marketplace that close countries from the global network? Most difficulties originate within a country; these are addressed in more detail in the next sections. Even in countries closed in the past, telecommunications deregulation and privatization have spurred private-sector initiative and capital to finance and support global Internet access. Diveo Broadband Networks offers high-speed Internet connection in urban centers of Brazil and Argentina. IBM Sri Lanka has about 25 points of presence scattered around the island so that virtually any citizen has local access to a global Internet connection via Singapore. The towers of the electricity grid in Ghana and neighboring countries are being used to hang telecommunications equipment that will access the Internet.

However, there may be some countries where private initiatives are lacking and so is the foreign private sector. There international programs of assistance help to finance global and regional Internet connectivity. The Leland Initiative of the US Agency for International Development (USAID) is networking 20 African nations; other programs are supported by the ITU and the World Bank. All this makes it increasingly difficult to argue that basic access to the Internet is unattainable for a country, or that it represents the most important hurdle to more fully developed usage of the Internet and electronic commerce.

Competition Policy, Information Aggregation, and Network Legacies

The Internet reduces substantially the economic frictions in the market-place thus allowing entry of new firms, new ways to fragment the production process, and new ways to bundle products to meet the needs of buyers. However, frictions remain: There is only so much screen space on a PC or on a mobile phone. Human inertia can be another friction. Incomplete privatization of domestic services industries and government regulation of the marketplace can affect the conduct of firms in the global marketplace. In conjunction with Metcalfe's law, such frictions can generate uncompetitive corporate behavior, which suggests that there is an important role for competition policy.

The strategy that a firm might take for presenting Web sites and their information to the user is a potential area of government concern. Portals (AOL, Yahoo, Sina, StarMedia) serve this function. A user can also "bookmark" a Web site that he or she visits frequently. How valuable is it to be the "first mover"—either in establishing a site that offers a particular product, service, or information, or in being the first portal to offer access and information aggregation to users? First movers do have advantages, but their power to keep out new entrants, and therefore the potential for uncompetitive results, is reduced by the technology itself. A site that does not meet the demands of the user has competition that is only one or two mouse clicks away.

On the other hand, human inertia to change can allow less desirable sites and portals to persist. Government policy toward both Internet entry and competition between Internet and virtual sellers can tip the balance. First movers reap the initial revenues, which tend to enhance capital market access, both of which enable first movers to finance development of superior products and services to keep them on top.

The key issue for competition authorities is whether sites or portals actively try to subvert the technological ability that allows users to change. For example, while AOL 5.0 added many useful features, it also made it difficult for users to connect to other portals. However, AOL's behavior was altered not by government intervention but by the demands of the users, who forced the company to make AOL 5.0 interoperable with other systems.

A second concern for competition authorities is strategic alliances between Internet portals and favored sites or products, or between ISPs and telecommunications and media companies. For example, a portal or information aggregator can favor one site or one firm simply by choosing strategically where to put the link on the screen. The favored firm then typically gives kickbacks to the aggregator based on the activity the aggregator directs to the site. If the aggregator is owned by or owns a telecommunications company (see chapter 3) or if the aggregator owns a media company, there is the potential for concentration of power and uncompetitive behavior. Thus the description of free-wheeling competition and easy access to a global Internet marketplace by even the smallest firm in the remotest country may be questionable. How much should policymakers worry? What should they do?

There are two ways the marketplace itself can correct these potential problems. The first depends on the continuing advance of technology.

For example, *bots* or *web crawlers* like mySimon.com search all Internet sites for the lowest price of a particular product. Such companies return to the user a list of sites by price; the lists can also include ancillary information like tax liability or delivery details. This technology reduces the power of incumbents and limits the role of strategic alliances, at least with regard to prices. While it is difficult to program a bot to include everything a buyer might want to know, such as quality, customer support, or method of production, a buyer who is choosy can initiate human-directed Internet searches.

The second way to allay concerns over uncompetitive practices depends on the diversity of businesses and consumers in the Internet marketplace. Even if there are some gains to being first into a market, there are infinite new markets to be the first into. Once the key access and usage infrastructures are in place, small businesses and those from developing countries can create products for individual consumers as well as reach out to the global marketplace. Of particular interest to developing countries, incumbents from the industrial countries are not likely to be interested in smaller markets, thus leaving opportunities open for local entrepreneurs who know these markets best. (See chapter 9 for examples of local entrepreneurs with global reach.)

There is another possibility for uncompetitive behavior: In many countries the service infrastructures on which the network depends are not fully private or enjoy partial or complete monopoly power. In some countries there is no competitive access to the telecommunications markets. Since network effects do give incumbents an advantage, competition authorities must be vigilant to prevent hoarding of bandwidth or cross-subsidization on the back of public-sector network infrastructure. Similarly, the legacy of state-owned companies can affect cross-border competition. Partially privatized firms often generate supranormal revenues in the domestic marketplace, which can be used to purchase private competition in the open marketplace.

It may be necessary to apply existing competition policy on both domestic and international fronts. On the domestic front, a first strategy is more rapid privatization and deregulation. Competition policy that requires full disclosure might be appropriate, such as demanding arms-length pricing or breaking the link between the ISP and the public telephone network are other points of government intervention. On the international front, consultations among domestic competition authorities are needed, although these are not always successful. (Part Two of this book reports on cases where jurisdictions of government authorities overlap in the global marketplace. Part Three addresses ways to improve the environment for cross-border and intergovernmental discussions about overlapping jurisdictions).

The objective of government policy is ultimately to foster an environment where economic activity and value-creation is directed less to *creating* the network and more to creating an interoperable framework of technologies and policies that in turn encourages businesses and individuals to *use* the network, making it more valuable to all participants.

Government Guidance and the Economics of Imperfect Markets for Information

Information collection, aggregation, and use underpin the value of the Internet. The market for information is prone to imperfections of three types: incomplete markets, asymmetric market power, and pure market failures. Each of these imperfections has analogs in other areas of economics where they are perhaps more familiar.

The first imperfection—incomplete markets—has been recognized in the financial markets. Seminal work by Professors Arrow and Debreu showed that the prices quoted in financial markets would not perfectly reflect all available information and would not properly price risk unless there was a financial instrument that paid off in every possible financial circumstance. But financial instruments for some risky circumstances may not exist. Data on financial outcomes, which are necessary for financial intermediaries to price risky circumstances, may be hard to obtain, particularly if the event is rare. Potential buyers of these financial instruments might not see their value because the occasion where the instrument would be valuable hardly ever happens. The costs of transacting in illiquid markets with few buyers and sellers may deter financial intermediaries from creating some financial instruments. In the Internet marketplace, if there are incomplete markets, the pricing and treatment of information by those who supply it and those who demand it will be imperfect.

The second imperfection—asymmetric market power—has an analog in negotiations, particularly in the literature on union bargaining. An individual worker has little power to negotiate pay and working conditions vis-à-vis a larger firm, particularly if the worker has few unique skills and can be easily replaced by someone else. A union effectively collects workers into a group which then has more power to negotiate with the firm, since if a whole group of workers were to strike, the cost to the firm would be much greater and its ability to replace the whole group quickly would be much smaller. With asymmetric market power, individuals' demands about how the Internet works may be ignored by the relatively fewer firms that collect the information.

Finally, the third imperfection—pure market failure—has as its apocryphal example "The Tragedy of the Commons." In England in the 1800s, farmers grazed their cows on common land. Too many cows and too much grazing on the common land ruined the grass. Even if the farmers recognized the source of environmental degradation (their collective activity), no one farmer had the incentive to not graze his one cow on the common land (since some other farmer would just put two cows out to graze). Yet each farmer was worse off for failing to value properly the common resource. The social value of the commons exceeded the sum of the private valuations of the commons.

This problem can exist even if there are complete markets in the Arrow-Debreu sense, and even if power among the participants in the marketplace is symmetric. There is no way for the market as a set of uncoordinated individuals to properly price or value this spillover, a public good.

The Internet marketplace has elements of all three market imperfections: Incomplete markets may arise through the human factor—users may not know what information is being collected about their activity on the Internet, or how it is being aggregated and used. Asymmetric power can arise from differences in market power between firms that collect and aggregate the information and users in the marketplace that provide the information. Pure market failure occurs when the market mechanism fails to account for a difference between the private and the social costs or benefits of a transaction—in this case, the collective value of information obtained via the Internet and other activities diverges from the value that each individual puts on his or her contribution to the pool of information. Indeed, network effects absolutely imply that there is a difference between the social and the private value of information on the Internet.

The previous section argued that the private-sector solution to achieving *technical network accessibility* has been good. What about the private-sector solution to imperfections in the Internet marketplace specifically for information? Is there a rationale for government intervention to correct some or any of these imperfections?

The example of using personal data on the Internet makes notions of market imperfections more concrete, and sets the stage for alternative policy approaches to improve how the Internet marketplace for information functions.

When a visitor clicks on a Web site, a computer program known as a "cookie" can collect information from that visitor—information that escalates in detail as the complexity of the visitor's activity on the site increases. This information may include name and e-mail address and place and type of work; it may also include the pattern of an individual's movements on the Internet ("clickstream behavior"). Other databases, including phone directories, financial services credit histories, car registration, electric bills and so on, can be aggregated and cross-referenced with the online behavior. Data mining companies like DoubleClick, Microstrategy, and Experian harvest, analyze, and sell the information for marketing purposes, among other activities.

Individuals may want to limit the collection, combination, and sale of their personal data, but they face several difficulties in doing so. First, some visitors do not know what is being collected online or what is in off-line databases; the firms themselves may not really know. Demanding that more detailed information be given to the individual as to the potential uses of these data, or offering greater choice in how much data need be revealed, may not help users better control the flow of information. Individuals may not know what their privacy preferences are. They may not be able to value them properly anyway.[6] In the Arrow-Debreu sense, policies on privacy do not "span the set" of desired information flows. Consequently, the markets for personal data are incomplete.

Second, there is asymmetric power between the collector of information and the user who is providing the information. Because there are relatively few portals and firms, and many users, firms have relatively little incentive to meet the demands of any single user. An individual can choose to not use the Internet (equivalent to the worker striking the firm), but that does not improve the outcome for either the firm or the user. Both lose the benefits that come with network participation.

Perhaps the most important market imperfection is pure market failure. Because collecting information on individuals is part of the value of the information itself (as discussed in the context of network effects), firms will want to collect information from everyone, even when users as a group would like less personal data collected. In the "commons" sense, the collected value of information to the firm is greater than the sum of the private valuations of information. From the perspective of society, society values privacy more than does the private firm.

What can government do to rectify any of these imperfections? Broadly, there are two strategies: A government can *mandate* a standard for collecting and using private data. For example, the EU Privacy Directive requires adherence to a standard in the use of personal data of EU residents by firms outside as well as inside the European Union. A *market-oriented* approach (for example, the US) encourages innovation by firms to close the market imperfections—to self-regulate by offering a range of services.[7]

Is there a winner (in an economic sense) between the US and the EU approaches to solving the problems of market imperfections and market failure? The economic "theory of the second best" shows that the market solution (the US approach) and the mandated solution (the EU approach) cannot be ranked in terms of which one comes closer to achieving the highest level of general well-being. In neither case will the needs of all individuals be met; nor can we be sure that society's needs are met.

On the one hand, the market approach yields an incomplete set of policies for meeting the privacy preferences of each individual. Some

---

6. Users of iWon.com are being paid (or at least may be) to reveal clickstream behavior. Do they know what information is being absorbed? Are they being paid enough? Do they care?

7. Both the EU approach and the US approach are discussed in greater depth in chapter 8.

individual privacy demands will not be met. And, by definition, if there is a pure market failure (of the "spillovers" or "public-good" type), the market cannot achieve the best outcome by itself. A freewheeling, market-oriented policy might lead to individuals who are concerned about the use of their information on the Internet refusing to log on. If users balk, the value of the network to everyone is by squared lower (network effects working in reverse).

On the other hand, the mandated solution assumes that each person has the same privacy preference as is determined by the government directive. Because people are heterogeneous, some individual privacy demands will still not be met. In this case those left out would probably be willing to disclose more in order to get more tailored products and services. A mandated policy of "one-size-fits-all" could lead to too little information collected and therefore too little Internet use by buyers and sellers who demand a high level of tailored service. The value of the Internet for everyone is again reduced.

One critical difference between the market and the mandated strategies is that with the market approach, firms continue to get incentives to try to satisfy individuals' privacy demands, particularly if those demands are communicated to the firms with enforcement measures as back-up. The incentives come in part from the very network benefits that are lost if the privacy policy is insufficient and users defect. Under the government-mandated approach, the private sector has fewer incentives to innovate to resolve market imperfections—and the enforcement issues remain.

Beyond the theory of these alternatives and how they work within the domestic marketplace, an even more important issue for global electronic commerce is the overlap of government jurisdictions and the potential conflict between a national jurisdiction and a cross-border economic activity in the global marketplace. Will the mandated approach create a barrier to cross-border trade, and with many governments and many strategies, yield a sort of Balkanization that limits the global reach and global benefits of electronic commerce? Or can the mandated and the market approaches be made interoperable so that the benefits of the network accrue to all?

Finding an interoperable policy approach that nevertheless is heterogeneous matters. Governments can, and perhaps even should, disagree on the degree of intervention in the marketplace. That is, societies do differ in their preferences for degrees of government intervention to achieve privacy, consumer protection, content filtering, and so on. To the extent that policymakers are elected to represent these views, diversity in the amount of government intervention into some areas of electronic commerce could be appropriate. Diversity appears to be inevitable in any case. The objective of policymakers should be to ensure that this diversity in approaches to governance becomes a niche opportunity for private firms to devise ways to bridge the different approaches, rather than a barrier to cross-border electronic commerce. A set of "best practices" would help to ensure that both domestic and international benefits are achieved.[8]

The Human Factor, the Institutional Factor, and the Pace of Technology

In the midst of the emerging technological and market capabilities of the Internet, there are the human and the institutional factors. People ultimately are at the heart of the marketplace and are the focus of many government objectives; governments are composed of agencies and institutions that already have functions. There are potential clashes between the pace of humans and institutions and the pace of technology. On the one hand, technology can outpace the ability of people and governments to respond to and implement it. In this sense technology moves too fast. On the other hand, human expectations can outpace the implementation of technology. In this case, technology moves too slowly. How do these human and institutional factors affect policy choices?

Too much hype about what the Internet and electronic commerce *can* offer runs the risk of overreaching what it *does* offer. Some people, particularly those outside the United States but also some groups within, find that the Internet does not offer them interesting or relevant content or products. The language is wrong, and there is nothing that matches their cultures or desires. For them, the Internet has little immediate value. This first impression poisons the waters for further exploration. How can these disappointed explorers be transformed into entrepreneurs, so that they and others like them find a more congenial and interesting environment— so that they become part of a community of users with common interests and therefore become part of the global network?

Getting individuals online and creating entrepreneurs require the infrastructures of services, standards, and laws that create an environment of efficiency, certainty, and trust.

A somewhat different problem arises when people hear about the great technological breakthroughs made possible by the Internet, but the technology fails under the weight of demand. A famous example was when Victoria's Secret, an upscale lingerie house with lovely models, hyped their new online fashion show and was so swamped with activity that the site server crashed. Another example is the failure of online banking thus far to deliver seamless bill-paying services because most companies that issue bills cannot process individual electronic transactions. In this

---

8. A set of "best practices" (or maybe a presentation of "avoidable outcomes") will be a sequel to this primer.

case, expectations for what the technology can (and ultimately will) do outpace the current implementation of the technology.

Finally, in many places around the world, the pace of technology exceeds the pace of adaptability. Governments may want to embrace technology, but it still takes time to put infrastructures in place. Coordinating the policy changes necessary to move forward quickly and comprehensively is very difficult within the often fragmented fiefdoms of government agencies or between the various legislative bodies. Perhaps worse, policymakers may hope that electronic commerce can be the "silver bullet" to kill problems ranging from slow economic growth to fiscal imbalance to a trade deficit without the hard work of changing the fundamental infrastructures and legal framework. In society at large, people may be slow to recognize the benefits of using the Internet; or they may be too burdened by their daily lives to invest in developing the human capital needed to work with the technology.

Within government, an "e-commerce czar"—a minister without portfolio—could embody the necessary cross-cutting, synergy, and vision and be the motive force within government to keep momentum going. This person also could be the international voice for the government.

For the people, policymakers have the responsibility to make sure that institutional inertia does not stop the virtuous cycle, where use of technology enhances the further uptake of technology, with the result of greater well-being. Proactively, using the Internet for human capital development is a strategic point from which to start this virtuous cycle—a cycle, moreover, where human capital development itself also improves how societies use the Internet.

II

ELECTRONIC COMMERCE INFRASTRUCTURES

Introduction

The three service-sector infrastructures of communications, finance and payments, and distribution and delivery comprise many of the technologies and processes that create the Internet marketplace.[1] The infrastructures themselves are not new, although their technological make up changes almost daily, with the rapid evolution of third-generation wireless telecommunications and satellite capabilities, Smart cards and online currencies, and overnight airfreight and digital delivery. Because the Internet and electronic commerce push out the technological frontier of these services sectors, they are increasingly important for a country's general economic welfare.

Electronic commerce highlights the synergies between the services sectors. Its fast pace, global reach, and information rich-environment requires that progress on upgrading all these infrastructures proceed comprehensively. Moreover, since the Internet significantly tightens the value-added chain of production and distribution, addressing only one of these infrastructures in policymaking is not enough to even maintain a country's current level of international engagement: There should be a sense of urgency about upgrading the services infrastructures. The next three chap-

---

1. Although a bit dated, *The Economics of Electronic Commerce: The Essential Economics of Doing Business in the Electronic Marketplace* by Soon-Yong Choi, Dale O. Stahl, and Andrew B. Whinston (Macmillan Technical Publishing, Indianapolis, IN), 1997 has very detailed discussions of the "nuts and bolts" of telecommunications and financial services infrastructures. *Building Confidence: Electronic Commerce and Development*, UNCTAD 2000, has excellent discussions of how electronic commerce affects operations in financial services and transport and delivery.

ters discuss how the Internet and electronic commerce affect these infrastructures and what the new technologies demand. They also address what policymakers can learn about the consequences of policy initiatives (or the lack thereof).

3

Infrastructure: Communications Systems

Fixed-line and wireless telecommunications form the backbone through which most Internet traffic travels. The communications infrastructure is therefore crucial to the growth of the Internet, in particular of value-added services such as media-rich content and electronic commerce. Policymakers can lay the foundation for a high-quality, fairly priced, and technologically up-to-date telecommunications infrastructure by introducing into their countries a combination of privatization, competition, and independent regulation. Where applied, such a policy framework has resulted in increased telephone ownership, lower prices for local calls, and higher network quality, thus increasing the ability of individuals and businesses to use the Internet.

Rapid change in the IT sector and the growing convergence between telephones, PCs, and TVs pose additional challenges for communications policymakers. The widespread delivery of the Internet via satellite and cable is not far away. TVs and wireless telephones are joining PCs as common tools to connect to and surf the Web. New technology can break down voice, text, and video into data packets that can be routed over the Internet, allowing individuals to talk locally or internationally via their Internet connections.

Communications policies must be flexible to adapt to this rapidly changing environment. Policymakers need to address not only the current state of competition, but also how these changes and growing convergence affect existing market participants and new entrants. Perhaps most important, policymakers should work with the private sector to ensure the interoperability of standards and protocols, so that all the sections of the Internet highway can link seamlessly.

The Current Environment

Basic telecommunications data as gathered by the ITU show that many countries still lack the state-of-the-art communications infrastructure needed to support and encourage Internet traffic (ITU 1999). A number of the world's lower-income countries, including most of sub-Saharan Africa, have less than 1 telephone line per 100 inhabitants (this measure is known as "teledensity"). Even several upper-middle-income countries, such as Malaysia and Mexico, have less than 20 lines per 100 inhabitants, compared to over 65 lines per 100 for much of Western Europe. Particularly troublesome is that many countries with low teledensity experienced only single-digit percentage growth in the number of main telephone lines between 1995 and 1998. There it can take several months or even several years for a company or an individual to get a new telephone line, a direct constraint on growth.

A second direct constraint is the price of a local telephone call. ITU data show that the cost of connecting to the Internet varies substantially by country, in large part because local telephone charges are so different (see figure 3.1). For example, in the United States, an individual pays about $20 per month for unlimited Internet access, with minimal or no per-minute local call fees. In China, almost half of the $65 per month in access fees is local call charges (ITU 1999, A-30, table 9). These charges can make Internet access affordable only to an elite few, especially in countries with lower per capita GDP. For example, in Uganda monthly Internet access charges are 107 percent of monthly income; in Mozambique, 29 percent of monthly income. By contrast, in the United States and Australia, Internet access fees account for less than 2 percent of monthly GDP per capita (ITU 1999, 31). Ongoing research by the OECD has confirmed that those countries with local call charges had lower Internet host penetration than countries without such charges.

In some countries, ISPs are mitigating high local call charges by offering no-subscription-fee Internet accounts. Typically, the ISPs form alliances with telecom providers to share local call charges; they also generate revenue by selling online advertising and tracking their customers' movements ("clickstream behavior") on the Web. Freeserve in the UK was one of the first ISPs to implement no-subscription-fee Internet access country-wide. Now other ISPs from around the world are following Freeserve's lead. While these ISPs offer an attractive option for many consumers, the access—in large part because of local call charges—is anything but free. Per-minute charges create a disincentive for individuals to take the time to explore ("surf") the Internet to discover what information or goods or services companies on the Web have to offer.

The impact of the time-tolled call, particularly where connections are slow, should not be underestimated. Individuals paying access fees based on their connection times often use the Internet only to read and send

Figure 3.1 Internet monthly access prices for 20 hours of off-peak use, selected economies (US dollars)

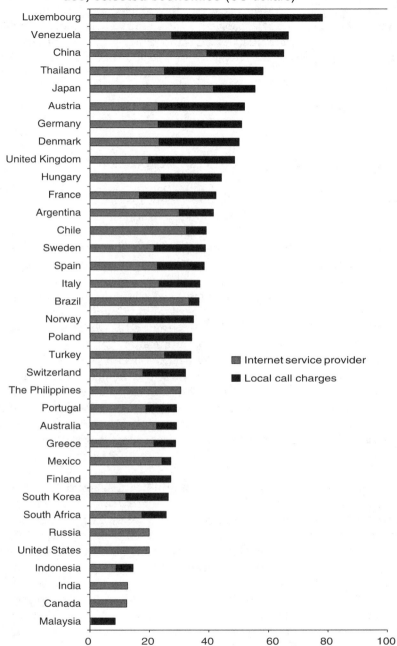

Source: ITU 1999.

electronic mail. As long as per-minute fees continue, users must pay to browse through the goods, services, and prices available online. Imagine, for instance, a library where readers had to pay by the minute, or a mall that charged window shoppers by the hour! These charges create a disincentive to using the Internet for information-gathering or electronic commerce—precisely those areas where the Internet offers the greatest efficiencies and economic benefit. Per-minute charges also limit the ability of companies to research what other businesses are doing on the Internet, and to investigate what market niches remain to be exploited.

Privatization, Competition, and Regulation

Policymakers can reduce or eliminate these local call charges, thereby encouraging Internet use, by introducing into the telecommunications sector a combination of privatization, competition, and independent regulation. Such a policy framework also promises to increase teledensity and enhance universal service, and make the sector more technologically up-to-date.

Empirical and anecdotal research by the World Bank and academic and private researchers demonstrates that privatizing public telecommunications offices (PTOs), introducing fixed-line as well as wireless competition, and creating an independent telecommunications regulatory body can significantly improve the telecommunications sector (see table 3.1). Such policies are strongly correlated with increases in per capita telephone mainlines, public payphones, and connection capacity, with decreases in the price of a local telephone call (Wallsten 1999, 1; Wellenius et al. 1992). For example, in Latin America and Asia, the teledensity in countries with privatized telecommunications grew twice as fast during the first five years after privatization as in countries that did not privatize (Petrazzini 1996, 37).

These policies also promote a telecommunications sector that is more technologically up-to-date, including greater network digitization and higher service quality. For example, countries in Latin America with privatized and/or competitive telecommunications sectors have had more digitization than those countries with monopoly, state-owned PTOs. Also, a study of the OECD countries revealed that liberalized telecommunications markets offer consumers higher service quality, as measured by the number of faults cleared by the next working day, the number of unsuccessful local calls, or the number of faults per 100 main lines. With the introduction of competition into OECD telecom markets, there has been a 97 percent reduction in waiting time to get telecom service, 15 percent lower call failure rate, 39 percent fewer faults per 100 lines, and 34 percent lead in the number of phones digitized (Petrazzini 1996, 40-1).

Table 3.1 Projected benefits to users from competitive telecom services in 2010, and cumulative gains, 1997-2010[1]
(billions of dollars)

	Cost savings 2010	Quality benefits 2010	Total gains 2010	Cumulative gains 1997- 2010[2]
Income level				
Low	10	15	25	177
Middle	25	25	49	346
High	50	25	75	523
Total	85	65	149	1046
Region/country				
European Union[3]	27	14	41	288
Latin America	9	9	17	120
East Asia and Pacific	12	18	30	211
Japan	19	10	29	201
South Asia	3	5	8	56
Rest of world	14	10	24	169

1. Excludes nations presumed to be competitive: the United States, Canada, UK, Denmark, Finland, New Zealand, and Sweden.

2. Calculated by straight-line cumulation of benefits over the 14 years, inclusive, starting with zero in 1997 and ending with $149 billion in 2010.

3. Refers only to the less competitive European nations: Austria, Belgium, France, Germany, Ireland, Italy, the Netherlands, and Spain.

Source: Gary Hufbauer, based on 1995 data. First printed in Petrazzini (1996).

Privatization alone, however, will not maximize improvements in the telecommunications sector, and can sometimes have deleterious effects. Indeed, privatization without competition, which occurs when a government grants a newly-privatized PTO exclusivity, can lead to higher connection prices, especially if government subsidies for local calls are removed. In Mexico, for example, local telephone call charges rose 1,065 percent in early 1990 because of the privatization of Telmex. Similarly, in Argentina charges rose 258 percent as the state-owned PTO prepared for privatization (Petrazzini 1996).

But the introduction of competition along with privatization almost always leads to lower prices and higher service levels. Chile, for example, introduced competition into its domestic and international telephony in 1994; this brought about rapid modernization of the telecommunications network, new services, and prices that are among the world's lowest.[1] Indeed, by that year local telephone call charges had dropped by an

---

1. See Wellenius (ND). It is important that Chile also introduced competition in data, value-added, and cable TV services and private networks in the late 1980s.

average of 36 percent from late-1980 levels (Petrazzini 1996, 32-33). Similarly, the 1998 sale of a majority stake in El Salvador's PTO to France Telecom, as well as the auction of a second cellular license to Telefónica of Spain, has produced a flurry of activity within El Salvador's once-sleepy telecommunications sector. In fact, it now takes only a day or two to get a new phone line in El Salvador, compared with up to 6 *years* previously, and the entire country is covered for cellular service.[2]

In almost all countries seeking to privatize and introduce competition into the telecommunications sector, the benefits have been shown to be greatest when there is an independent telecommunications regulator. The World Bank has been active in working with policymakers in developing countries to establish such bodies (Wellenius et al. 1992). Independent regulation is particularly critical to guard against a monopoly telecommunications provider extending its rent-seeking behavior into the Internet. For example, in Morocco the telecommunications provider, IAM, recently started offering Internet access to subscribers at rates believed to be below cost in order to gain market share, a move that threatens to put the country's many private ISPs—which must rely on IAM's infrastructure—out of business. The telecommunications regulator, a fairly new body with limited technological expertise, will need substantial enforcement capacity to correct IAM's recent behavior so that Internet delivery will remain competitive in Morocco.[3]

External enforcement of competition in the telecommunications sector is now possible with the World Trade Organization's (WTO) Basic Telecommunications Agreement. The agreement binds signatories to certain regulatory principles as well as investment access commitments. It requires countries to establish an independent telecommunications regulator and provide transparent rules for the use of scarce commodities such as broadcast spectrum. Where a country's regulator is weak, for lack of funding, human capacity, or political reasons, outside countries can seek redress through WTO dispute settlement procedures.

Convergence and Interoperability

Privatization, competition, and independent regulation are necessary so that the fixed-line and wireless telecommunications infrastructure can support and encourage the growth of Internet traffic. There are additional challenges facing policymakers, given rapid technological developments and the growing convergence between telephones, PCs, and TVs. Satellites

---

2. Field research conducted by Sarah Cleeland Knight February 2000. It still costs roughly $0.80 per hour to call locally in El Salvador.

3. Field research conducted by Catherine L. Mann and Sarah Cleeland Knight, September 1999.

and cable now complement fiber optics and copper lines in forming the backbone of the Internet. Wireless telephones are in some countries more popular than PCs for using the Internet. It is becoming more common for individuals to use Internet connections to talk on the telephone.

Current communications regulations, conceived for the public switched telephone network (PSTN), may not be well equipped to adapt to such technological change and convergence. Regulatory flexibility is needed to ensure that new market entrants as well as existing participants can be competitive. Policymakers also need to work with the private sector to ensure that standards and protocols link all the sections of the Internet highway.

One example of how technological developments strain existing regulations is the emergence of Internet telephony, or voice-over Internet services. Companies like Cisco Systems (CPN: the Cisco Powered Network) have made it possible to break down voice, text, and video into data packets that can be routed over the Internet. As a result, voice communication can travel through the Internet from computer to computer, computer to telephone, or even from telephone to telephone, anywhere in the world.

While the quality is still relatively low compared to traditional voice connections, Internet telephony is much cheaper to deliver, making it a popular alternative especially in those countries where calls are costly and service less than first-rate. As a result, a number of Internet telephony providers have sprung up, including NetVoice, IPVoice, eYak, and Net2-Phone—the last of which charges less than 10 cents per minute to ring any telephone in the United States from overseas. Traditional providers are also jumping on the Internet telephony bandwagon: AT&T and Sprint are both starting to offer such services in Asia (*Business Week,* 13 September 1999, 34). As a result, Internet telephony is expected to grow from less than 1 percent of global telecom traffic in 1999 to 17 percent by 2003 and more than 30 percent by 2005 (*Business Week Online,* 1 May 2000). (See figure 3.2.)

Some countries, however, are trying—rather unsuccessfully—to protect their PTOs by banning competitive delivery of Internet telephony services. For example, Poland's telecom ministry is trying to crack down on Internet-relayed international calls that circumvent the state-controlled PTO by threatening fines or even the withdrawal of telecommunications licenses (*FoxNews.com,* 12 January 2000). Internet telephony is also banned in India, although several companies are providing it anyway, so that individuals can call the United States for less than a tenth of the traditional service rates (*Times of India,* 27 January 2000). Similarly, Telófonos de México has been trying to stop the Internet telephony services offered by AT&T and British Telecommunications (*Business Week Online,* 1 May 2000).

Instead of trying to block the inevitable growth of Internet telephony, governments should embrace this new, potentially more efficient commu-

Figure 3.2   The growing importance of Internet telephony

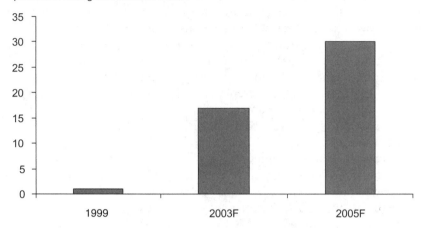

percent of total global telecom traffic

Source: Business Week Online, "The Talking Internet," 1 May 2000.

nications service. Internet telephony's prices are much lower, but so is its quality; thus, it is likely to be a net addition to rather than a substitute for traditional voice traffic, especially in developing countries. It is also difficult to enforce a ban on Internet telephony, especially once the calls have been patched on to the PSTN (ITU 1999, 112-17). Internet telephony could even be an attractive addition to a PTO's bundle of communications services.

Internet telephony is just one of a number of technological changes spurring the convergence of telephones, PCs, and TVs. Such technological change requires policymakers to make communications regulations more flexible, to encourage new solutions, approaches, and innovations.

Today, individuals and businesses access the Internet using a variety of interfaces, from hand-held devices like Palm Pilots to mobile telephones. The build-out of these interfaces is occurring at different speeds in different countries: Relatively high mobile phone penetration in Japan and Europe is driving the private sector in those areas to reconfigure Web pages to fit the smaller screens. In China, where TV penetration is relatively high, companies like Microsoft are offering WebTV, a service that allows individuals to surf the Internet from their televisions. In contrast, in the United States the focus is on media-rich content delivered through PCs. Rather than choosing to support one technological "winner" among these different interfaces, policymakers should encourage interoperability, so that the value delivered to users is maximized. Such interoperability will increase the value of all interfaces rather than render one or more of them obsolete.

One example where policymakers should work with the private sector to increase interoperability is in bridging the different standards for wireless connections. Currently the world is divided in its use of wireless telephone standards: GSM (global system for mobile communications) is the dominant standard for much of the world except North America, with an estimated 215 million users. In the United States, CDMA (code division multiple access) and TDMA (time division multiple access) dominate. As a result, most subscribers in the United States cannot use their mobile phones in Europe or Asia, vastly limiting the benefits to users who travel abroad. The private sector is moving closer to achieving interoperability between the different standards: In early April 2000, for example, operators and providers of CDMA, TDMA, and GSM began collaborating on the GSM Global Roaming Forum, an international organization open to all industry organizations (*PR Newswire*, 7 April 2000). Governments should support such efforts in every way possible so that interoperability is not stymied by inefficient regulation or bureaucratic process.

Conclusion

With such rapid technological change and convergence, government regulation or intervention that (even by mistake) limits new entrants or system interoperability will put a country behind the technological frontier and limit the value of the network for both businesses and individuals. Private sector consortia like Symbian, a joint venture among Ericsson, Motorola, Nokia, Psion, and Matsushita working toward standard technology for wireless Internet delivery, will increase the number of users of the Internet highway, as well as the benefits they derive. Such standards can be a valuable foundation for new business development, especially where the private sector is small or nascent. As a result, companies can concentrate on creating value-added Internet services like media-rich content and electronic commerce, especially those that target niche audiences, without having to reinvent the wheel.

The interoperability of standards and protocols is an important complement to the other changes to telecommunications regulation required to encourage use of the Internet and electronic commerce. Privatization of PTOs; competition in fixed-line, wireless, and other forms of Internet delivery; and the presence of an independent regulatory body can work together to create a high-quality, fairly priced, and technologically up-to-date telecommunications infrastructure that supports the growth of Internet traffic and electronic commerce.

4

Infrastructure:
Financial Sector and Payment Systems

An efficient and sound financial structure is the second service-sector infrastructure critical for the growth and development of electronic commerce. Such a structure is in fact a key ingredient for general economic well-being. A country's financial system intermediates between savers and investors and helps allocate and discipline capital to yield economic benefits to both individuals and the economy. The financial system is also the conduit for monetary policy, which affects the overall level of a country's macroeconomic activity. Domestic policies that encourage a deep and resilient financial system support economic development. Global forces and the liberalization of financial systems, including through electronic commerce, can augment and support these objectives, although policymakers need to be wary: The pathway is not without potholes.

Electronic commerce directly influences the financial structure of an economy in several ways. First, just as for businesses that produce goods, electronic commerce affects the range of products that financial intermediaries offer. It affects how businesses and buyers interact with each other. Since electronic commerce is global, financial intermediation is more likely to involve cross-border transactions and nondomestic institutions. Second, financial intermediaries interact with each other and with the central bank via payments systems. The faster pace and the greater international component of electronic commerce place greater demands on a country's financial plumbing.

More broadly, the multiple components of the financial system—banks and nonbank financial intermediaries and markets—play a very important role in supporting the development of firms that, on the one hand, participate in the global value-chain of production and, on the other, innovate electronic commerce products to best meet the needs of local users. Government policies that influence financial intermediaries and the range of financial products will materially affect the development of electronic commerce in a country.

Finance, Development, and Electronic Commerce

The questions of how finance and development are linked, and what impact international competition might have on domestic financial markets are not new. However, the results of an increasing body of research on these questions have implications for how policymakers might use electronic commerce to help create a financial environment conducive to development, and moreover, how an environment conducive to electronic commerce also supports financial sector development.

Development of the financial sector, particularly where there are clear legal and accounting systems, improves long-run economic performance by raising productivity growth (Beck, Levine, and Loayza 1999; Levine, Loayza, and Beck 1999). At the same time, higher income tends to be associated with a deeper and more resilient financial system that includes a rich array of both bank and nonbank institutions and markets (Demirgüç-Kunt and Levine 1999). This type of financial sector can better withstand economic volatility and downturns.

Competition, domestic or foreign, makes the financial sector better at disciplining capital to achieve higher economic rewards with greater efficiency. Argentina demonstrates that domestic financial institutions remain active in the domestic marketplace even after the market is opened to foreign competition (Claessens, Demirgüç-Kunt, and Huizinga 1998; Clarke et al. 1999; Denizer 1997). The domestic institutions have unique knowledge of the domestic marketplace, allowing them to thrive by adding value to local firms and consumers. This combination of international reach by some institutions coexisting with local reach of domestic institutions is a feature of the Internet and electronic commerce more generally. (see chapter 1).

On the other hand, evidence from other countries, including Turkey and Morocco, finds that domestic banks can remain collusive even after local and foreign competition is allowed, with deleterious effects on domestic financial intermediation and growth.[1] The Internet and electronic commerce enable lower-cost cross-border financial activities that may not yet have been liberalized sufficiently by foreign presence and domestic

---

1. Denizer 1997; field research by Catherine Mann in Morocco, September 1999.

entry; thus, it can play a part in improving financial and overall economic performance. As discussed in more detail in chapter 8, even if countries have not explicitly liberalized the financial sector through their commitments in the WTO under the General Agreement on Trade Services (GATS), they can allow the liberalizing features of cross-border financial transactions via electronic commerce to move toward greater liberalization without going back to the negotiating table.

Electronic Banking and Financial Services

Electronic commerce technologies affect individual financial institutions in a number of ways, which together push them to alter the mix of services they offer. Electronic commerce technologies significantly reduce the cost of providing financial services, but they also turn traditional products offered by financial institutions, such as some loans, into commodities. For example, a 1997 study by Booz Allen (corroborated in 2000 by Arthur Andersen) suggested that a transaction at a teller window costs a bank $1.07, an automatic teller machine (ATM) transaction $0.27, and an Internet banking transaction only $0.01. At the same time, margins on some loans, particularly those backed by real assets such as homes, are falling. Competition by lenders for the right to offer loans to borrowers who fill out standard forms for standard loans has become intense. For securities trading as well, full-service brokerages charge $150 for executing a trade, but online brokerages like E*trade charge only $10 (ITU 1999, figure 3.7).

On the other hand, electronic commerce technologies and lower transaction costs allow financial institutions to treat clients individually. In this age of online mortgage applications and stock trades, financial institutions can retain their relationships with clients by creating bundles of services unique to the needs of individual clients. Such bundles can include traditional savings and checking accounts that can be tracked and updated electronically, as well as online bill-pay. For example, about 90 percent of German consumer bank Web sites offer online transactions. Rather than use the cost savings from the Web sites to expand beyond the local environs, these institutions are consolidating their relationships with their traditional customer base at the city and village level (BlueSky International, 12 July 1999; field research by Catherine Mann, June 2000). Similarly, the range of services brokerages must offer to keep customers rises as difficulties in executing trades falls.

Online banking developments in developing countries show some technology leapfrogging, although the importance of securing customer trust is paramount. Banks in some developing countries have been at the forefront in providing online banking. Brazil's Banco 1 offers a full range of bank services over the Internet, and Brazil is one of the few countries where individuals can "bank" with the government (that is, pay their taxes) over the Internet In Mexico, 5 percent of Internet subscribers use Internet banking services, with 95 percent of those citing convenience, 67 percent reputation of the bank, and 63 percent attractive fees as the reason. Of those not using the services, 45 percent wanted to try Internet banking, but it was not available through their bank. Yet 39 percent of nonusers had security concerns, and about 30 percent thought the situation was too new and wanted to wait and see (ITU 1999, 53, figure 3.8). In short, customers generally want to do Internet banking but also want their financial operations to take place in a secure environment with an institution they can trust.

Increasingly demanding customers mean that financial institutions must continually enhance the services that they offer. For example, use of online banking services via PCs in the United States is expected to triple from 7 million households to more than 24 million households by 2004. But many new users are discontinuing their online banking services. In fact, over one-third of on-line bank users in the United States discontinued their accounts between July 1998 and July 1999 because the services were too cumbersome and insufficiently comprehensive to be worthwhile.[2] To reap the cost savings, and to develop relationships that create value to both customer and bank, online banking services must be user-friendly and meet customer needs, which may require an extension of the traditional bounds of "financial services."

The fragmented relationship between customers, their bills, and the banks that clear their payments stands in the way of a greater uptake of electronic commerce, Internet banking, and a more efficient financial services sector. In Sri Lanka, customers take payments in cash directly to businesses like the telephone company or the utility company: Only if they directly deliver the cash do they receive a receipt. Although domestic banks in Sri Lanka have telephone banking in place and are gearing up to offer PC banking, the population remains unwilling to use these services in part because they do not get a receipt, and often payment is delayed.[3]

In the United States, a different problem arises because so *few* transactions are cash-based. Whereas a debtor household or business might do its banking online, the creditor may not bank online, or at least not through the payer's bank. Therefore, there is no direct link between the payer and the payee. An effort to consolidate bills in a clearinghouse is a good example of the principal of network effects (see chapter 2): Chase Manhattan, First Union, and Wells Fargo are building an alliance of 11 banks (which presumably account for a large share of both payer and payee

---

2. Based on research by GarnterGroup's Dataquest, Inc. and CyberCitizen Finance, a division of Cyber Dialogue.

3. Field research by Catherine Mann, Sri Lanka, October 1999.

accounts) into a bill-clearing network. Bank customers would have a single site to use and the alliance will do the back-office operations necessary to present bills on the site and then transfer payments at a designated time (*Infobeat*, 23 June 1999).

Whereas on-line bill presentment and payment seems straightforward, significant difficulties have arisen and no service is currently considered acceptable. This case offers a good example of where expectations of what technology should be able to do exceeds what it currently can do. In addition to technical challenges associated with bringing together multiple parties, there remain issues of security and trust. In some cases, online bill payments are not made in a timely fashion, so that banks make money on the "float" between the time that the payer requests the transfer and the payee receives the funds.

Payment Vehicles and Security

Beyond electronic banking or electronic brokerage, the financial sector is intimately involved in the broader realm of electronic commerce in its role as enabler of online payments for transactions between businesses, consumers, and governments. The fast-paced global environment of both the electronic and physical worlds demand that financial intermediaries offer easy-to-use payment tools that allow rapid electronic funds transfer across borders. However, the more anonymous real-time business environment also demands a high degree of client verification as well as security and authentication of funds transferred. Financial partners or payment vehicles that cannot deliver both these services will not be competitive. Are there tensions between the need for speed and the desire for secure, verifiable transactions? Can security and speed be put on a virtuous cycle where technology designed to enhance the one also enhances the other? What if this does not happen?

Speed is crucial. Electronic commerce operates in a 24-hour, 7-day a week ("24/7") environment. Increasingly it is composed of digitally delivered inputs and outputs, where offline cash-on-delivery simply is not an option. The efficiencies and cost reductions promised by electronic commerce, particularly B2B, will not materialize without an online payment vehicle.

Moreover, Internet businesses must authorize transactions through payment institutions (e.g., banks or credit card companies) in real time so as to allow immediate delivery of digital products. A financial system that cannot provide this will stymie the development of electronic commerce and of the economy generally. Speed of authorization and clearing is also important at the macro level: The shorter the time between authorization and actual payment, the more efficient the transaction and the lower

Figure 4.1 United States preferred consumers' online payment methods (percent)

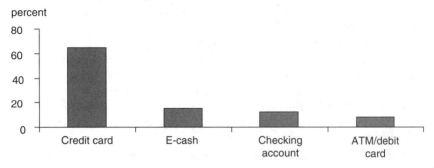

Source: The Economist, 19 February 2000, E-cash 2.0, 68, using data from Jupiter Communications.

the institutional risk (see more discussion of payment systems in the next section).

Although there are a number of online payment techniques (see figure 4.1), about 80 percent of electronic commerce transactions currently use credit cards. The international credit card is currency-neutral; it is recognized in nearly every country, which is of particular value in global electronic commerce. Consequently, in the near term, countries where credit or debit card penetration and usage are low may be less able to achieve maximum benefits from global electronic commerce, unless an alternative, equally interoperable mechanism is available. On the other hand, online verification, fraud, and charge-backs are becoming more serious, with particular relevance for small and medium enterprises (SMEs) in both industrial and developing countries. If the credit/debit card mechanism is to remain the premier method of on-line payment, these problems must be resolved.

Credit-card penetration varies widely by country for various reasons including both culture and policy. In many countries, such as China, consumers prefer cash transactions, in part to avoid audit and tax trails; credit card usage for electronic commerce remains low, even as usage of the Internet (such as for e-mail) has risen sharply. Consumers are also concerned about the security of their card numbers online, particularly if they are not protected from liability in the case of fraudulent use of their card. In the United States, the cardholder is liable for $50 if a card is lost or stolen, and is usually not liable for any fraudulent transaction. In contrast, in Taiwan and El Salvador, the cardholder is liable for the full amount of any fraudulent purchase and must go to court to obtain redress. In some countries, such as Sri Lanka, banks put very low limits on credit cards, in part to limit the development of a credit culture and in part to limit exposure to fraudulent use.[4]

Where there is aversion to credit cards, other on-line and Internet payment mechanisms are taking shape. In Sri Lanka, IBM is teaming up with a company in Malaysia to develop a secure on-line debit mechanism (direct debit to the bank account using the bank routing number and a PIN authorization). IBM plans to guarantee redress in case of fraud—an interesting blurring of the distinction between a product and a financial services company. American Express "Blue" card comes with an on line "purse" and hardware to securely debit the smart card. A person using a cell phone in Finland can buy soda from a vending machine, and the charge will show up on the phone bill.

Finally, in some countries, the additional charge for international credit card services can be quite high, as much as 5 to 7 percent. Whether these charges are passed on to the buyer or absorbed by the seller, the price differential undermines incentives for electronic commerce. In Bulgaria, for example, the service charge may be high because of currency risk, as well as the inability of credit card companies to prosecute fraud cases.

The government in some countries is intervening with regard to fees, although perhaps not at the source of the problem. In Bulgaria and Taiwan, policymakers are setting up a domestic credit card clearing facility that would offer lower fees on cards issued by domestic financial institutions. They argue that the lower fees are possible because the domestic clearing and issuing institutions will be better able to prosecute fraud, avoid losses, and manage foreign exchange exposure than international companies.[5]

Such government-backed projects, by reducing the spread in credit-card transactions, could in theory help the country by jump-starting electronic commerce. The problem is how to ensure that the symbiosis between domestic financial institutions and the clearing facility does not hinder the integration of the financial institutions into the global environment. Taiwan is planning to partially privatize its domestic clearing facility. The competitive value remains in doubt, however, given the low penetration of foreign financial institutions in Taiwan. In the end, the worry is that although the domestic facilities may not charge high clearance fees, the financial institutions that are members will not be operating in an internationally competitive way. Either way, businesses and consumers do not benefit from globally competitive financial intermediation.

It is clear that security for financial transactions is the sine qua non for electronic commerce. Without security, on-line payments simply will

---

4. Field research by the authors Catherine Mann in Taiwan and China; Sarah Knight in El Salvador and Catherine Mann in Sri Lanka, August 1998.

5. Field research by the authors and colleagues in Taiwan, August 1998; Bulgaria, October 1999.

disappear and many of the benefits of electronic commerce will not be achieved.

Most discussions of security focus on the potential for theft of credit card numbers. But equally important, and receiving greater attention now, is the potential for a legitimate credit card holder to use a card fraudulently on the web. For example, Mohamed Mustafa & Shamsuddin Co. (a department store in Singapore) was one of the early adopters of on-line selling in June 1998. However, in under three months, while the store had made on-line sales of S$2 million, credit-card fraud cases accounted for S$300,000 to S$500,000 (US$174,900 to US$291,500). Cardholders purchased and received goods, and then "charged-back" the transaction. (See below)(Yee 2000). Verification of the buyer by the seller is thus part of the security question.

What is the problem that sellers face? Suppose an online company receives a buy order with a credit card number. Although the number is encrypted (making the transaction secure from the buyer's standpoint), if the seller does not verify that the buyer was authorized to use the card, the seller is liable for the full amount of the transaction should the buyer defraud the company by charging back the transaction. If the seller has sent the products already, the seller loses out on both the value of the products and the remittance to the credit card company. Because international electronic signature technology is not fully developed, the seller must verify through either signature or through other means (such as matching address of billing and parcel delivery) that the buyer is authentic and authorized. Mustafa's no longer accepts on-line payment, but has fallen back to e-mail ordering, clearance, and then delivery. In the United States, some small electronics companies have been caught by the fraudulent buyer, the lack of authentication, and the charge-back liability to the credit-card companies. (*Business Week*, 4 March 2000.)

For small countries and SMEs to truly benefit from global electronic commerce they need global reach. Thus, security and authentication protocols have to protect them as both buyers and sellers and not be so expensive as to preclude their participation. Faster authorization from the firm to the credit clearing house will not solve the problem of authentication. Electronic signatures would allow authentication to travel electronically just as quickly as the authorization to buy and the funds to transfer. However, approaches to electronic signatures differ. Mutual recognition or common strategies have not yet emerged. Until they do, the financial infrastructure will be hobbled in its ability to deliver the services necessary to support electronic commerce.

Credit/debit-card companies clearly have an interest in ensuring that transactions are secure and authorized; indeed the major companies are important investors and users of the protocol Secure Electronic Transactions (SET). Yet this mechanism does not appear to meet the needs of users. Businesses and buyers are seeking other mechanisms that more cheaply enable cross-border electronic commerce. If they succeed, the position of the credit card could erode. Chapter 8 discusses security and authentication in more detail.

The Monetary Foundation of the Economy

Finally, financial intermediaries function as part of the monetary foundation of an economy under the direction and supervision of the central bank and regulatory authorities. Electronic commerce impacts the economy's monetary foundation and the conduct of the central bank, most notably in payment systems and also potentially in foreign exchange management (UNCTAD 2000; Group of Ten 1997.)

Full efficiency and realization of the benefits of electronic commerce depend on the rapid payment and settlement of accounts: The "plumbing" or payment-system relationships between the payment institutions (e.g., independent credit-card companies), financial intermediaries, and the central bank need to be efficient. If there is one clearinghouse for transactions, the most efficient use of that facility is to clear only the net transactions between the parties. This is the approach used most commonly by central banks and their domestic banks and by credit-card companies around the world.

Electronic commerce increases the demands on these clearing facilities. First, clearing needs to be speedy (because transactions are digital) and in real time (because transactions are 24/7). Thus the standard approach of settling accounts every day at, say, 4 p.m. exposes the financial system to "daylight" risks. Real-time gross settlement (RTGS) of transactions eliminates these exposures among intermediaries and the central bank, but requires much greater security and stronger technologies. Yet without RTGS, exposures representing uncleared transactions can build up at one point in the system, potentially destabilizing individual institutions and possibly the overall financial system if an institution becomes bankrupt between settlement periods. Without RTGS, exposures that build up during the day implicitly represent a subsidy to those with open "debts" to the clearing facility and a tax to those with open "loans" to the facility, unless a fee is charged or rebated in real time on those open positions— clearly something requiring very advanced technology.

If all transactions between a clearing facility, financial intermediaries, and businesses were domestic, a daylight bankruptcy could be handled with relatively little stress to the overall economy. However, because electronic commerce is global, these transactions will involve foreign exchange. Daylight exposures could represent a risk to the foreign exchange reserves of a country (particularly a small country), and in any case can pose difficulties to end-of-day management of foreign exchange through the central bank. While RTGS will not reduce the magnitude or volatility of intraday foreign exchange transactions, at least the central bank will not be surprised at settlement. Such surprises have been the source of much financial and macroeconomic distress, ranging from the Herrstadt Bank failure, to the failure of Penn Central securities, to the collapse of the Korean won in 1998.

This discussion of the need for real-time clearing, points to the near-term challenges facing governments that wish to maintain controls on foreign exchange usage in order to husband foreign exchange reserves. Full participation in electronic commerce for firms and consumers in these countries will be more problematic. Some countries allow exporters greater access to international exchange than other businesses (Morocco, for example). This strategy could limit the use of electronic commerce by indigenous small businesses that import in order to produce for a market niche in the external or even the domestic market. Saffron producers in the poor southern part of Morocco, for example, could retain more of the profits from the sale of saffron by developing a Web site to market their product internationally. To build this business, however, the saffron producers need imported hardware, web-design software, and perhaps marketing expertise; the present restrictions on foreign exchange may make it all but impossible to bring this to fruition.

A second problem of macroeconomic financial management that many developing countries face is the desire to maintain a closed capital account but an open current account. This strategy is made more difficult by electronic commerce because Internet transactions are not transparent to authorities. For example, government authorities cannot verify whether an on-line purchase was of computer software or a stock certificate. No product is delivered, and tracing the electronic trail to a bank yields relatively little information. In Sri Lanka, the authorities have approached this problem using both limits and voluntary compliance. Credit cards can be used to purchase anything from abroad, but the US dollar value is constrained by the relatively low SL rupee limits on the cards. In addition, the central bank has told domestic banks to remind their customers that purchases of foreign financial instruments are not allowed.[6] The authorities do recognize that these approaches are only buying time to put domestic and international clearing capabilities on a more solid footing.

Digital cash (chits created by selling on the Internet that can be used to buy on the Internet) can be created by agreements between firms and financial institutions. In some respects, digital cash simply continues the trend toward disintermediation of financial activity from traditional banks. Digital cash could become a new source of money and credit in

---

6. Field research by Catherine Mann, October 1999.

an economy, just as changes in ATM and "sweeps" technologies[7] have affected fractional reserve banking and the conduct of monetary policy. Digital cash could one day change the velocity of fiat money created by the central bank and may change the leverage that the central bank has over economic activity through instruments of monetary policy; it should be considered in the monetary policy process. (Group of Ten 1997) While many believe that digital cash will at some point be significant, it has not yet caught on. Barter, cash, and credit are firmly entrenched as the means for engaging in commerce and electronic commerce.

Digital cash, money laundering, and other cash-transfer capabilities are more easily available to more people and businesses via the Internet and electronic commerce; they may be undertaken by financial subsidiaries and nonbanks outside the regulatory sphere. The issues are not new, particularly since global capital markets have been electronic-based for some time. Nevertheless, since the Internet presents a new venue, a review of supervision is warranted. As has been the case in the past, policy coordination discussed in the context of domestic and multilateral oversight bodies will help avoid forum-shopping (GAO 1999).

Conclusion

In sum, the banking and payment systems need to be able to process transactions in real time, both domestically and in multiple currencies on international markets. One way to jump start this internally is to encourage participation in the local market by foreign financial institutions that already have this capability. The technology and knowledge transfers are important to improve domestic activities. Moreover, the partnership between international institutions with technology and local institutions with local expertise brings the domestic institutions into the global network of financial institutions.

As discussed further in chapter 8, allowing foreign competition via electronic means in the domestic financial marketplace is one way to achieve greater domestic competition. Many countries have only limited commitments for financial liberalization in the GATS. Electronic finance will enable domestic firms to access global capital markets for the benefit of the domestic economy. Therefore, countries should look upon electronic finance as a way to achieve global standards without using resources by a return to the WTO negotiations table.

---

7. ATM—and "sweeps" technologies—which allow banks to sweep their reserves holdings into interest-earning assets overnight and on weekends—alter the money demand function.

5

Infrastructure: Distribution and Delivery

Distribution and delivery round out the service-sector infrastructures critical to the development and growth of electronic commerce. In some ways this infrastructure is the most important, for distribution and delivery make possible the nexus between the electronic and the real-world marketplaces. While the electronic or digital delivery of goods and services is becoming more common, many on-line purchases must still travel via the physical world to their final destination.

What makes distribution and delivery critical is that all of the benefits and efficiencies engendered by the use of electronic commerce in purchasing—particularly lower costs and just-in-time production and ordering—can be quickly eroded if those purchases face inefficiencies in transit. Exorbitant costs, long delays, and damaged or lost shipments now plague electronic commerce purchases, particularly when they must travel internationally. Such inefficiencies signal to policymakers that if electronic commerce is to grow unimpeded and the investments that companies and countries make to get themselves electronic commerce-ready are to bear fruit, distribution and delivery when structures need to be modernized.

The Internet and electronic commerce can help solve the problem of how to improve distribution and delivery. Electronic commerce can reduce costs in terms of both time and error in paper work. Information flows between shippers, buyers, sellers, and financial partners can be improved.

The changes needed are not unlike those for telecommunications and financial services. Privatization, competition, and independent regulation together can reduce shipping costs and increase service. Such a policy framework can also help to improve a country's general economic health. But it may be more politically difficult for policymakers to introduce these changes into distribution and delivery because this area tends to be one of the most protected. Yet if left convoluted and inefficient, distribution and delivery could hinder not just the growth of electronic commerce but also a country's participation in the evolving global value-added chain of production.

Why Distribution and Delivery Are Important

Distribution and delivery are central to a country's macroeconomic health. Improvements to the infrastructure of distribution and delivery, which include the transport and postal infrastructure, are positively correlated with productivity gains. Also, value-added for the sector accounts for a sizeable percentage of total GDP and employment.

As growth increases, demand grows for distribution and delivery services, especially in developing countries. At the same time, because foreign aid for improvements to this sector are decreasing, creating the environment where the private sector can shoulder the burden of transport construction is crucial.

Consider these statistics:

- At the macroeconomic level, there is a positive correlation between the transport infrastructure and productivity. Not surprisingly, vehicle-intensive industries benefit most in terms of productivity from improvements to the transport sector, including road building (Fernald 1997).

- Value-added by transport is estimated to account for 3 to 5 percent of GDP, and 5 to 8 percent of total paid employment (World Bank 2000).

- Demand for transport, especially road transport, is growing one and a half to two times faster than GDP in most developing countries, though the percentage of transport infrastructure financing covered by foreign aid is decreasing (World Bank 2000).

Improvements to distribution and delivery not only enhance productivity but also create incentives for private sector investment. As the value-added chain of production becomes increasingly global, aided by technological advances, it is essential that the real-time processing of orders and fulfillment be precisely coordinated with distribution and delivery. This is particularly important in industries with numerous and complex steps along the value-added chain.

Where production, and distribution and delivery are not coordinated, the private sector loses the incentive to innovate and invest in new technologies. In Sri Lanka, for example, inefficiencies in customs clearance and air cargo make it more difficult for apparel producers to move to producing the higher value-added, upmarket designs demanded by stores in Western Europe. A partnership between the private sector, which is willing to invest in electronic commerce technologies, and the government, which needs to speed customs procedures as well as improve road and air facilities, would yield significant benefits to a country that depends on textiles and apparel for 10 percent of GDP and 40 percent of exports.[1]

Electronic commerce increases the importance of distribution and delivery to a country's economic health. As more companies from different sectors move to integrate electronic commerce into their production, the more global and tighter the value-added chain will become. Countries with sleepy, inefficient distribution and delivery systems will not be able to meet the private sector's need for fast turnaround and inexpensive transit. They risk being left behind in the globalization of production as well as the growth of electronic commerce.

While the importance of distribution and delivery to an economy tracks the growth of electronic commerce, the Internet can diffuse improvements to this sector throughout the economy (see figures 5.1 and 5.2). Customers anywhere in the world can now track their shipments over the Internet; even low-cost truck lines, discount air carriers, and ocean vessels offer services similar to those of high-end carriers like United Parcel Service (UPS) (*Wall Street Journal*, 4 November 1999, A1). Electronic bills of lading speed transactions between freight forwarder, carrier (air, sea, rail, or road), importer's agent, importer's bank, customs, and exporter's bank.[2] (*Journal of Commerce*, 21 June 1991, 1.)

At the same time electronic commerce, in particular B2C, creates new challenges for distribution and delivery. In physical stores, it is the customer who handles and pays for order fulfillment (by choosing the goods and paying for them at the cash register) and delivery (by transporting those goods home), at the expense of the customer's own time. In electronic stores, however, it is the seller's responsibility to coordinate order fulfillment and delivery. Even Wal-Mart is having a difficult time adjusting its logistics geared for store-based transactions to deliver on-line orders to individual customers (*The Economist*, 26 February 2000).

Many companies are responding by outsourcing their electronic commerce distribution and delivery. Retail operations can outsource to companies like Fingerhut and Bechtel that specialize in order fulfillment. Cisco Systems is working with Fed Ex to merge input orders in transit from factories in the United States, Mexico, Scotland, Taiwan, and Malaysia so

---

1. Field research by Catherine Mann and colleagues in Sri Lanka, October 1999.

2. The legality of electronic signatures is critical to make electronic bills of lading work (see Chapter 8).

Figure 5.1 Distribution of leading Internet applications in the global freight transport market

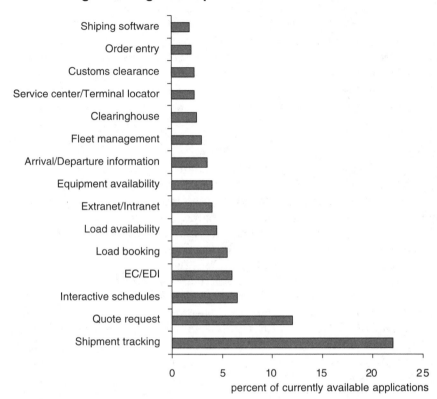

Source: UNCTAD (2000), 47.

that the parts can be assembled directly at the customer's location, saving Cisco considerable sums on warehousing (*Wall Street Journal,* 4 November 1999, A1). Similarly, Toshiba determined that it was losing market share to Dell Computer because it could not deliver custom-ordered computers as quickly; by outsourcing assembly to FedEx, it regained market share.

These efficiencies can be erased or even eliminated where competitive distribution services are lacking and high-end, rapid delivery companies like DHL, Fed Ex, and UPS or local counterparts are limited or prohibited altogether. One example of how the efficiencies of electronic commerce can be eroded by the inefficiencies in distribution and delivery is in El Salvador, where on-line buyers typically have items shipped to a post office box in Miami, where private courier companies like Gigante Express consolidate shipments for delivery to buyers. These buyers have benefited

Figure 5.2 Internet use in freight transport by region based on application count (percent)

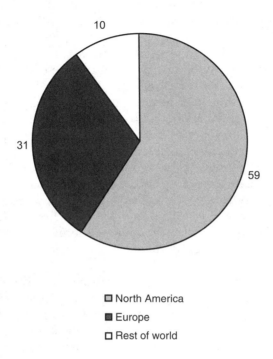

☐ North America
■ Europe
☐ Rest of world

Source: UNCTAD (2000), 49.

from the on-line global marketplace, but have had to sacrifice prompt delivery.

Policy Changes for Distribution and Delivery

Distribution and delivery for retail electronic commerce purchases often entail high shipping costs, long delays, and even missing or damaged products. Policymakers can work to improve the distribution and delivery sector, thereby encouraging the growth of electronic commerce, by following a general policy framework of privatization, competition, and independent regulation. It has been widely shown that such policies tend to reduce distribution and delivery costs and improve service.

Of all the service-sector infrastructures important for electronic commerce, perhaps the most difficult for policymakers to liberalize is distribution and delivery, precisely because it is the most protected. Protection discourages private investment. Indeed, as of December 1998, the transport sector in all developing countries accounted for only $14 billion in private sector investment, compared to $53.1 billion for the telecommunications sector, and $26.8 billion for the energy sector (Rogers 1999). Latin America and the Caribbean accounted that year for more private sector investment than any other region, in large part because of a general opening of service-sector infrastructures.

But private investment in distribution and delivery is increasing as many developing countries open up competition. The World Bank has documented the benefits that countries are experiencing from private provision of distribution and delivery services. In Colombia, for example, privatizing road maintenance has reduced costs by 25 to 50 percent. Labor costs are 50 percent lower in privatized rail services in Argentina and Brazil. Competitive franchising in bus operations has reduced operating costs by 25 to 40 percent in European countries like the UK, Denmark, Finland, and Sweden. In Venezuela the withdrawal of protection from state-owned monopolies has reduced shipping costs by 30 percent (Gwilliam 2000).

But there are many areas in the infrastructure of distribution and delivery where protection still exists and competition is limited. These areas vary by mode of transport and by region. It is up to policymakers to ensure competition exists along all modes. This is especially important for the fulfillment of electronic commerce purchases, which usually travel across national borders and use multiple transport modes.

One area for caution is the cross-subsidization from a distribution or delivery sector that remains protected to one where competition is increasing. Six years ago, UPS filed a complaint with EU competition regulators and the US-EU International Competition Policy Advisory Committee alleging that the German post office, Deutsche Poste, was using revenues from the sale of government land ($3 billion in 1998 alone) and from very high first-class mail charges to acquire private logistics, express and parcel companies that compete directly with UPS and other carriers (*Traffic World*, 31 May 1999; *The Economist*, 13 May 2000, 67-80). Moreover, although Deutsche Poste has invested substantial sums in e-commerce ventures (buying 10 percent of GF-X, an on-line freight exchange whose other owners include Lufthansa and British Air), it apparently has been losing money on its parcel freight business for years.

In Morocco, Fed Ex has to pay the state-owned post office a fee for every package the company receives or sends.[3] Also, the post offices in many countries, including the United States and Japan, are moving into

---

3. Field research by Sarah Cleeland Knight, 15 September 1999.

e- commerce offerings like on-line bill payment that compete directly with the private sector (OECD 1999b).

Digital Delivery

The digital delivery of inputs and final products is becoming increasingly important for electronic commerce, and it offers special challenges for policymakers. In particular, certainty and trust—especially in the preservation of intellectual property rights—is critical if electronic commerce is to grow unimpeded. (See chapter 7 for further discussion of intellectual property protection.)

The private research firm Forrester projects that as soon as 2004, one-quarter of Internet purchases will be delivered by digital download (Spiegel *E-Commerce Times*, 24 January 2000). The digital delivery of products like music and software is already common, and the private sector is working on other products for digital distribution. These products hold substantial benefits for developing countries in particular. For example, electronic books can enhance education in poorer and remote areas. And since prices for electronic technologies generally fall quickly, even the poorest of school districts might soon have better access to cutting-edge information.

Apart from intellectual property protection, key policy concerns that could hold back ubiquitous digital delivery are authentication and the treatment of digitally delivered products in trade negotiations by members of the WTO. These issues are also discussed in more detail in the next chapters.

Conclusion

Policymakers need to confront inefficiencies in distribution and delivery by ensuring that the sector is competitive across all modes. Active competition, both domestic and foreign, backed by independent regulatory agencies, can help policymakers circumvent the political obstacles to removing protections from this heavily entrenched sector. Only with low shipping costs, speedy delivery, and excellent service can the physical distribution of goods bought over the Internet grow unencumbered. Countries should use GATS 2000 as a starting point for analyzing their distribution and delivery systems.

III

OPPORTUNITIES AND CHALLENGES FOR GOVERNMENT AND POLICY

Introduction

On the one hand, the Internet and electronic commerce offer a great opportunity for government to reduce costs, streamline operations, and return higher benefits to taxpayers. The Internet can improve communication with citizens. Governments may be better able to perform key functions of human capital development using new technologies and the new environment. On the other hand, the current approach to some of these functions—for example, the current regime for raising revenue—may be pressured by the technological innovation, global reach, and information-rich but fragmented environment of the Internet and electronic commerce.

Governments also play a very important role in establishing the environment of certainty and trust that is key for the Internet to flourish and electronic commerce to yield both macro- and microeconomic benefits. Standards, protocols, laws, and regulations—such as technical communications and interconnectivity standards; security protocols; laws on electronic signatures, certification, and encryption; and privacy and content regulations—help to create certainty and trust for the purchase and sale of products over the Internet.

Some issues relevant for this environment of security and trust are not new. Standards for technical equipment have always allowed business fully to exploit new products and new markets, and economic activity has always proceeded more efficiently and smoothly when contracts are specific and businesses and consumers feel that they are protected from fraud.

But electronic commerce brings new trust issues to the forefront. It is now more difficult for countries to enforce their own standards, protocols, regulations, and laws with respect to e-commerce transactions, both because the Internet is transnational and because today's technology limits the ability of government to regulate electronic commerce. Moreover, many policymakers worry that attempts to enforce existing regulations on the Internet might curtail the growth of these new technologies. It is not always clear, therefore, what combination of legislation and private sector action maximizes the benefits of the Internet and electronic commerce.

Underlying many of these concerns, too, is a fundamental disquiet posed by electronic commerce: How much does this new way of trading internationally undermine national sovereignty? The Asian financial crisis, environmental catastrophes like Chernobyl, and the interplay of nuclear weapons with economic forces all demonstrate the constraints that governments face in exercising power in today's interdependent world. The Internet exacerbates this reality. It is redefining the powers and behavior of governments. Local, national, and international governments and forums and the private sector, both business and consumers, are grappling with issues ranging from taxes to privacy, from security to content, from consumer protection to intellectual property rights. These issues only begin to scratch the surface of what the electronic world implies for governance.

6

Government Operations: Tax Regimes and Administration, and Services

The basic economic activities of government are to raise and redistribute revenues and to provide public services. We can think of these activities as comprising the "business" of government. Just as private businesses are reaping efficiency gains from the Internet and electronic commerce, so too can government increase the efficiency of what it does as a business. Similarly, just as private firms are examining how electronic commerce alters the parts of the value-added chain that affect their core businesses, so too should government think about how to use electronic commerce to improve service to citizens. What is most important for governments is that increasingly, the jurisdiction of government authority is different from the economic marketplace.

Taxation and Tariffs

The evolving Internet marketplace has some important attributes (see chapter 2) that matter for tax regimes: global reach and value creation through information, product bundling, and production fragmentation. These factors will put pressure on existing tax regimes. Governments can ignore or try to offset these pressures. But, a more proactive approach, which is the approach being taken by the private sector in its activities, is to consider how the fiscal system might need to evolve. A final factor of importance, particularly for taxes, is that there is greater mobility and potentially greater economic anonymity for participants in this marketplace.

Global reach implies a great overlap of national jurisdictions. International coordination of tax policies, though not necessarily harmonization of tax rates, will likely be necessary in the future. Governments need to consider carefully how best to target the tax (and other parts of the fiscal) system to meet citizens' needs and social objectives of redistributing income. This may imply a fiscal system more focused on individuals and less on the corporation.

Hand in hand with generating *value added from information* and new markets is that value creation will be increasingly complex; it may be difficult to determine how or where value is created. Both value-added taxation of transactions and direct tax systems that depend on defining permanent establishment of corporations will fit poorly within the emerging reality of economic activity.

Finally, *greater mobility* of firms, potentially making transactions more difficult to trace, or even anonymous, put a greater premium on increasing the incentives for voluntary compliance and reducing the incentives for forum-shopping, both within and across jurisdictions.

On the plus side, the Internet and electronic commerce have great potential for reducing the cost of tax administration and for increasing the ability of the government to serve its constituents. Tax burdens could be lower on account of the greater efficiency of fiscal administration.

How Governments Have Responded

Death and taxes, or the death of taxes? It should come as no surprise that the question of how the Internet and electronic commerce will affect taxes and tariffs has received early and intense policy attention. Most analyses of electronic commerce, trade, and tax address how to implement existing regimes in the more complex e-commerce environment. This is understandable because business tax accountants, trade negotiators, and government revenue authorities have to deal *now* with the questions of, on one side, what duties do I owe to whom, and, on the other, how much revenue are we likely to collect.[1]

Governments generally do not want to take precipitous action. Maintaining a tax and tariff environment with clear rules is important for businesses, consumers, and government. But policymakers see the potential for a premature (and, they believe, undesirable) liberalization of trade and an erosion of their revenues. Governments have responded in both international forums and in their own marketplaces, inconsistently, and without foresight. This incremental approach increases the likelihood that

---

1. See *International Tax Review*, September 1999, for a review of how the following countries and regions are interpreting existing tax law in electronic commerce: Australia and New Zealand, Canada, Germany, India, Ireland, Israel, Japan, Latin America, the Netherlands, Singapore, South Africa, and the United Kingdom.

the evolving system will be distorting, with incentives to avoid or evade that will affect both domestic and international business and consumer strategies.

Government Discussions in International Forums: WTO, OECD

Governments have taken explicit action to keep electronic commerce free from customs duties. At the WTO Ministerial in Geneva in 1998, the members agreed to a temporary moratorium on imposing customs duties on electronic commerce and products delivered electronically. The decision was in large part a recognition that the rapid evolution of the Internet, particularly the greater use of digitized information, was blurring the traditional distinction between goods and services—a distinction of great importance under WTO rules and domestic tax regimes (further discussed below).

Since 1997 the OECD, in conjunction with nonmember governments and private groups representing business and tax accountants, has been analyzing how electronic commerce might affect international and domestic taxes. The outcome of that effort was "Tax Framework Conditions," which reaffirms five principles that guide governments generally in applying taxes: neutrality, efficiency, certainty and simplicity, effectiveness and fairness, and flexibility.[2] Tax neutrality and perhaps fairness appear to be the overarching principles as governments face e-commerce, although their interpretations of neutrality are not consistent (see discussion below).

The OECD's initial conclusion was that, generally, existing domestic and international tax systems could cope with the networked world (OECD 1997a). The indirect taxation areas targeted for further examination were cross-border application of consumption and value-added taxes, particularly the varying treatment of goods and services. In the area of direct taxation, the OECD's Model Tax Convention (the basis for many bilateral international tax treaties)[3] was generally thought to apply, with further analysis targeted at how electronic commerce might be treated under the rules of permanent establishment, how transactions might be defined as either business profits or royalty income, and how transfer-pricing rules might be affected. In fact, these areas targeted for additional OECD analysis are exactly the areas where governments are trying to extend existing tax law to e-commerce transactions, leading to inconsistent treatment of transactions, within and beyond countries' borders.

---

2. See http://www.oecd.org//daf/fa/e com/e com.htm#top e commerce.

3. Many countries have used the OECD Model Tax Convention as a blueprint for tax treaties that apportion responsibility and revenue to avoid double taxation of income earned through foreign investment. See http://www.oecd.org//daf/fa/treaties/treaty.htm. See also: http://www.oecd.org//daf/fa/material/mat 07.htm#material Model for the most recent information on the model convention.

Treatment of Indirect and Direct Taxes

Most countries have not faced the fact that applying customs duties or indirect taxes to cross-border sales will be increasingly difficult. In some countries, such as Morocco, tax authorities believe that their net is dense enough to capture transactions that should generate either a tariff or a domestic tax. In others, such as in Taiwan, the tariff implications of digital downloading are understood, and they are considering whether to set up mechanisms to apply tariffs to digital products, even though they acknowledge that international transactions of services are not subject to tariffs now.[4] For right now, research suggests that little revenue has been lost so far (UNCTAD 2000, Goolsbee 2000, and Mattoo and Schuknecht 2000). So governments have time to consider an approach that recognizes and works effectively with the changing economic environment.

The US states and the EU Commission are examples of tax authorities and jurisdictions that have started to make explicit recommendations for how to apply sales and value-added taxes to e-commerce transactions. Neither body fully recognizes that domestic decisions have cross-border implications. Inconsistent tax treatment of transactions between the United States and the European Union already has surfaced. The approaches taken by these jurisdictional units points out the challenges to be faced by other policymakers as electronic commerce expands.

In the United States, when Congress passed the Internet Tax Freedom Act it mandated review of the implications of electronic commerce for domestic sales taxes. The Gilmore Commission (see box 6.1) recommended that digital products downloaded over the Internet (software, books, or music) should not be taxed—and in the interests of tax neutrality, their tangible equivalents also should be tax-exempt. The issue of taxing services delivered over the Internet did not come up with the Commission because generally services are not taxed.

In contrast, the EU tax authorities are drawing a bright line between goods and services and to a greater extent than the United States already have drawn Internet transactions into their tax orbit. All electronic transmissions under the general term "soft goods," including downloaded software, digitized books, or architectural drawings, are services that should be taxed at the appropriate value-added tax (VAT) rates.[5] While the EU ruling would seem to simplify and increase certainty, in fact it does not because there are so many different rules for VAT taxes on services.

Moreover, the Europen Union places transactions under the purview of GATS in the WTO (WTO 1999). (As discussed below, the United States and other countries have effectively delayed characterizing these transac-

---

4. Field research by Catherine Mann in Taiwan, August 1998, and in Morocco, September 1999.

5. For an overview of the treatment of e-commerce transactions see http://europa.eu.int/scadplus/leg/en/lvb/l31041.htm.

Box 6.1 The US and domestic sales taxes: The Gilmore Commission

The Internet Tax Freedom Act took effect on October 1, 1998, and kept domestic Internet transactions free from any new taxes for three years; existing sales or use taxes apply, although they are difficult to enforce. The act remanded the question of how or whether domestic state and local sales taxes needed to be changed to an Advisory Commission on Electronic Commerce composed of business, government, and consumer representatives (the Gilmore Commission). When the life of the Commission ended (March 2000), members did not reach the required two-thirds majority to formally recommend a course of action to the US Congress. A simple majority called for a five-year extension of the moratorium on new taxes and simplification of domestic sales taxes, among other things. The Commission also recommended that digital products downloaded over the Internet (software, books, or music) should not be taxed, and, in the interests of tax neutrality, that their tangible equivalents also would be tax-exempt.[1]

Despite the obvious point that any decision about the treatment of cross-state taxes might affect the treatment of cross-border taxes or the effectiveness of international trade and tax agreements, it was not within the mandate of the Gilmore Commission to consider international transactions or taxes. So it did not. Meantime, Congress, in advance of the WTO Ministerial in Seattle, passed a non-binding "sense of the Congress" resolution that encouraged the US administration at the Seattle negotiations to try to make permanent the cross-border moratorium on customs duties for Internet transactions. The legislative language seemed to ignore the fact that domestic taxation of Internet transactions (as through sales taxes) represented a quite similar issue.

---

1. See Patricia Fusco. 2000. (31 March) http://Internetnews.com/ec/news/print0,,4_331801.html and Jeri Clausing. 2000. Foes of Internet Tax Ban Vow to Fight On, *New York Times*. http://nytimes.com.library/tech/00/04/cyber/capital/04capital.html (4 April).

---

tions for the purpose of WTO rules.) The EU approach highlights the inter-relationship between decisions in the trade and in the tax arena on how to treat e-commerce transactions.

Further, the European Union has proposed that businesses both within and outside the European Union apply, collect, and remit VAT taxes on products (including software, books, and music) purchased or downloaded from the Internet by non VAT-registered entities (usually individuals) (Andrews, *New York Times*, 2 March 2000).[6] It has suggested that non-EU firms should establish their tax identity within an EU locality in order to determine which rate of tax applies when they sell products B2B.[7] In the interests of tax neutrality, the EU approach implies that a

---

6. The amount of "lost" tax revenue from cross-border sales appears to be minuscule. Of greater likely import is the argued disadvantage of bricks-and-mortar stores vis-à-vis online merchants who have not had to collect VAT.

7. Document of the EU Commission regarding electronic commerce and indirect taxation: http://www.europa.eu.int/scadplus/leg/en/lvb/l31041.htm.

cross-border tax on sales of digital products should be collected by the foreign firm and remitted to the national authority rather than have a cross-border customs duty collected by an EU customs agent. This approach yields a unilateral and extra-territorial application of a national tax law.

Though sales and use taxes have received the most attention, properly accounting for the global distribution and origin of business income was an ongoing tax issue facing policymakers in both industrial and developing countries even before electronic commerce complicated matters further. Under the OECD Model Tax Convention, the authority to tax income in a particular country is limited to income earned by a "permanent establishment" in that country. International income tax treaties are designed to allocate income among the parties to the treaty and to avoid double taxation. However, many non-OECD countries do not subscribe to this convention, are not participants in international tax treaties, and view income earned by any assets in their country as falling within their tax jurisdiction (Maguire, *International Tax Review* September 1999, 3-12).

Moreover, countries do not classify income earned (business profits or royalty income) consistently. In March 2000, the OECD Technical Advisory Group (TAG), which included OECD member governments, nonmember governments, as well as business advisory groups, tabled for comment the Treaty Characterization of E-Commerce Payments.[8] It does not resolve the issues, although it presents the majority and minority views on how to treat e-commerce income. (Note that the TAG's mandate was simply to interpret existing tax codes, not to modify the tax code.)

How do some country practices accord with the TAG review? The EU application of VAT to all soft goods transactions does not accord with the TAG majority view, in which these transactions would generate income that would be taxed as business profits. In Israel, taxation depends heavily on the rights that are conferred when the digitized product is used, which follows the spirit if not necessarily the details of the majority view (Katz, *International Tax Review* September 1999, 65-6). In India, where payments for the use of online information, technical support, and software used to access a database would all be treated as royalty income subject to withholding taxes in India rather than the country of the multinational, the system appears to follow the TAG minority view (Basu and Visser 1999).

How Should Governments Be Responding?

Policymakers have made few changes to their tax regimes in light of e-commerce transactions. They have taken the existing tax regime as a

---

8. See http://www.oecd.org//daf/fa/treaties/tcecommpay.htm.

given; electronic commerce has been shoe-horned into that regime, while at least nominally following the OECD principles. Already this effort has created different treatment of e-commerce transactions inside and across borders. As electronic commerce becomes pervasive, governments must rethink their tax and trade regimes.

So how should they be thinking about modifying their tax and tariff regimes? On the trade side, there is a rising tension between the simple division of all transactions into goods or services. On the tax side, there is a rising tension between the domestic bounds (and legislative authority) of most tax regimes and increasingly global economic activity.

Tariffs in a Networked World

Electronic commerce poses a true challenge to the organizing framework of the WTO[9]—the classification of all cross-border transactions into either the General Agreement on Tariffs and Trade (GATT) or GATS. If this classification is maintained, should electronic commerce and digitized products be classified into GATT or GATS? The European Union advocates the latter; the United States (along with most other countries) remains agnostic.

Although this classification issue seems clear, questions remain. Products purchased electronically but delivered physically (such as books from Amazon.com) would appear to be subject to WTO rules on trade in goods: the same tariff would apply to the book whether purchased over the Internet or not, although on small-package imports, enforcement might be difficult. An architectural blueprint delivered electronically would continue to be classified as a service, where generally tariffs are zero. A non-tariff barrier, such as a professional license, might prevent this service from being offered if it were delivered physically, as by mail, but enforcing the barrier over a downloaded drawing might be difficult (as would enforcement of VAT on services as noted above). And consider software downloaded from the Internet, which may or may not exist on a hard medium such as a CD-ROM. Is this a good or a service? Would customs agents even know that a transaction on which a tariff should be paid had happened?

Applying taxes on both domestic and cross-border transactions causes even deeper confusion. The WTO moratorium on customs duties did not reach inside any country to apply to taxation of domestic sales over the Internet. Nor did it address how income earned over the Internet should be taxed. But, "domestic" tax systems are now applied in one way or another to cross-border transactions. For example, VAT systems apply taxes differently to cross-border transactions, depending on whether the

---

9. Electronic commerce and the WTO are explored more fully in Mann and Knight (2000). See also WTO (1997).

Box 6.2 Indirect tax systems

The VAT is a tax on supplies of goods and services applied at all stages of the production process. It is charged by the supplier and then credited by the users of the inputs in the course of doing business. Because each transaction leaves an invoice path, the VAT system essentially relies on double-entry bookkeeping by VAT-registered businesses on both sides of a transaction. The final consumer, not being a VAT-registered entity, ultimately pays the tax. Some businesses, such as financial intermediaries, find it difficult to get credit for VAT, so ultimately the financial institution pays the tax.

The US sales tax system is different in that final users (usually buying at retail) pay the taxes, usually on tangible property only (with exceptions), not on services. Business inputs generally are exempt from the tax. The administrative burden of the sales tax system comes principally from the 30,000 different tax rates that apply depending on location. Tax ignorance, rather than tax avoidance or evasion, is a real issue.

The goods and services tax used in many developing countries and in Canada and Australia is applied at the point of sale and collected by the seller. In the current economic environment in many countries, it is administratively straightforward, which enhances its popularity with governments. However, to avoid the distributional consequences of such a regressive tax (and of the US sales tax as well), there is often an extensive schedule of exceptions to the tax, including food, clothing, public transportation, and so on.

transaction is an import or an export.[10] Direct tax systems must determine how to tax income earned by a business in more than one country so as to avoid double taxation.

Thanks to the Internet, governments have had to grapple with how to mesh their domestic and international taxes and tariffs in a much wider range of cross-border transactions. For example, following the EU approach, if all e-commerce transactions are services, classified under GATS, they all should be taxed the same way. To do otherwise would imply inconsistent VAT treatment of electronic transactions within and outside countries. The approach the European Union has therefore taken effectively "harmonizes up" tax rates in order to maintain tax neutrality. In contrast, the Gilmore Commission embraced a bias toward lower tax rates by recommending that selected electronic soft goods and their tangible equivalents be sales-tax free. This "harmonizing down" may generate inconsistent tax treatment of purchases over the Internet and through other means of products not explicitly exempted. Over time, this approach could yield lower tax rates as more products are exempted.

Indirect Tax Regimes in a Networked World

Many tax systems depend on indirect taxes, such as sales taxes, VAT, or goods and services taxes (GST) to raise a substantial share of government revenues (see box 6.2). In the OECD, all the countries except the United

---

10. Importers include the VAT but exporters receive a credit.

States have or will soon have a VAT/GST system. In the countries of the European Union, VAT revenues account for about 30 percent of total tax revenues. In states in the United States, sales and goods taxes account for about 12 percent of total revenues, but can reach much higher percentages. In developing countries, VAT and GST systems are the mainstay for raising revenues.

Fifty years ago, VAT was simple to administer and audit. But times have changed, and VAT has not. International transactions were the first hurdle. Since VAT is supposed to raise revenues *within* a country or region, exporters receive a VAT credit rather than forward the tax burden to customers abroad, and imported products are assessed VAT so as not to have a tax advantage over domestic competitors (OECD 1997b, 16).

Services transactions are the next hurdle. They fog the clarity and simplicity of the VAT system. For many services, VAT is collected by the supplier on the presumption that the customer needs to be relatively near to receive the services. However, for intangible or intellectual services (copyrights, licenses, advertising, professional and consultant services and financial transactions) VAT is already paid by the customer. A customer who is not VAT-registered is supposed to declare the transaction and pay the tax (OECD 1997b, 15-9). Certain types of service firms, including financial intermediaries (and looking forward, possibly ISPs) often cannot recover VAT so they pay it as if they were the final consumers.

If digitized products are treated as services, VAT gets more murky. For products like books and music, VAT treatment as a good yields lower tax rates than VAT treatment as a digital product classified as a service. On the other hand, if the digital product is downloaded from a site outside the VAT jurisdiction (for example, the European Union), no VAT gets paid unless the customer declares and pays it.[11] So one product and one tax regime yield three possible tax rates—hardly the OECD goal of "neutrality, efficiency, certainty and simplicity, effectiveness and fairness, and flexibility."

These examples are simple: E-commerce transactions are becoming much more complex. For example, ISPs are the "portal" or starting point for many activities on the Internet. ISPs could end up playing tax collector (as the delivery man does with flowers) or paying the service VAT themselves (like financial intermediaries). Clearly the incentives are to move ISP activities offshore so as to blur responsibility for paying the VAT, and indeed some European ISPs have set up in low-tax jurisdictions.

The sales tax issue facing the United States yields additional examples of tax strategizing. BarnesandNoble.com incorporated as a separate business entity from the parent stores so as to avoid "nexus" (or physical presence) and the requirement to collect sales taxes on all its sales through the

---

11. Pending the acceptance of the proposal of the European Union, discussed earlier.

Internet. However, because the entities must remain separate, business synergies and brand extension cannot be exploited. For example, someone who buys a book online (because they like the additional features of book reviews available online) cannot go and pick up the book at a local store branch.[12]

The Internet marketplace characterized by cross-border trade in information-rich products will increasingly strain the VAT system. Economic transactions created from a variety of international and domestic locations make it increasingly difficult to apply the credit-invoice method of accounting for VAT at each stage of the value chain. There is no value chain; this is a *network* creating value. Or, how should VAT be applied to a continuous stream of services? For example, how should Bloomberg's real-time access to stock-market data streams, international financial reporting, and on-line discussion topics be classified under VAT?

Cross-border services are particularly murky because they often incorporate both a domestic and a foreign element: data-processing or consultant services, for example. The burden of VAT on transactions will be increased with the complexity of production. For example, "build to order" computers get parts and inputs from numerous sources, some have preloaded software, and the final assembly may be done by the delivery firm. VAT administration in this case will be hugely complex. Governments must look at other ways of raising tax revenues.

Direct Tax Regimes in a Networked World

The other major form of taxation is direct taxation of corporations and individuals. In the United States, income taxes account for 60 percent of total federal tax revenues, with about 80 percent of that coming from individuals. Generally, income earned by US firms and individuals are taxed at US rates regardless of where the income was earned—this is *residence-based* taxation. Developing countries to varying degrees also depend on income taxes, including taxation of income earned by nonresident firms operating in the country—*source-based* taxation.

Because source- and residence-based taxation in the global context must yield double taxation of some income, tax treaties attempt to allocate income earned to the source and the residence according to "permanent establishment" and give tax credits to minimize double taxation (Lukas 1999, 26-7; Sher 1999). Value creation in the global networked marketplace will increasingly strain the definition of permanent establishment, making the allocation of income increasingly difficult. The threat of double taxation increases, too, along with the incentives for noncompliance, particularly by mobile firms.

---

12. IBM "e-business solutions" division has a clever advertising campaign that plays on the potential synergies between online and on-site stores that could be exploited by IBM software. It is clear that software is not the only hurdle.

The definition of a permanent establishment rests on two foundations: (1) fixed place of business or physical presence,[13] and (2) dependent agents who, among other activities, can conclude contracts on behalf of the corporation as a normal course of business. "Permanent establishment" runs into trouble in the networked world. First, the information-based and network-based creation of products means that physical presence is much less important as a criterion for participating in value-creation (consider software code). Second, the mobility of information-based firms not only undermines physical presence but also calls into question the characterization of dependent agents. Finally, the complexity of Internet marketplaces (consider the virtual auctions and exchanges for B2B transactions) challenges the notion that there is a single "head" to the organization that could help define either physical presence or dependent agent.

Most practical attention to this question has focused on Web sites and servers: do they constitute physical presence if located within a country or do they constitute a dependent agent even if they are not located in a country but are "open for business" there? There is no consensus yet, but arguments revolve around the range of activities available on a Web site and the extent to which a server is tied to a firm.

Servers control data flow among computers on a network. Web sites are the presentation of information or locus of activity for a firm. Data flows can be initiated by the server and the Web site (for example, targeted advertising) or by the user (for example, information-gathering). Do these activities represent permanent establishment?[14] If the server or Web site merely broadcasts information or advertising, it does not contact the purchaser, but the purchaser contacts the Web site, which then contacts the server. In this case, it would seem impossible that the physical location of the server or the Web site would constitute a dependent agent or nexus.

Looking forward, however, what if the server can individually target a consumer in another country? Does this change the notion of permanent establishment, dependent agent, or nexus? Consider two buyers in the same country who digitally download the same product from the server. One buyer was contacted by the server in a targeted effort; the other happened upon the Web site and downloaded the product. How can it make sense (and what kind of incentives result) when the two purchases are treated differently for tax purposes? One can imagine a service where the server would automatically route purchases through the least-taxed environment, much as call-back telephone services re-route and reduce telephone charges for callers in countries with high telephone tariffs.[15]

---

13. However, facilities for inventory or for collecting information do not confer physical presence.

14. The analogy in the context of US sales tax is nexus.

15. Two other issues for the direct tax of corporate earnings are treatment of royalty income and transfer pricing. Income earned from sales and that earned from licenses or royalties are taxed at different rates, and the nature of network transactions that give rise to royalty

In the end, the complexity of Internet products challenges the formula for allocating income according to how much value was created or income generated by certain geographical locations and types of transactions. Trying to fit Web sites or servers or royalties into the existing definitions of permanent establishment or character of income is just putting a finger in the dike. As Internet products and activities increasingly are composed of information and intellectual property, the character of income will be even more difficult to determine. As technology increases the range of delivery devices and the web presence for Internet activities to telephones and TVs, permanent establishment will be eroded. Governments must look at single tax rates for all types of business income and for ways to avoid having to allocate income to different countries.

Trusted Third Parties and Shoring Up Existing Tax Systems

The characteristics of the Internet marketplace challenge the foundations of both main tax systems. VAT cannot adequately handle information-rich products, and is administratively cumbersome for global transactions and bundled value-added. Direct tax regimes that depend on concepts like permanent establishment to allocate income will come under stress because Internet transactions are so complex. Both systems will be confounded by the mobility of firms.

Can technology itself be used to shore up the existing system? Governments could use the Internet's information-tracking capability to track the origin and destination of each transaction or each element of a product bundle, and apply the appropriate tax. Would this violate other rights of the citizen? Would it require extraterritorial reach of the taxing authority or lead to trade barriers at borders?

Several proposals being considered to improve the yield of existing tax regimes rely on private software and trusted third parties (TTP) to stand between the buyer and seller to calculate, collect, and remit the tax to the appropriate jurisdiction. In the United States, the Gilmore Commission reviewed this proposal in its investigation of alternatives to state sales-tax administration. The European Union proposed a narrow variant when it argued that international credit card companies should collect and remit VAT taxes. The Indian Central Board of Direct Taxation has suggested that an international organization be set up to "detect commercial and

---

income differs by country. The higher information content of network products highlights these disparities and creates incentives for tax avoidance.

Transfer pricing on the Internet is potentially a larger issue, but not necessarily as a form of tax avoidance. Transfer pricing, or more generally the pricing of transactions at non-transparent, non-arms-length rates, is more likely for complex information-based products where network effects are a key component of prices. Or consider auctions where prices are endogenous to the number of participants in the market. For more on practical analysis of transfer pricing rules, see Rolph and Niederhoffer (1999).

financial transactions on the Internet." More broadly, a World Tax Organization could be the venue for discussing these and other issues (Tanzi 1999).

While technology and TTPs could be the tax collector, to do so with sufficient depth and care would yield a lot more information about the details of the transactions and the activities of participants than when the retail store or delivery truck driver collected the VAT; an individual's identity and purchasing habits would be in the hands of a TTP. The information collected by TTPs for tax purposes could reveal proprietary business strategies or alliances (terms of each sale and who with). At least some of the TTPs would have to have international reach, since the most difficult aspect of e-commerce taxation is cross-border activities.

Depending on TTPs to administer taxes raises issues going far beyond the tax regime, on which governments already disagree. First, having a private institution administer taxes should give governments pause. If TTPs work for electronic commerce, why not privatize the whole tax system? Second, what would be the jurisdiction of TTPs? They would operate on behalf of a government, yet outside its political jurisdiction. Therefore, international agreements as to the scope of their activities would be required. Third, what about enforcement? With a multilateral authority like the WTO, countries have found inside-the-border interference to be anathema[16]—and the objective of this entity would be to tax! Finally, the TTP would have to be paid. History shows that when private entities are paid to raise public funds, it is difficult to come up with politically or economically "incentive-compatible" contracts.

Moreover, there are already differences between the European Union and the United States (and other governments as well) over the cross-border transfer of data, particularly personal information. In the international tax context, the European Union would have to allow the TTP to collect such data. Yet the European Union has already significantly restricted the collection of such information for commercial purposes. In contrast, the United States allows these data to be collected for commercial use, but prevents the US Internal Revenue Service (IRS) from collecting it as a matter of course (see the discussion of privacy in chapter 7). The conflicts over what data would be collected for tax purposes could impact business strategies, much as tax differences now do.

The TTP approach exemplifies a common theme in the policy arena: issue convergence and policy overlap. Whereas technology could help a TTP to improve the working of current tax regimes, privacy policy would dampen the desire to adopt this approach. More generally, policy

---

16. Consider the difficulties in Seattle in November 1999 on issues of labor and the environment. Competition policy, another "inside-the-border" issue, has regularly been rejected as not within the purview of the WTO.

approaches to one issue increasingly impinge on how governments pursue policies on another issue. Policy choices are increasingly interdependent.

Towards an Alternative Tax Regime

The new international marketplace is network-driven and information-rich. Value is created around the globe in complex, real-time interactions. In contrast, tax and tariff laws are based on domestic jurisdictions, simplistic notions of the value chain, and contiguous production and consumption. The systems are static, founded on rules formed incrementally by case law or infrequent multilateral negotiations. So far most governments treat electronic commerce as just another way to engage in trade, not something that will warrant a change in policy.

The validity of domestic-based tax systems increasingly is being pressured by the global environment and a new economy that is dynamic. Policymakers must take a proactive stance and think about what an international tax system might look like. Now is the time—when what is being done on the Internet and through electronic commerce is still relatively easy to understand—to seek the most efficient and effective way to raise government revenues. VAT is not the answer; neither are direct taxes allocated on the basis of permanent establishment or on residence (see box 6.3). Soon electronic commerce will generate ever more complex interactions of media, people, information, and things. The current incremental strategy will yield an increasingly rules-driven and fragmented system that invites evasion and forum-shopping, is costly to administer, and does not support the maximum benefits that can be achieved with Internet-based commerce. Governments must rethink their tax regimes.

Government is in the business of raising and redistributing taxes and providing public services. That business will continue. Policymakers should take the opportunity now when the challenges are "big enough to see, but small enough to solve" (Leavitt 2000) to chart the direction toward a simpler, fairer, and more liberalizing approach to taxation and tariffs.

These observations lead us to examine a significant source of income for raising tax revenues: labor compensation. How does the global network impact its taxation? Among the sources of income to tax, labor wages has probably been the least affected by the Internet and electronic commerce. Labor, by and large, remains within the same political jurisdiction as the tax authority.[17] How much it pays its labor is one of the economic transactions that a firm keeps close track of, even in the Internet marketplace. Labor income can be taxed using methods that include reporting, audit, or declaration.

---

17. This is not to say that labor cannot move; but it is relatively less mobile than firms, particularly at the margin of electronic commerce.

Recognizing the increasing complexity of allocating income, a residence- based system has been suggested, among others by the United States in one of the earliest concept papers addressing the issue.[1] Residence would be defined as where the firm most central to the bundled product maintains its "strongest ties." This concept is murky; does it mean residence of incorporation, in which case tax avoidance through havens becomes a likely problem. Moreover, countries, ranging from Australia to India and South Africa that depend on source-based direct taxation of income for tax streams would lose revenue under a residence-based scheme, unless an adequate tax-transfer mechanism could be implemented. Many governments see the residence-based scheme as unfair and too favorable to the US because of the high percentage of multinational firms, and increasingly high-tech Internet firms, that are resident in the United States but create products using value-added from around the world.

International cooperation to allocate tax revenue is an obvious requirement for such a system, but having the United States effectively hold the pursestrings for another government creates difficulties. Moreover, the residence-based scheme does not solve the inherent difficulty of accounting for different sources of value-creation when the value-added derives from a global network of inputs. The foundation for allocating tax revenues must depend on something other than trying to break down the production process to determine how much value was added at what point and in which location.

---

1. US Department of the Treasury (1996).

Taxing wages does not solve all problems. Wage income is only one source of labor's remuneration. Increasingly in the United States, for example, stock options and other benefits and bonuses are part of the employment package. Differential treatment of stock options between the United States and the European Union has already affected the behavior of labor and encouraged it to become more mobile across the Atlantic.

Cross-border information flows of wage and benefit statements from international firms raise privacy concerns. Moreover, a firm must be willing to comply with an extraterritorial request for information, although this is less onerous than actually collecting and remitting taxes. International cooperation among governments and firms remains paramount.

The questions of fairness and compliance inevitably arise when labor income is taxed relatively more than capital income. Tax evasion of both labor and capital income taxation in many countries is why they have chosen the VAT, GST, or tariff systems. These are not new issues, but the reduced ability to tax value-added, transactions, or corporations raises the stakes for finding appropriate answers and charting a course toward changing tax regimes to reflect the new realities.

A superior outcome can be achieved if governments recognize that the Internet and electronic commerce warrant a regime shift. New ways of creating value and jurisdictional overlaps will demand more international cooperation and new tax regimes that raise taxes on the bigger targets (income, not transactions) and at the ultimate source of value (people, not firms). Along with the objective of tax neutrality, this should engender a downward bias for tax rates on transactions and a global low rate on corporate earnings. Broad based and progressive taxation of personal income can generate sufficient income for government programs, and can be more socially aware and progressive, as well as administratively less burdensome.

Government Administration

Government as a big business has a lot of "customers." Even where a government is streamlined, it has a large labor force, is a big spender, and interacts in many ways with its citizens. Streamlining administrative costs, improving the efficiency of procurement, and making communication with citizens as well as other governments more transparent are ways the Internet and electronic commerce can improve the relationship between governments and its constituents.

Administration

Many countries have already put information about government structure and services online. Increasingly they are using Internet technology and electronic commerce to streamline paperwork and payment processes within agencies, between agencies, and between the government and its citizens. This use of the Internet and electronic commerce can be a powerful force for building the infrastructure that supports private electronic commerce. In addition, it can help foster confidence in electronic commerce. But whereas the government may indeed play a key role in jumpstarting Internet usage, it should be willing to relinquish its position to private firms as they offer superior services.

Providing information about government agencies and activities online can help coordinate federal and sub-federal missions. In Morocco, the Ministry of Information Technologies is putting information about all federal ministries and departments online (including all business regulations) and is installing computers in regional government offices to make this information accessible to the public. Heads of the main sub-federal units (the Wali) are considering whether to connect their regional headquarters "downward" to provinces and prefectures as well as "upward" to the federal site. Not all levels of government are convinced of the benefits of information-sharing (indeed, an individual bureaucrat's power can be constrained by openness of information on the Internet).

Government Web sites can improve communication between government and citizens. In Bulgaria, the government Web site includes the text of all laws as well as pending legislation.[18] All agency directors have e-mail boxes—and apparently they even answer their mail! In other countries, addresses but no links are available. In still others there are e-mail links, but no one answers the mail. The promise of the Internet for improving the relationship between government and its citizens is in its capability for interactive two-way communication, in contrast to papers or TV broadcasts, where information generally flows only one way.

Governments can also partner with private firms that have built regional Web sites. AfricaOnline was founded in 1994 by three Kenyans who had studied at US universities, then returned to Kenya to open ISPs with operations in Kenya, Côte d'Ivoire, Ghana, Tanzania, and Zimbabwe, and links to businesses in and local information about Swaziland and Uganda. On the private sector part of their Web site, there is information about businesses as well as NGOs and aid agencies. On the official links, there is information about the economy, links to chambers of commerce, and so on. The links to the Côte d'Ivoire site are in French, the official language.

Government experimentation with Internet and electronic commerce can reveal weaknesses in key infrastructures that support electronic commerce (as well as economic development more generally). Within government, one agency's desire to use the Internet and electronic commerce might be stymied by another agency's regulation of infrastructure. This can be a powerful force generating change within a government. Two years ago, the agency for tax administration in Taiwan began making tax forms and information available online; the objective was to get citizens used to using the Internet and to eventually file taxes online, ultimately lowering the cost of tax administration. However, the first year of the experiment, it took so long to download the information and forms and the telephone charges were so expensive that a person who used the online method ended up being "taxed" to pay their taxes on-line.

In contrast, the Brazilian government has paved the way for on-line filing using secure connections and easy payment: typing http:// www.receita.fazenda.gov.br takes the tax payer to a simple tax preparation site where personal information can be typed in, and taxes paid via bank card. The ability of the Brazilian banking system to facilitate these transactions was a prerequisite for electronic commerce by the government.

A different problem has faced tax authorities in Sri Lanka and Morocco, for example. Internet technology in both countries could significantly reduce the cost of tax administration, which at present is based mostly

---

[18] Field research by Randy Hartnett in Bulgaria, October 1999, and Catherine Mann and Sarah Cleeland Knight in Morocco, September 1999.

on paper and pencil. In Sri Lanka, a high fraction of the tax revenue raised is needed to administer the taxes, so there is a real potential for efficiency gains; in Morocco, the myriad special excise taxes create a fragmented tax system that invites evasion and abuse and is costly to administer. In both countries, additional efficiency gains and enhanced transparency would come from linking domestic tax systems with the customs systems.

The main barrier to moving forward is the shortage of human capital to modify existing systems and to write software. The Sri Lankan tax ministry is seriously understaffed. The Moroccan tax authorities have the hardware but would be helped by having a "best practices" manual sourced from experience by other developing countries on how to apply electronic commerce to the tax system.[19]

A partnership between private business and government projects can help bridge the human capital needs and may jump-start government use of the Internet. One strategy is to create an elite consulting service to the government for information technology—an "IT strike force." While it would be best to source the team from the domestic economy, some members of the group could come from abroad, funded by international agencies. This consulting group would work with tax agencies within a country to bring their operations online, and then train agency staff to take over once the consulting team has gone.

The advantage of the IT strike force is two-fold: (1) Government agencies often find it difficult to compete with private-sector salaries—particularly as the IT sector starts to develop within a country and as people who are trained have opportunities abroad. (2) Most government agencies do not want or need a large permanent IT staff. A strike force can "connect" the agency, train the people, and then move on. Even better, the strike force could help ensure that the systems of various agencies are interoperable.

Procurement

B2B electronic commerce is reducing costs and increasing efficiency in resource use in private-sector manufacturing by 10 to 50 percent (see chapter 2). Why shouldn't government get the same benefits? The Internet and electronic commerce offer several ways that government procurement can be made more efficient and transparent.

First, simply putting online information about upcoming procurements, with contract specifications, enhances transparency. Moreover, embedding well-functioning search engines within a procurement site enables small and medium firms to more actively compete with large firms. Going

---

19. The electronic commerce roundtables sponsored by UNCTAD are helping developing countries learn from each other what are the most successful approaches to common challenges.

further, putting winning bids and performance evaluations online raises the professionalism of government procurement as well as of the firms that satisfy the contracts, and helps citizens see for themselves how the business of government is conducted. Finally, putting government administration of procurement online can be part of a virtuous cycle that strengthens other key infrastructures, such as telecommunications and financial intermediation. All this increases the likelihood that government (and thus the taxpayer) will get its money's worth, and that the process is fair and open.

For example, the Taiwanese government is putting its register of upcoming government contracts on its Web site. The Mexican government is putting $25 billion of government contracts out for bid on compra*net*. Mexico's site will include information on competing bids (*Business Week*, 1 November 1999). Chile wants to procure everything from paper clips to toilet paper through its Web site. The pressure by the government to benefit from electronic commerce may push ahead the telecommunications deregulation process (*Latin Trade*, March 2000, 38).

As the private sector builds e-commerce capability within a country, the government gains a powerful partner to further efficiency and openness in procurement and administration. In the United States, for example, two years ago, the Defense Logistics Agency (which is responsible for $900 billion in procurement for defense forces worldwide) constructed EMall for small-ticket purchases (under $2,500). The procurement officer goes to EMall, finds the part or product that s/he needs, orders it, and receives it the next day, rather than filling out a paper form, mailing it, waiting for another procurement office to ask firms for bids, and then waiting for the part to arrive. EMall streamlines the process so much that in 1999, the cost of some of these purchases was cut in half (*Washington Post*, 5 April 2000, 5).

A private sector firm, FedCenter.com, has since opened a procurement site especially for business-to-government sales. It includes vendor descriptions (whereby firms can identify themselves by geography or targeted groups, such as small, women, or minority-owned business), as well as links to the Federal Acquisition Regulations. On another private sector site, GovWorks.com, the government purchaser can look for auctions, which can reduce procurement costs even more. These private and government sites that occupy different parts of the market space are linked to each other.

To maintain competition and incentives for further private innovation, it is important that the government-initiated sites and the private-sector sites operate on a level-playing field and work to complement each other. In Singapore, for example, a private-sector site and a government portal are both vying for the market for procurement of office products and recruitment services (Levander, *Asian Wall Street Journal*, 25 October 1999).

Some governments are big sellers as well as big buyers. At China-TradeWorld.com, foreign businesses can buy everything from shoes to tools from any of 180,000 state-authorized firms. This site also contains trade and financial news from the official Chinese Trade Ministry, English translations of Chinese laws, and translation services (Hillebrand, *E-Commerce Times*, 28 February 2000). Looking forward, it will be important that Chinese authorities allow small private enterprises to trade with business abroad, rather than acting as the sole portal and authorizing agent for e-commerce trade between China and the rest of the world. China's concern is that poor quality and performance of some firms could undermine buyers' interest in Chinese products. This is a legitimate issue, but can be addressed though private-sector certification rather than state certification (see chapter 7).

Over time, as both the government and private-sector firms integrate electronic commerce into their operations and strategies, and as necessary financial and telecommunications linkages are enabled, private-public partnerships will bridge Web sites. Over time, the private sector can play a more major role in government administration. In the United States, egovnet.com, and in the UK, ecommerce.iosis.net, are private-sector sites that present current regulations, for example for professional licensing, and allow professionals to renew their licenses online by linking to the appropriate governmental (federal or subfederal) site. In the United States, for example, GovWorks.com offers a range of activities for the individual-to-government relationship, such as the ability to pay parking tickets, real estate taxes, and so forth.

Even if only information about administrative guidelines is available online, it increases the likelihood that such guidelines will be administered fairly by local authorities. For example, foreign businesses desiring to start activities in Morocco have complained about obscure regulations and of the near-requirement to hire a local facilitator. Because the Moroccan government would like to encourage new enterprise (both foreign and domestic), it is moving to put the regulations for business activities online so as to enhance transparency and regularize administration. This is also giving the government the opportunity to review its guidelines to determine whether they still serve their intended purpose. The WTO government procurement agreement is a framework for information transparency and fairness (see box 6.4).

Communication

The Internet greatly increases the capability of a government to communicate with its citizens and of governments to communicate with each other—enhancing cohesion within political boundaries and defusing cross-border conflict. Government could become more responsive to citizen concerns and better explain the rationale for government policies.

Box 6.4 The agreement on government procurement in the WTO

Government procurement of products and services for its own purposes is an important share of total government expenditures, usually estimated at 10 to 15 percent of GDP. It thus has a significant role in domestic economies.

While governments usually try to get the best value for their money through open and nondiscriminatory procurement regimes, sometimes they try to use the procurement process to achieve other domestic policy objectives, such as promotion of local industries. This kind of discrimination may be overt, as when it is mandated by statute, or more covert, as when foreign products and services face barriers in trying to compete for government business. Typical barriers are set up through selective tendering, technical specifications, and, most commonly, lack of transparency in tendering procedures, including contract awards.

Government procurement of both goods and services was effectively omitted from the multilateral trade rules. Discriminatory government procurement does cause international trade distortions; there is increasing awareness of its trade-restrictive effects. Also growing is the desire to close these gaps in trading agreements. The first steps to bring government procurement under international trade rules were taken in the Tokyo Round of Multilateral Trade Negotiations. The Agreement on Government Procurement (GPA) was, however, amended several times before it was signed when the WTO was established on 15 April 1994.

The GPA establishes rights and obligations among its members with respect to their laws, regulations, and procedures for government procurement, of which the cornerstone is nondiscrimination. Article III:1 states that parties are required to give the products, services, and suppliers of any other party to the agreement treatment "no less favorable" than what they give their domestic products, services, and suppliers. The GPA also permits parties to modify this if certain procedures are followed (article XXIV:6). The agreement does not apply to all government procurement; exceptions are allowed for developing countries in certain situations (article V) and for noneconomic reasons such as national security, public morals, public order or safety, human, animal or plant life or health, and intellectual property (article XXIII). Thus, not all WTO members are bound by the agreement, making the GPA "plurilateral."

Source: The WTO Web site, http://www.wto.org.

Many governments in developing countries have begun to provide more information on government activities on the Internet. This helps reduce the costs of communicating (of particular value in large countries) and helps to forge common bonds among citizens who are far apart.

Of course, some governments are concerned about the communication capabilities of the Internet. China and Singapore, among others, try to selectively filter information for their citizens. But censoring the Internet is difficult, and it could erode the increased transparency and trust that should be the outcome of government online.

The Internet improves communication among countries within a region, often to help promote discussion of common concerns. For example,

USAID's Leland Initiative is working to increase communications among policymakers in East African countries on common approaches to technology uptake as well as to assist in democratic institution-building. The Eizenstat Initiative focuses, among other issues, on water usage by countries in Mediterranean Africa. SIDSnet (the Small Islands Developing States Network) brings together 42 nations to discuss common issues, such as tourism, energy, ecology, and resources (Human Development Report 1999, 60).

The promise of the Internet is that a government will be able to do more for its citizens at less cost. By increasing the effectiveness of government activities, the quality of the relationship between government and its citizens should increase: importantly, citizen well-being generally will be enhanced. A key caveat is that technology alone cannot promote well-being: people remain the key ingredient. Using technology to create a virtuous circle where it reduces costs, raises awareness, and supports skills, which in turn leads to more effective use of technology, is the ultimate objective of government intervention. (A complete discussion of this topic is in chapter 9.)

7

Government and the Environment of Certainty and Trust

Mancur Olsen, the Nobel prize-winning economist, addressed the legal foundations for market development in his last book, published after his death (Olsen 2000). He noted that when legal foundations are lacking, economic transactions tend to be anchored in spot markets in time or geography. To encourage economic transactions to take place beyond spot markets, to where time or space separates the transaction, requires a promise that after one half of the transaction is complete, the other half will occur in the future or at some other place. As discussed in the context of the economics of the Internet marketplace, an essential force for value creation comes from exploiting such markets in time and space. Olsen's remarkable insights support the critical importance of legal foundations for electronic commerce—without ever mentioning the Internet!

Fostering this environment of certainty and trust requires governments to both intervene and forbear. On the one hand, government must put into place the framework: the codification of rules, enforcement, and consistent application. On the other hand, government need not intervene to determine what technological solutions might best fill the legal frame. It is not the job of the law, but of technology, for example, to derive the means to ensure the validity of electronic signatures, although case law may tell which technological solution best achieves the legal objective.

But is the legal framework sufficient to create the certainty and trust needed to encourage the growth of electronic commerce? Or is government intervention necessary to ensure that users will indeed use the Internet and gain its benefits? And under what jurisdiction do laws and regulations operate? Electronic commerce is global; legal jurisdictions, unless agreed to multilaterally, are local or national.

Legal Framework

In order for electronic commerce to flourish, a commercial legal framework needs to be in place to recognize, facilitate, and enforce electronic transactions worldwide. Most laws and policies governing the physical world apply generally to the Internet, even if they were written before the advent of electronic commerce, though some modification may be necessary. Countries anxious to promote electronic commerce may be tempted to write laws and regulations specific to electronic commerce. Instead, general commercial law, including contract rights and intellectual property protection is needed to promote development; it can then be adapted if necessary to accommodate electronic commerce.

National and international efforts to date have been directed at building the legal and technical infrastructure—the validity of contracts, protection of intellectual property, and standards and protocols—to ensure the interoperability of the Internet. Recognizing the global reach of the Internet and of electronic commerce implies an international approach, since contracts will not be enforceable if only one country recognizes the legal validity of an electronically signed contract. Similarly, intellectual property will not be adequately protected if only a handful of countries provide copyright, patent, and trademark protections; computers will be unable to communicate unless there are standardized interfaces connecting networks that permit interoperable applications.

One approach that promotes international coordination is drafting model laws and uniform rules, conventions and treaties, and technical standards and protocols. To the extent that countries adopt similar legal and technical bases—either through government agreement or private sector acclamation—potential conflicts are minimized. Governments can use these tools to inform national laws and policies. For example, the United Nations Commission on International Trade Law (UNCITRAL) has adopted model legislation for international contracts and is working on uniform rules on electronic signatures; the World Intellectual Property Organization (WIPO) has drafted new treaties; and international groups, both government and private, are promoting standards and protocols.

National efforts need not be identical—either in law or through technology applications—but they must be internally consistent and internationally interoperable. Divergent national approaches resulting either from the failure to adopt legal protections or from raising barriers, will adversely affect electronic commerce to everyone's detriment.

Some countries, including the United States and the European Union, have legislative bodies that must pass and implement legislation at both federal and subfederal levels. Tensions can result from differences in the pace of legislative change at the two levels, as well as cause tussles over jurisdiction. These problems within countries and legislative regions are the precursor to similar issues to be played out globally. Observing how the United States and the European Union face these issues can be insightful. Much of this section therefore will examine the United States and European Union as representatives of alternative approaches to both jurisdictional overlap and the need for policy interoperability.

Commercial Code and Contracts

National and international efforts now underway to address legal rules for electronic commerce are primarily adapting contract law. UNCITRAL has been the focal point for efforts to develop model legislation to guide the use of international contracts in electronic commerce. While specific contracts between parties could resolve legal issues raised in conducting business electronically, UNCITRAL concluded that relying on local law was unsatisfactory. As a result, it adopted the Model Law on Electronic Commerce in 1996. This is a set of internationally acceptable rules and principles to guide states in removing legal uncertainties arising in the electronic environment.[1] The UNCITRAL model law, endorsed by business groups like the International Chamber of Commerce, has been enacted by a number of countries.

In the United States and the European Union, the operational unit for commercial law is at the subfederal level. Within the United States, the Electronic Signatures in Global and National Act of 2000 embodies the general principles of the UNCITRAL Model Law, but state law has jurisdiction and must be revised. The National Conference of Commissioners of Uniform State Law, the American Law Institute, and private sector groups like the American Bar Association, are promoting the Uniform Electronic Transactions Act (UETA). UETA relies on existing principles of contract law; its objective is to establish legal equivalence between electronic records and signatures and paper and signed documents; it is the first comprehensive effort to adapt state law to electronic commerce. However, not all states have signed on, nor must they, making elusive the common contract framework necessary for the growth of electronic commerce.[2]

In contrast, the European Union, in response to concerns that existing national rules on the formation and performance of contracts were inconsistent, proposes to establish a coherent legal framework for the develop-

---

1. The model law has rules to validate and recognize contracts formed through electronic means; set requirements for contract formation and governance of electronic contract performance; defines the characteristics of a valid electronic writing and an original document; provides for the acceptability of electronic signatures for legal and commercial purposes; and supports the admission of computer evidence in court. See http://www.uncitral.org.

2. As of April 2000, 7 states had adopted UETA and 27 more had legislation pending. In facilitating a uniform domestic legal framework for electronic transactions, UETA may provide an international model.

ment of electronic commerce within the Single Market. The European Parliament formally adopted the Directive on Electronic Commerce on 4 May 2000, and member states must implement it within 18 months from publication in the Official Journal of the European Union.[3]

Will mandates at the federal level yield standardization where common approaches and certainty are needed? Not necessarily. On the one hand, the Directive provides that electronic commerce service providers are subject to national laws of the *country of origin*, which implies that such business activities need not be consistent with the laws of 15 different member states. On the other hand, the Commission's proposed regulation on jurisdiction and enforcement of judgments in civil and commercial matters[4] provides that in international on-line contract disputes, a consumer can seek redress *in his/her own country* if the seller approached the consumer through ads. This draft directive could require companies to comply with 15 different sets of consumer protections. Thus, even mandating a "federal" or EU-level directive does not necessarily standardize approaches. Efforts to address the inconsistencies between the EU directives are underway (Mitchener, *Wall Street Journal*, 22 November 1999; Greenberg, *E-Commerce Times*, 1 November 1999).

The US and EU examples show that there are two types of inconsistency that governments need to consider in trying to promote certainty: One is between legislative bodies at *different levels of government*; the second is across functional bodies or agencies *within a governmental level*.

Security: Encryption and Authentication and Certification

More than 80 percent of companies indicate that security is the leading barrier to expanding electronic commerce with their customers and partners. After the February 2000 hacker attacks paralyzed several popular Web sites, surveys showed that nearly 60 percent viewed the attacks as a "watershed event" for US electronic commerce, 65 percent would be more cautious when doing business online as a result of the attacks (Information Technology Association 2000), and 70 percent were not comfortable providing credit-card information over the Internet (Center for Democracy and Technology 1999). It is not just the consumer who is concerned: The May 2000 Love Bug virus cost companies billions of dollars

---

3. The directive addresses treatment of electronic contracts, the definition of where operators are established, transparency and information requirements for operators and commercial communications, liability of intermediary service providers, dispute settlement, and the role of and cooperation between national authorities. See Directive on Certain Legal Aspects of Information Society Services, in particular electronic commerce, in the internal market (Directive on Electronic Commerce) at http://www.ispo.cec.be/commerce/legal/legal.html.

4. A revision of the Brussels convention.

as their internal computer systems crashed and communications were disrupted.

Security implies that consumers and businesses can be confident that

- communications and data are safe from unauthorized access or modification,

- sellers and buyers are who they say they are, and

- both the individual transaction mechanisms and the overall network are secure.

Promoting secure systems and certifying the authenticity of parties to a transaction are essential to a climate of trust for the purchase and sale of products over the Internet.

While a range of technologies, techniques and protocols promote secure Internet transactions, the primary ways to establish security and trust on open networks has been through two major technology applications—encryption and authentication.[5] Authentication techniques, including digital or electronic signatures and certification mechanisms, help to ensure the origin of the data (authentication) and verify whether data has been altered (integrity). Encryption helps to keep data and communications confidential.

How has electronic commerce changed the environment and put a higher premium on security? The Internet uses an open, nonproprietary protocol that allows for more global marketplace participation, from large to small firms and consumers, as well as multiple jurisdictions. It operates much more quickly, requiring that money and products be transmitted or mailed simultaneously rather than sequentially. It is also more anonymous, with fly-by-night companies potentially operating outside the reach of authorities.

Encryption

Encryption is widely regarded as the most promising answer to the problem of securing electronic transactions. Lawrence Lessig, an expert on the legal aspects of the Internet, asserts that "encryption technologies are the most important technological breakthrough in the last one thousand years" (Lessig 1999). Encryption is the transformation of data based on the operation of mathematical algorithms, which reduce messages to a set of numbers that can be decoded only by those who have the algorithm

---

5. Early examples of security protocols for online transactions like using credit-card information over the Internet were Netscape's secure socket layer (SSL) and the secure electronic transaction (SET) protocol adopted by credit card companies, but both were only partial solutions to the security problem.

key that created the coded text.[6] Encryption represents the locks and keys of electronic commerce, enabling individuals to keep data and communications confidential as they are transmitted over the Internet.

Electronic mail, on-line banking, Internet credit-card purchases, electronic taxes, and medical records all use some form of encryption technology. As more businesses and individuals come online, the need for strong, reliable encryption technologies will increase. Its use is likely to become ubiquitous.

The widespread use of encryption, however, raises fundamental law enforcement and national security problems. The same technology that guarantees secure and private transactions for consumers can also be used by criminals and terrorists to hide their illegal activities. Intelligence gathering by governments for national and foreign policy purposes depends on access to information. The more data encrypted, the more difficulty intelligence agencies have in collecting information. Because of these legitimate and competing objectives encryption policy has been one of the most contentious electronic commerce-related issues within the United States, and between the United States and other countries. Encryption policy exemplifies the problem of both overlapping jurisdictions as well as issue convergence—that is, policies broached by one government will impact another—and second, even within a country, policymaking objectives overlap so that policies to achieve several objectives cannot be made independently.

In an attempt to balance national security and domestic law enforcement concerns with the need for security and trust in electronic transactions, the United States had restricted exports of "strong" encryption.[7] Export controls have been the primary means to limit the proliferation abroad of encryption technology that intelligence and law enforcement groups find difficult to break. Within the United States there are no restrictions on the use or strength of domestic encryption, in part because of the US domestic political culture.[8]

Other governments face the same commercial, security, and law enforcement concerns, but their approaches differ. Many countries (including France, China, Israel, Russia, and South Africa) restrict domestic use of encryption products. Laws in Singapore and Malaysia require

---

6. For a detailed explanation of encryption, its applications, and types of encryption, see http://www.rsasecurity.com/rsalabs/faq/1-7.html.

7. The strength of encryption—how easy it is to break the code—depends on the algorithm: The greater the number of possible keys, the longer it will take to crack. DES, the data encryption standard, is 56-bit encryption, which means that 100,000,000,000,000,000 keys are used. Adopted in 1976, it remains the official US standard for encryption today. See Singh (1999).

8. Some members of the law enforcement community do want to restrict the domestic use of encryption (arguably a more effective means of control than export controls).

users to disclose their encryption keys or face criminal penalties (Clausing 2000b). Earlier this year, China announced plans to ban companies from buying products containing foreign encryptions, and to require foreign firms to register their software with the government. The change in US policy (see box 7.1) means that other countries that had depended on the United States to prohibit the export of strong encryption are now considering domestic controls.

Because of the tensions between the law enforcement, security, and commercial communities, multilateral coordination of encryption policies has been limited, although there has been discussion in the OECD. Its 1997 Guidelines on Cryptography Policy offer basic principles for formulating national policies to secure electronic commerce transactions; in 1999, OECD produced an Inventory of Controls on Cryptographic Technologies. The primary international instrument for export controls on encryption products is the Wassenaar Arrangement, an informal group that coordinates the export control policies of 33 nations. Because of the significant national security implications of encryption, the United States discouraged international institutions from addressing the issue other than through the Wassenaar Arrangement.

As one of the earliest users of the Internet, with an industry at the forefront of encryption methods, the US experience is worth reviewing to see how the problem of issue convergence played out. Several lessons emerge from how the United States tried to reconcile the competing interests of law enforcement, security, and commercial gain.

First, the attempt to restrict the proliferation of strong encryption abroad failed. In fact, it encouraged foreign firms to create their own encryption products—firms that the US government cannot directly regulate and which compete directly with US companies.

Second, the attempt to mandate a specific technological outcome—key escrow, key recovery, or recoverable encryption—was largely unsuccessful. The fact that some firms did respond to the pressure and produced recoverable products shows, however, that government actions can still influence the market, even when the policies are not successful. However, influence fell far short of an optimal solution.

Moreover, this experience offers evidence that governments should work to facilitate technologies that meet public policy *objectives*, rather than try to mandate a technological *outcome*. Given the competitive world economy, government restrictions without multilateral agreement are bound to be futile.

Third, there were (and continue to be) costs to government intervention. In this case, government actions actually impeded the growth of electronic commerce, since time and money were spent trying to push the market in a different direction from where innovation and the global industry were moving. US firms lost market share.

Box 7.1 US encryption policy

The evolution of US encryption policy over the past decade provides an example of government efforts to reconcile the competing objectives of national security and law enforcement with the desire to promote electronic commerce.

US policy has been characterized by one attempt after another to mandate the development and use of a specific type of encryption application. In 1993, the US government announced the "Clipper Chip," which would be attached to a telephone and protect private communications. It used a key escrow system whereby two keys would be deposited with two separate government agencies, which law enforcement officials could access under certain circumstances. Predictably, industry and privacy groups rejected the proposal.

In 1995-96, the government revised its policy several times to relax export controls, provided that a key was escrowed with a USG-certified agent, not the USG. It also established the basis for a "public key infrastructure" system, which many experts believe could ultimately provide the basis for a secure environment. The administration finally settled on a policy that allowed the export of 56-bit or longer encryption, but only if US companies committed to develop "key recovery" products. Such products would permit the recovery of encryption keys, thereby allowing law enforcement officials access to the text of the communication under legal authorization. The administration's efforts amounted to a type of industrial policy in which the government leveraged firms' need to export to promote a technological solution that was optimal for government.

The policy of trying to mandate key recovery encryption engendered strong opposition from US high technology firms, who feared that export controls would result in competition abroad from companies not subject to comparable restrictions. At the time, US companies had most of the world market share in encryption technology. Privacy advocates also opposed the policy as an unwarranted intrusion on individuals' rights to ensure the privacy and security of their electronic communications. In addition, a blue-ribbon panel of the National Research Council issued a report in 1996 detailing the growing vulnerability of computer networks in the information age and the importance of encryption; it recommended the relaxation of export controls.[1]

(*continued next page*)

Finally, how encryption unfolded is a useful reminder that, in an age of revolutionary change, new thinking on issues like national security is essential. Important concerns about Internet technology can often best be addressed and potentially fixed by modifications to the same technology. This is clearly a task for the private sector. While it is appropriate for governments, on behalf of society, to identify needs and set public objectives, government regulation is likely to hinder optimal solutions.

Encryption is potentially the answer to the most difficult public policy issues related to electronic commerce, especially privacy. Encryption technologies can put decisions in the hands of users, letting them choose the degree of security or privacy their values require. The proper role of governments seeking to promote electronic commerce is to encourage the development and widespread use of this critical technology.

On the other hand, traditional societies or countries more concerned about domestic law and order and fundamental national security than is

Box 7.1 (*continued*)

In the face of mounting business and privacy opposition, and Congressional threats to eliminate encryption controls entirely, the United States significantly relaxed its policy in early 2000 to allow for the export of any encryption product regardless of strength to most customers with some minor exceptions. The policy shift, characterized by US government officials as helping business and promoting electronic commerce, was seen by many as a repudiation of US efforts to mandate a specific type of technology, but was nonetheless welcomed by high tech firms and US allies.[2]

Although the United States eventually was forced to abandon its policy, the attempt was not without costs. Whereas US companies making encryption products had few competitors in 1993, today there are many encryption firms—Brokat in Germany and Baltimore Technologies in Ireland among them—that have experienced phenomenal growth, due in large part to US restrictions. Despite industry opposition to the key recovery policy, many firms did actually develop products with recovery features built in, especially software firms.[3]

1. National Research Council Computer Science and Telecommunications Board (1 May 1996).

2. Secretary William Daley in US Department of Commerce, press release, "Commerce Announces Streamlined Encryption Export Regulations, 12 January 2000.

3. Lessig, 1999, 52. Included in the list of companies that produce recoverable products are IBM, Network Associates, the owner of PGP, and Cisco as part of a router.

---

the United States are likely to resist the widespread use of encryption by their citizens. International discussions may help alter their view of the balance of benefits of the global network against the limitation of domestic jurisdictions. These discussions may also make clear the limited effectiveness of domestic approaches.

Authentication and Certification

Electronic or digital signatures[9] are used in electronic transactions to identify parties, authenticate messages and information, and verify that data have not been altered. Authentication techniques, which include digital or electronic signatures, can be implemented through different technologies depending on the needs of the parties and the transaction. Such methods are not new—passwords and other means have been used for years in EDI transactions—but today there are a wide variety of authentication methods.

---

9. Authentication includes digital signatures and other forms of electronic signatures—terms have been used interchangeably, creating confusion. The differences are the subject of international discussions, but for simplicity, *authentication* refers to the larger class of electronic applications whose function ranges from identification and authorization to legal recognition, thereby covering electronic signatures as well as other technologies.

Authentication techniques linking individuals and entities in the electronic environment are less meaningful if they are not accompanied by certification mechanisms. Certification authorities (CA) or other certification methods are independent means of verifying transactions and parties in the electronic world. A CA establishes trust by authenticating the identity of participants to an on-line transaction, providing legally-binding proof of messages sent over the Internet, and verifying the integrity of the information exchanged. Numerous private companies provide these certification services, as they have for years, without the benefit of legal protections or government approval.[10]

Internationally, the issue of authentication has been broached primarily in three different venues: UNCITRAL has been dealing with the legal issues, OECD the policy framework, and standards bodies like World Wide Web Consortium (W3C) and the International Organization for Standardization (ISO) on the technical standards. The private sector has contributed significantly to these bodies, including through the International Chamber of Commerce's GUIDEC—General Usage for Internationally Digitally Ensured Commerce—which provides definitions and best practices to facilitate a global framework to ensure commerce over electronic media.[11] As with encryption, a key issue in the context of authentication and certification is technology neutrality: Because the Internet is so dynamic, it is important that policymakers not codify a particular technological solution into standards or laws.

UNCITRAL has been drafting uniform rules to support the use of electronic signatures, as well as reviewing the legal aspects of digital signatures and certification authorities. Because authentication technologies evolve rapidly, the UNCITRAL Working Group adopted a technologically neutral approach to avoid excluding future technologies from the scope of the uniform rules. The draft rules, therefore, cover all forms of electronic signatures and authentication techniques, and address standards that certification authorities should meet.[12] Similarly, the OECD affirmed a nondiscriminatory approach to electronic authentication, and members have committed to amend laws and policies that may impede specific electronic authentication mechanisms.

However, the fact that such rules are not binding has led the United States, Japan, and France to call for an international convention on elec-

---

10. The US government has supported legislation to protect CAs from liability, believing that legal protections would encourage more widespread use of certification mechanisms.

11. http://www.iccubo.org/home/guidec/guide.asp.

12. Also addressed in the draft are the principle of party autonomy, presumption of signing and originals, duties and responsibilities of signature holders and CAs, and recognition of foreign certificates. See http://www.uncitral.org/en-index.htm for the Draft Uniform Rules on Electronic Signatures.

tronic transactions. A binding convention would embody principles of party autonomy and technology neutrality in choosing electronic authentication methods, as well as establish minimal rules that prohibit paperless records and signatures from being rejected in court simply because they are electronic.

In 1998, OECD countries adopted a Declaration on Authentication for Electronic Commerce at the Ottawa Ministerial Conference. The declaration stated principles encouraging the formulation of electronic authentication policies with minimal government regulation, technological neutrality, and party autonomy. The OECD has also addressed international interoperability and mutual recognition of CA. This is important because certifications issued in one country might not be recognized in another, especially if some countries require licensing and will not accept certifications from unlicensed foreign CAs. The OECD also prepared an Inventory of Approaches to Authentication and Certification in a Global Networked Society. Their survey found that most countries have taken one of two approaches: Comprehensive measures enabling digital signature technology, or a minimalist technology-neutral approach that simply establishes the legal validity of any kind of electronic signature.

The technical aspects of authentication and certification have been addressed by the W3C in its project to use digital signatures and certificates and other technologies comprehensively to help users find effective ways to represent digitally signed assertions and endorsements that extend beyond the identity and integrity functions. Meanwhile, the ISO and Internet Engineering Task Force have been working on technical standards development.

As with taxes (chapter 6) and contract law, nations that have both federal and subfederal jurisdictions are challenged to achieve consistent domestic solutions given the overlap in jurisdictions. The US and EU approaches represent two alternative strategies.

At the federal level in the United States, Congress passed legislation in June 2000 to establish a uniform national framework for electronic transactions. The legislation grants electronic signatures the same legal force as traditional paper signatures, endorses a technology-neutral standard for electronic authentication, provides that federal rules will not preempt state law covering electronic agreements, and provides certain legal protections for consumers.[13] For their part, the states have enacted or are working on legislation recognizing the validity of electronic signatures, with most states having adopted minimalist enabling proposals to ensure that electronic signatures are not denied legal effect simply because they are electronic.[14]

---

13. The Electronic Signature in Global and National Commerce Act 15 is expected to be adopted in 2000. See Olender (2000).

14. Forty-one states have taken some action to address electronic transactions. See Internet Law and Policy Forum (2000a).

The European Union has taken a different approach. Prompted by concerns that differing national standards, as well as a lack of mutual recognition, could fragment approaches to electronic commerce and on-line services within the European market, the European Union drafted initial measures on digital signatures in 1997. The proposal was modified and adopted in 1999 as the Directive on a Community Framework for Electronic Signatures, which establishes rules for security and liability for transactions in all the member states. While the European Union's objective is to recognize electronic signatures as legal irrespective of the technology used, the Directive may in fact create a preference for particular types of electronic authentication and a presumption that electronic contracts signed using the government-endorsed methodology are legally binding (Pincus 1999).

Many countries now have laws relating to electronic signatures, and even more have proposals pending. Such measures are increasingly important to the growth of electronic transactions, especially since many countries still require prior written agreement for contracts to be valid between parties not in the physical presence of each other.[15]

The most common approach, generally adopted before 1999 by countries such as Argentina, Colombia, Germany, Italy, South Korea, and Malaysia focuses on digital signatures only and a regulated approach to CAs. Similarly the Indian Parliament in May 2000 passed legislation to establish the legal validity and enforceability of digital signatures and electronic records. More recent initiatives like those in Mexico and Canada in April 2000 may indicate a trend toward addressing electronic authentication and certification issues more broadly and flexibly, rather than just endorsing digital signatures.

In sum, disparate approaches to electronic signatures can create obstacles to electronic commerce.[16] Clearly, there are differing standards on multiple levels—state, national, and international. Some entities—subfederal as well as national—have adopted measures favoring digital signatures to the exclusion of other technologies.

Given that the market has not coalesced around one authentication method, and given the pace of technological change, prescriptive legislative approaches to security, authentication, and certification are not optimal. They undermine the network benefits of global electronic commerce. Policymakers should provide a flexible legal framework that makes electronic signatures valid, and allow the market to choose the technical means of meeting consumer and business security needs.

---

15. Such is the case in Mexico, which necessitated the May 2000 amendments to its Civil and Commercial Codes regarding electronic transactions. See http://bakerinfo.com/ecommerce.

16. The OECD is surveying its members regarding national laws and regulations that may act as obstacles to the use of electronic signatures. The results, which are likely to be available late this year, could spur activity to harmonize national approaches.

The lack of a uniform international framework for electronic authentication and certification may well be slowing the widespread use of electronic signatures. As electronic transactions using authentication methods become more commonplace, problems with inconsistent approaches are likely to increase if key issues such as mutual recognition across borders are not addressed. International discussions like those in the OECD and technical bodies should be expanded to include more countries so as to promote consistent authentication principles and interoperable policy internationally. It is important that the private sector actively engage with policymakers to ensure interoperability of both technological solutions and policy approaches.

Standards

As noted previously, standards and protocols are an important part of a legal framework for electronic commerce that promotes an environment of certainty and trust. Standards may be national and international as well as formal and informal means to ensure the interconnectivity of computer and telecommunications networks. Collectively, these technical specifications allow different products and services to work together so users around the world can communicate independent of the type of computer, ISP, or network used. "In effect, the global information infrastructure will be a federation of heterogeneous networks operating via standardized interfaces for the interconnection of networks and which allow applications to be run across them with seamless interoperability." (Arzano 1997).

How standards are developed varies from informal dialogues among industry representatives like the Internet Engineering Task Force (IETF) and W3C, to international bodies such as the ISO, the ITU, and the Internet Corporation for Assigned Names and Numbers (ICANN). For the most part, the private sector has led the way in setting the standards for electronic commerce, aware as it is of the danger of prematurely locking in standards that can be overtaken by technological advances and market preferences.

The standards process is necessarily dynamic, continually evolving as technology itself changes. Adaptability and dynamism is key:

> If several years ago, a standard-setting body or a government agency had sat down and tried to define electronic commerce standards or structures, no person, no matter how enlightened, could have hoped to envision the future and develop protocols to serve all the needs that have emerged. . . . No standard-setting body could hope to replicate the innovations that will be introduced according to the demands of commerce itself (Hillebrand 1999a).

Examining the approaches of the United States, the European Union, and Taiwan offers insights on why different sets of policymakers choose one type of intervention over another. These alternative approaches may yet yield interoperable outcomes.

The US government has consistently promoted the position that the marketplace, not governments, should determine technical standards (A Framework for Global Electronic Commerce 1997). While encouraging the private sector to take the lead in setting standards, the US government informally works with industry, primarily through the Commerce Department's National Institute for Standards and Technology (NIST). NIST is a neutral forum for bringing together broad industry representation and facilitating the dialogue necessary to address standardization.

This informal process of dialogue with industry stands in marked contrast to the EU system. With a long history of regulatory barriers as a result of the diverse manufacturing standards within European countries, the European Union relies on more formalized structures and a centralized process to help set European standards. As a result, European countries have tended to dominate the ISO process. American companies have expressed concern that European countries may be using the standards-setting process to favor European manufacturers. But US firms gain global recognition and reach when they conform to ISO standards. So, it is the neutrality of the standard-setting body that is at issue.

In some countries, such as Taiwan, the government has thought it desirable to choose among standards that are being set by the private sector internationally and exhort domestic entities to adopt that standard. The belief is that this approach will save time and effort for the domestic private sector, which can then expend its energies on innovation in other areas.[17] To the extent that there is an internationally agreed standard, this approach—where the government informs the domestic private sector of the outcome of the international contest—may be valid. Once a country reaches the international technological frontier, this approach is less viable.

The balance is between interoperability and dynamism. Interoperability need not mean that single, uniform solutions are applied to electronic commerce (Pincus 1999a). Local requirements dictate differing implementation, but the more interoperable these different approaches are, the more electronic commerce will be facilitated. Industry representatives have worked effectively in international standards-setting organizations to set voluntary standards. To achieve network benefits (discussed in chapter 2), the private sector has a strong incentive to set standards to enable interoperability as well as dynamic change. Government-mandated approaches tend to remove incentives for private-sector innovation. Consequently, policymakers should facilitate private-sector efforts within an

---

17. Field research by Catherine Mann and colleagues, August 1998.

international, voluntary, and consensus-based environment. They should not mandate standards for electronic commerce.

Intellectual Property

Generally, the architects of intellectual property protection laws must balance the need to protect intellectual property that is expensive to produce but easy to replicate with the desire to promote competition and further innovation.[18] Characteristics of the Internet and electronic commerce—information rich, network effects, global reach, rapid technological change—accentuate the importance of and challenges to intellectual property protection.

Consequently, an analysis of intellectual property protection must proceed along several fronts at once. Intellectual property law needs to address the *extension* of protection to materials transmitted over the Internet, as well as the delivery mechanics. It needs to address the *scope and length* of protection for business methods used to conduct electronic commerce and to collect information into databases. While the way forward for policymakers is convoluted and murky, suggesting a considered approach, technology and businesses are galloping forward at breakneck speed. Will the pace of technology and business obviate or undermine policymakers? Or will policymakers misjudge the extent, scope, and length of protection needed to support innovation, impeding the growth of global electronic commerce?

Intellectual property protection for software related to the Internet and electronic commerce is increasingly exposing issue convergence and jurisdictional overlap. For example, the approach to intellectual property protection affects other policy concerns, including consumer protection. In addition, just when international cooperation on intellectual property protection has started to bear fruit in the context of WIPO and WTO Trade Related Intellectual Property (TRIPS), such agreements may be so broad as to stifle the dynamic e-commerce environment and, in particular, the prospects for developing countries and new business.

Although e-commerce policies across the board are in a state of flux, policies for protecting intellectual property are in a particularly dynamic phase. Several examples will help show the different angles that policymakers must face and address. These examples suggest that a single approach that covers all types of intellectual property related to electronic commerce will be very difficult to craft.

---

18. See Keith Maskus (2000) for a remarkably comprehensive analysis of the economics of intellectual property, subsequent policy issues, and empirical analysis.

Why Raise the Issue of Intellectual Property?

As discussed in Part One, information is an increasingly important component of the product bundle, and information, by itself, has the attribute that it is noncontestable (the information can be used by more than one person without being used up). As discussed in Part Two, digital delivery of perfect copies is increasingly possible and indeed desirable. Looking at intellectual property law and electronic commerce through this lens, the enormous potential of electronic commerce cannot be realized without assurance that a seller's intellectual property will not be stolen, and that buyers are confident they are obtaining authentic products. Clear and effective copyright, patent, and trademark protection are necessary to protect against piracy and fraud on the Internet (see box 8.4 for more discussion).

On the other hand, interoperable computer methods that build on existing platforms for electronic commerce increase the value of the network to everyone. Indeed, such open standards and protocols have spurred the exceedingly rapid development of the Internet and electronic commerce thus far. Similarly, because of network effects, information can have increasing value, as more people have access to it, use it, and augment it (consider an auction site, for example). Therefore, IP protection that limits the ability of firms to create interoperable software will constrain the value of the whole network, as well as keep out new firms and participants. This kind of intellectual property protection could not only slow the growth of electronic commerce generally, it could exacerbate the divide between early adopters and later entrants.

Issues for Transmitted Materials

The issue of intellectual property for transmitted materials is probably more clear-cut, in that the nature of electronic commerce and the availability of new technologies make it relatively easy to circumvent controls and to widely distribute illegal duplicates. Consequently, this issue was the first that national and international bodies addressed. However, there are still numerous questions about the reach of this protection.

In December 1996, under the auspices of the WIPO, nations joined to create the foundation for strong IP protection on the Internet. Two treaties updating the Berne Convention—the WIPO Copyright Treaty and the WIPO Performances and Phonograms Treaty—were negotiated. These treaties require adequate and effective protection for copyrighted works and sound recordings in cyberspace, including the communication, reproduction, and distribution of electronically transmitted data. Both treaties cover technological protection, copyright management information, and the right of communication to the public. The treaties also permit countries to implement provisions in accordance with differing national legislation, and provide for exceptions to rights in certain cases that do not conflict with a normal exploitation of the work and do not unreasonably prejudice the legitimate interests of the author (e.g., fair use). The treaties will enter into force upon ratification by 30 states.[19]

However, key elements of implementation of these agreements were not addressed in the new WIPO treaties, including third-party liability, application of the fair-use doctrine, and limitation of devices to defeat copyright protection. In these three areas, the pace of technological change is forcing signatories to figure out how to adjudicate protections within the realm of intellectual property itself, and moreover, how to balance IP protection and other protections with policy mandates, such as consumer protection.

For example, what rights and obligations are associated with having links to sites that facilitate decoding of copyrighted data? Can companies that link to other sites be prosecuted for violating a law, even if the company itself does not violate any law? The case at issue now in US courts is software (DeCSS) that decodes the protective devices that limit the copying of DVD format material (Kaplan 2000).

Are companies violating fair use doctrines when they cache information (hold it or replicate it so that it can more efficiently use Internet technologies as well as quickly deliver the requested information). Does it matter whether caching is on a satellite or a server?

Whose responsibility is it to properly account and pay for use if financial obligations result from digital transmission of copyrighted material? The Secure Digital Music Initiative (SDMI), an international consortium of 120 companies and organizations, has already crafted a specification for delivery of digital music that is interoperable with existing formats. SDMI is now working on a set of principles that will embrace interoperability of formats, ensure copyright and certification (via digital watermark), and also fulfill the desire to have unprotected formats.[20] It does not appear that SDMI would be the financial arm or watchdog, however. Instead, offshoots of existing financial clearinghouses (BMI and ASCAP) are strengthening their on-line presence.

Issues of Business-Method Software

Patent rights for software is a fundamental question.[21] Because of recent court decisions, US legislation, and new policies of the US Patent Office

---

19. As of 21 June, 2000, 18 nations had ratified the Copyright Treaty, and 15 had ratified the Performances and Phonograms Treaty. See http://www.wipo.int/eng/ratific/doc/u-page.doc. The United States ratified and passed implementing legislation in 1998 and deposited its instruments of ratification with WIPO in September 1999.

20. See http://www.sdmi.org.

21. For a legal perspective on these issues, see Groff (2000), http://www.gabar.org/ga_bar/febcov3.htm.

(USPTO) and the European Patent Convention that expand subject matter eligibility, business-method software is now the fastest-growing category of new patents.[22] In the fiscal year ended September 1999, computer-related software patent applications to the USPTO doubled to 2,600 and about 600 were granted. The potential for a proliferation of patents for basic e-commerce software, which already includes Amazon.com's One-Click feature, Priceline.com's reverse auction method, and Mobjob.com's group-buying technique, is viewed by Lawrence Lessig, one of the world's experts in Internet law, as "the single greatest threat to innovation in cyberspace." (Gleick 2000).

The economic issue is how to balance protection so as to maintain innovative activity with the potentially anticompetitive effects of such protection, which may be more severe in the e-commerce world because of network effects. In addition to this inherent difficulty, business-method patents expose the jurisdictional tensions between US and European national approaches and commitments and obligations under international agreements in TRIPs.

Specifically, TRIPs patent protection extends 20 years and allows reverse engineering of software; neither of these provisions makes sense for business-method software. On the one hand, reverse engineering allows new entrants to build on and augment existing platforms, which can yield the tailored approaches that benefit classes of users, and also furthers network benefits by ensuring the interoperability on which those benefits depend. But reverse engineering scuttles the very protection that is being granted.

On the other hand, nearly everyone agrees that 20 years is too long for business-method software; Jeff Bezos, CEO of Amazon.com, has suggested shortening patent life to 3 to 4 years. But because of the TRIPs provision, the United States has little incentive to change its own laws, and certainly no ability to change the length of patents agreed to in other jurisdictions (Sandburg 2000). The USPTO plans a "partnership roundtable" in summer 2000 to include the full range of stakeholders to discuss business-method patents.

Issue Convergence: Intellectual Property and Consumer Protection

Because it is so easy to transact business over the Internet, issues of intellectual property protection and consumer protection are colliding in both domestic and international jurisdictions. A US example is the Uniform Computer Information Transaction Act (UCITA), written under the auspices of National Conference of Commissioners on Uniform State

---

22. The relevant court decision was *State Street Bank & Trust Co. v. Signature Financial Group* in July 1998. The relevant US legislation is the American Inventors Protection Act of 1999. The European patent convention is expected to in effect legitimize patenting of business-method software later in 2000. For more discussion, see *The Economist* (18 April 2000), Horvath (1999), and Fried (2000).

Laws. The essence of UCITA is that software and other forms of digital information are neither a good nor a service but a transfer of a right to use intellectual property.[23]

Although still under legal review and comment, some argue that UCITA would void or weaken many of the consumer protections offered to buyers under existing defect and warranty laws. It would affect what buyers could do after having "bought" a product, since in effect they are not buying but renting it; for example, buyers would have to remove the software if they gave away their computers. Moreover, the vendor could under some circumstances void the software remotely—the mere ability to do so causes much angst among privacy advocates.[24]

An international example of how consumer protections and intellectual property are colliding is on-line sales of prescription pharmaceuticals. The "grey-market" trade in prescription pharmaceuticals is not new (Maskus 2000). However, reduced frictions between geographical markets, polar opposite governmental approaches to the pricing and availability of pharmaceuticals, and the increased anonymity of the Internet accentuate its possibilities. The US Customs service seized 4½ times as many packages containing prescription drugs in 1999 than in 1998; they confiscated abou2 million pills (Pear, *New York Times*, 10 January 2000). Nonetheless, the level of capture is small, pointing to the difficulty of sorting through the huge volume of international small-package flow.

This trade undermines the patent protection given to prescription pharmaceuticals. Moreover, some drugs are misbranded, which in itself undermines the value of the company when the drug does not perform as expected. However, there is also the fact that some drugs do not meet US quality standards or are illegal, putting consumers at risk. In some cases the imported drugs are identical in every way except price, with the price difference resulting from different government regulations of pharmaceuticals. On balance, the United States is more concerned with fraudulent activity and has proposed extending federal jurisdiction to on-line drugstores—but they have official jurisdiction over only US drugstores. There is no international consumer protection, and the international intellectual property protection is being ignored.

Trusted Environment

The legal and technical aspects of creating a predictable legal environment discussed in the previous sections are the necessary foundations for elec-

---

23. See the discussion of this distinction (between buying and renting) in the context of tax liability in chapter 6.

24. The governor of Virginia has signed UCITA into law; many other state legislatures are considering it. Some see the refusal to sign this legislation as an indication that these states

tronic commerce to flourish. Governments must therefore give them high priority in the near-term if electronic commerce is to take hold. Generally, these aspects call for consistent approaches by governments.

However, other aspects of establishing an environment of certainty and trust that governments will be forced to address—such as protection of individual privacy, consumer protection policies, and approaches to objectionable content on the Internet—are more complicated. How can the benefits of electronic commerce be balanced with the need to protect individual and societal values, for instance? Because a government's policies will be based on political culture, legal tradition, and values, issues of trust are more likely to generate differing national approaches—there is no "right" policy. Yet, national policies will require international coordination, as well as ways to resolve conflicts, if network benefits are to be enjoyed. Technology, too, is important in establishing trust, and empowering individuals to make choices about how much security, privacy, and access they desire.

To a great degree these issues of trust deal more with B2C transactions than with B2B transactions, where the fastest growth is expected. Therefore, it may be less urgent to address these issues than to put in place the basic legal and technical infrastructure. However, the promise of electronic commerce will not be realized unless consumers feel safe and secure.

To a greater or lesser degree, governments traditionally champion consumer interests as a result of the fundamental asymmetry of market power discussed in chapter 2. The point was broached there about how much the new environment of the Internet and electronic commerce might accentuate or reduce this asymmetry. On the one hand, the environment is more global, more anonymous, and faster paced, which might tend to accentuate the power of business over consumer. On the other hand, thanks to technological innovation, it has never been easier for consumers to get information about businesses and to "click" away from unresponsive ones.

The key questions are: Will a government approach that emphasizes self-regulation and technical innovation meet the demand for privacy, for consumer protection, and content? If the answer is no, how can the threat to electronic commerce posed by nationally mandated solutions be minimized? And how important is the human factor in these assessments?

Privacy

With the many benefits of electronic commerce comes the challenge of how to manage personal information. Electronic commerce creates information

---

are "unfriendly" toward technology companies. One way or the other, the patchwork quilt of legislation will undermine both consumer and producer protections.

trails that allow transaction information to be tracked, collected, and compiled, providing vast amounts of information about personal details of people's lives. While personal information has been tracked for years, through barcode scanners, credit cards, and the like, what is fundamentally different today is the ease with which data can not only be gathered and compiled electronically, but also manipulated and used. Data collection on the Internet has become widespread (and big business), with 92 percent of all commercial Web sites collecting some personal identifying information (Georgetown Survey 1998) (also box 7.2).

While the on-line market is still growing, consumers increasingly are concerned about the vast amounts of personal information available in the electronic world, and how it is used. In a recent poll, 85 percent of those surveyed cited the privacy of information transmitted online as the most important issue related to the Internet (overtaking censorship).[25] If consumers fear that the information they provide online may be used inappropriately, they will hesitate to participate, thereby slowing the growth of electronic commerce and limiting the many benefits of its full realization. How governments respond to this lack of consumer confidence—specifically, whether they adopt market or mandated policy approaches will have a significant effect on the future of electronic commerce.

Privacy stirs deep concerns. Some interest groups respond with moral outrage, noting that most countries in the world recognize privacy as a fundamental human right. The most recent constitutions specify rights to access and control of one's personal information (Privacy and Human Rights 1999). Some groups advocate that countries worldwide adopt comprehensive privacy and data protection laws.

In trying to produce better-tailored products, industry highly values the collection of information from everyone, and may undervalue the demands of users who want less personal data collected. But industry does not want to scare away users and reduce the network benefits. Groups like the Alliance for Global Business and the Global Business Dialogue on Electronic Commerce (GBDe) have called for a flexible approach to the protection of personal information, "including the acceptance of self-regulatory solutions and technological innovations that empower the user" (Global Business Dialogue 1999). The Transatlantic Business Council also supports industry-led, market-driven privacy protection principles, and suggests that national privacy protection allow for differences based on national political systems and local culture.

International Initiatives

Even before the advent of the Internet, the OECD in 1980 promulgated the Guidelines on the Protection of Privacy and Transborder Flows of

---

25. @plan (2000), Schwartz (*Washington Post* 20 May 2000, E1). Similar figures have come out of other surveys.

Box 7.2   The DoubleClick imbroglio and information gathering practices

The challenge to privacy today comes primarily from the advent of powerful technologies that allow an unprecedented amount of information to be gathered, stored, analyzed, and manipulated efficiently and inexpensively. Browsing the Web can divulge a significant amount of information to the Web sites visited, in most cases without the user's knowledge.

Profiling refers to the practice of aggregating information about consumers' interests and preferences gathered by tracking their movements online, and using the resulting profiles to create targeted advertising on Web sites. ID cards, advertisements, and Web bugs are means by which information is exchanged automatically when individuals visit Web sites.[1] A common practice is the use of "cookies"—data files that sites embed on a user's browser when users visit Web sites. Each cookie contains a tracking number, thereby identifying the computer, though generally not the user. However, if a user gives his/her name to a site during a transaction, or visits multiple sites that subscribe to the same tracking system, a common cookie can cross-reference information, thereby revealing even more personal information. Usually these processes take place without any notification of or awareness by the consumer.

This type of information-gathering has been ongoing for years. However, when the US firm, DoubleClick, the biggest supplier of on-line advertising, acquired Abacus Direct Corp., a database firm with information on millions of consumers gathered through direct mail marketers, and announced plans to target advertising to Internet customers, there was a strong public outcry.[2] The combination of the databases would link anonymous visits to a Web site with a person's real name and address. Even though DoubleClick asserted that the connection would only take place with the users' permission, privacy advocates argued that such permission was gained indirectly, and filed complaints with the US Federal Trade Commission. The states of New York and Michigan opened investigations; Michigan directed the company to suspend its practice of sending cookies to consumers' computers without their explicit permission and commenced legal action.

DoubleClick responded to the criticism and pressure by committing not to link personally identifiable information to anonymous user activity "until there is agreement between government and industry on privacy standards."[3] To deal with the public outcry, it also organized a self-regulating coalition of 26 Internet advertising firms known as the Personalization Consortium.[4] The consortium has drafted guidelines for fair access by individuals to their information, redress to change information, and criteria for options to allow users to "opt-in" rather than "opt-out" of providing personal information when visiting Web sites. Industry representatives are negotiating with regulators over new voluntary restraints on online profiling and reforms of information-handling practices on the Internet.[5] DoubleClick also appointed an independent privacy advisory board of prominent security and privacy experts, as well as consumer advocates to review the company's practices for potential privacy violations.[6]

The revelations concerning DoubleClick and similar information-gathering trends have focused greater public attention worldwide on the implications for privacy on the Internet. As a result, privacy and consumer advocates internationally have mobilized to push for greater legal protections for privacy, not only in the United States but also in other countries emphasizing self-regulation, such as Australia and Canada.[7] The Canadian government recently dismantled a database of information

(*continued next page*)

supplied by citizens to the government in large part due to public concerns for privacy, even though there were no known breaches of security.[8]

1. Andrea Petersen, "A Privacy Storm at DoubleClick," *New York Times*, 23 February 2000.

2. DoubleClick's announcement in June 1999 was not the first to generate such a response. In early 1999 Intel faced strong public criticism when it became known that its new microprocessors contained an embedded serial number that could be used to identify individual computers on the Internet; it was forced to offer software to disable the feature.

3. Chet Dembeck, "Online Privacy Inside and Out," *E-Commerce Times*, 25 April 2000.

4. See Laurie J. Flynn, "Web Privacy Group to Offer a Seal of Approval," *New York Times*, 3 April 2000, and Robert Conlin, "Industry Leaders Tackle Online Privacy Issue," *E-Commerce Times*, 5 April 2000. The Personalization Consortium is developing guidelines on the collection of data on users and their surfing activities and a Web seal program.

5. Glenn Simpson, "Online Advertisers Are Negotiating Deal on Privacy Rules with US Regulators," *Wall Street Journal*, 13 June 2000, 8.

6. Chet Dembeck and Robert Conlin, "Beleaguered DoubleClick Appoint Privacy Board," *E-Commerce Times*, 17 May 2000.

7. Adam Creed, "Australian Government Introduces Privacy Legislation," *E-Commerce Times*, 13 April 2000.

8. Steven Bonisteel, "Canadian Government Kills 'Big Brother' Database," *Newsbytes*, 30 May 2000.

Personal Data to embody established principles of fair information practices, and provide a basis for data protection that ensures the free flow of information (see box 7.3). While there is general consensus among OECD members on the validity of the principles,[26] there has been renewed concern about their implementation.

At their 1998 Ottawa conference, for example, OECD Ministers adopted the Declaration on Protection of Privacy on Global Networks, reaffirming their commitment to effective privacy protection and committing to "build bridges between different national approaches based on law and self-regulation."[27] The OECD also produced a comprehensive survey of national, regional, and international privacy mechanisms, both legal and self-regulatory instruments (OECD 1999c).

While the OECD has served as a useful venue for discussion among its members, the guidelines are nonbinding and countries have taken different approaches to the implementation of privacy protection. The

26. Citing their use in national and international instruments, the OECD decided in 1998 that it was "not necessary" to make revisions.

27. See "Progress Report on the OECD Action Plan for Electronic Commerce," 23 September 1999 at: http://www.oecd.org/dsti/sti/it/ec/act/paris_ec/pdf/progrep_e.pdf.

Box 7.3 OECD privacy guidelines

Collection Limitation Principle: There should be limits to the collection of personal data and any such data should be obtained by lawful and fair means and, where appropriate, with the knowledge or consent of the data subject.

Data Quality Principle: Personal data should be relevant to the purposes for which they are to be used, and, to the extent necessary for those purposes, should be accurate, complete, and kept up-to-date.

Purpose Specification Principle: The purposes for which personal data are collected should be specified not later than at the time of data collection and subsequent use limited to the fulfillment of those purposes or such others as are not incompatible with those purposes and as are specified on each occasion of change of purpose.

Use Limitation Principle: Personal data should not be disclosed, made available or otherwise used for purposes other than those specified in accordance with Paragraph 9 except: with the consent of the data subject; or by the authority of law.

Security Safeguards Principle: Personal data should be protected by reasonable security safeguards against such risks as loss or unauthorized access, destruction, use, modification, or disclosure of data.

Openness Principle: There should be a general policy of openness about developments, practices, and policies with respect to personal data. Means should be readily available of establishing the existence and nature of personal data and the main purposes of their use as well as the identity and usual residence of the data controller.

Individual Participation Principle: An individual should have the right:
 a) to obtain from a data controller, or otherwise, confirmation of whether or not the data controller has data relating to him or her;
 b) to have communicated to him or her, data relating to him or her within a reasonable time; at a charge, if any, that is not excessive; in a reasonable manner; and in a form that is readily intelligible to him or her;
 c) to be given reasons if a request made under subparagraphs *(a)* and *(b)* is denied, and to be able to challenge such denial; and
 d) to challenge data relating to him or her and, if the challenge is successful to have the data erased, rectified, completed, or amended.

Accountability Principle: A data controller should be accountable for complying with measures which give effect to the principles stated above.[1]

---

1. OECD, "Guidelines on the Protection of Privacy and Transborder Flows of Personal Data" (Adopted in the form of a Recommendation by the Council of the OECD on 23 September 1980), http://www.oecd.org/dsti/sti/it/secur/prod/priv-en.htm, 4-5. Twenty-eight countries and the European Union belong to the OECD.

methods/models, some of which can be mixed and matched, include (Privacy International 2000):

■ A comprehensive approach, generally with omnibus data protection legislation that governs the collection, use, and dissemination of personal information. Countries taking this line typically name a Commissioner for Privacy to monitor compliance (European Union, Taiwan, Hong Kong, and New Zealand).

- Coregulation, a variation of the comprehensive approach entailing industry enforcement with government oversight (Australia[28] and Canada[29]).

- Issue-specific legislation to protect certain areas, such as financial information, or restrict certain practices, such as unauthorized use of IDs and passwords (United States, Australia, and Japan).

- Self-regulation, in which companies and industry bodies establish codes of conduct (United States, Japan, and Singapore).

- Promotion of technologies and standards that allow consumers varying degrees of privacy and security, including encryption technology, smart cards, and the W3C's Platform for Privacy Practices (P3P) standard.[30]

More than 25 countries have adopted comprehensive legislation, and more countries are considering such laws (Privacy and Electronic Commerce 1998).

Governmental Approaches and Consequences

National approaches to electronic commerce generally reflect differing legal and cultural traditions. The United States and the European Union exemplify two alternative responses to privacy protection.

Relying on market mechanisms and self-regulation, the United States has taken a hands-off approach that emphasizes private-sector leadership and minimal government intervention. This market-driven, self-regulatory model has garnered support in Australia and Japan, among other countries.

The primary alternative is the more regulated model, the mandate approach. With a tradition of comprehensive legislation, the European Union has approached electronic commerce with a more regulatory stance and with a series of directives addressing specific issues. This mandated approach has been embraced in part by Canada, among others.

Either approach must, at some point, be enforced by government or the courts if it is to succeed in its objective of enabling an environment of certainty and trust.

---

28. Australia specifically restricts the government's use of personal information. See http://www.doc.gov/ecommerce/privacy.htm.

29. Canada also restricts the government's use of information. Canada is currently considering comprehensive legislation protecting privacy generally. *Ibid.*

30. The Platform for Privacy Practices (P3P) is a software that converts a company's privacy statements into a machine-readable format, allowing users to be warned if a site gathers more information than they are willing to divulge.

Is there a "best" approach to resolving privacy concerns? What happens in the cross-border context when two large trading partners take different approaches? The US-EU differences offer insights into what will become more pervasive questions of overlapping jurisdictions in the global context and is another example of issue convergence.

The Market-Oriented Approach: US Example

The market-oriented approach followed by the United States relies on a mix of legislation, regulatory enforcement, and self-regulation to assure the protection of personal privacy online. Federal and state sector-specific legislation (e.g., information related to children, medical records, or financial information) is combined with private-sector self-regulatory mechanisms. The US system polices self-regulatory commitments through the Federal Trade Commission (FTC). In 1999, the United States created the position of Chief Counselor for Privacy within the Office of Management and Budget to coordinate privacy policy throughout the government.

Self-regulatory efforts have sought user-friendly mechanisms for facilitating awareness and the exercise of choice online, for the adoption by the private sector of fair information practices and for dispute resolution. The objective is to ensure that consumers know the rules, companies comply with them, and consumers have access to personal information in a company's possession, as well as recourse when injuries result from noncompliance.

There has been substantial innovation among private-sector groups to respond to the demands for privacy online. The Online Privacy Alliance has led the way in protecting private information transmitted electronically. Companies and business associations have adopted guidelines for posting privacy policies online, and led a campaign to inform Internet users on how to shield their personal data on the Internet. Several organizations such as BBB*Online* (see box 7.4) and TRUSTe provide an enforcement mechanism through the use of Web site privacy seals. Codes of conduct, such as BBB*Online*'s Code of Online Business Practices, drafted in cooperation with consumer representatives and government, also give merchants guidance on consumer protections.

In the past year, 88 percent of commercial sites surveyed have posted privacy policies or statements, up from nearly two-thirds the previous year (US Government Working Group on Electronic Commerce 1999 and FTC 1998). Some Web sites also offer consumers a choice through click boxes of how much personal information to divulge, although the opting out feature has been criticized as too complicated for many on-line users. A variety of other methods to give users options for personal data disclosure are also in use or under development. However, with increasing public concern for privacy, and the evidence of both domestic and international fraud, the US model has come under greater scrutiny (see box 7.5).

Box 7.4 Industry self-regulation—BBB*Online*

Prominent among private-sector self-regulatory initiatives to promote trust and confidence on the Internet is BBB*Online*.[1] Launched in 1999 as a wholly-owned subsidiary of the Council of Better Business Bureaus (CBBB), the BBB*Online* program builds on the experience and long history of the CBBB in fostering ethical relations between business and consumers through voluntary self-regulation and education. The CBBB provides dispute resolution services, including mediation and arbitration, to corporations and customers, reports on how well companies protect consumers, refers cases of illegal practices to the FTC, and grants the over 250,000 local business members nationwide use of a BBB trustmark.

BBB*Online* has established similar services through its BBB*Online* Reliability and BBB*Online* Privacy Programs. Three difference seals—which are posted on Web sites—are awarded to companies meeting certain rigorous standards, such as a satisfactory complaint record, participation in BBB's advertising self-regulation program, and agreement to dispute resolution at the consumer's request. The Reliability program has enrolled more than 5,000 businesses, making it the most significant Web site trustmark program.[2] The Privacy program awards seals to businesses that clearly post privacy policies meeting rigorous standards, such as notice to consumers, disclosure, choice and consent, and security, and agree to consumer dispute resolution. The Kid's Privacy seal, part of the Privacy program, recognizes businesses that are in full compliance with even more extensive requirements concerning children's privacy online, such as obtaining parental consent before any personal information can be collected or used. The BBB*Online* trustmarks, which readily identify responsible online businesses, have become the electronic equivalent of the Good Housekeeping Seal of Approval for Web sites.

Seeking to internationalize and harmonize the online privacy seal effort, BBB*Online* recently announced a joint initiative with the entity responsible for privacy seals in Japan to develop reciprocal seals that will be easily recognizable by consumers in both countries.[3] Similar efforts are underway in Europe. BBB*Online* has also drafted a Code of Online Business Practices in cooperation with consumer representatives and government to give merchants guidelines to implement consumer protections.

While efforts like BBB*Online*, TRUSTe, and CPA Webtrust provide only a partial response to consumer concerns, they do hold promise as effective and enforceable means of business self-regulation.

---

1. See http://www.bbbonline.org.

2. "BBB*Online* Reliability Program Reaches 5,000 Businesses," press release of BBB*Online*, 16 May 2000. See http://www.bbbonline.org/about/press/051600.html.

3. "New Online Privacy Protection Tool to Transcend Borders," press release of BBB*Online*, 18 May 2000. See http://www.bbbonline.org/about/press/051800.html.

The Mandate Approach: EU Example and Cross Border Implications

European countries generally have comprehensive privacy systems with explicit laws requiring gatherers of data to register with government privacy offices. They prohibit or limit certain data uses, such as direct marketing, that are routine in the United States. In 1995, the European Union adopted the Directive on the Protection of Personal Information

Box 7.5 Changing US environment and emerging trends

As a result of the DoubleClick controversy and increased concerns about privacy on the Internet, a shift in public opinion is underway in the United States regarding the adequacy of the industry's self-regulatory efforts. The credibility and effectiveness of industry self-policing efforts have been significantly damaged, with some analysts predicting that government regulation of electronic commerce privacy issues is a "foregone conclusion."[1] The implementation of the Children's Online Privacy Protection Act in April 2000 (see Content section in this chapter), as well as financial services legislation, is seen by many as the first in a series of efforts to regulate consumer privacy online.

As a result of growing consumer concerns, numerous legislative restrictions on Internet privacy have been proposed by Congress and individual states. A House subcommittee recently approved a bill to establish a privacy commission (modeled on the Advisory Commission on Electronic Commerce that addressed the taxation issue) to examine online privacy, identity theft, and the protection of personal records as well as make recommendations on whether additional legislation is necessary.[2] Other legislation would require companies to disclose how they collect and use personal information or prohibit the disclosure of such information without consumers' permission; still other measures would create a new federal seal program to certify Web sites that adhere to fair information practices. Members of Congress even formed a Congressional Privacy Caucus to advocate for personal privacy. Underlying the proposals and new focus on privacy issues are public opinion polls that ranked the loss of personal privacy as the number one issue of concern regarding the Internet.[3]

In addition, the FTC has been more aggressive in promoting privacy, rapidly moving to center stage as the main US government agency addressing Internet regulation; electronic commerce has become the agency's primary concern.[4] Its role will be even larger when the US-EU privacy accord is implemented and the FTC is required to monitor compliance by US firms. The FTC has undertaken a number of initiatives, including a review of the information-sharing practices of health care Web sites, proposed rules for the protection of consumers doing business online with bank and other businesses involving the transfer of money, and establishing an Advisory Committee on Online Access and Security.[5]

Most notably, however, the FTC's position on the adequacy of the current system has changed. Until May 2000, the FTC supported a self-regulatory approach, recommending against new privacy legislation and greater regulation. However, even though new survey results show continued improvement in the number of Web sites that post privacy policies (90 percent), it indicated that only 20 percent meet FTC standards for adequately protecting consumer privacy.[6] With the release of its third report to Congress on the state of online privacy, the commission concluded that legislation is necessary to ensure adequate protection of consumer privacy online.[7] While applauding private-sector self-regulatory initiatives, the report concluded that "industry efforts alone have not been sufficient," and recommended a legislative framework for basic privacy protection for consumer-oriented Web sites.[8]

Even before the FTC decision, the Clinton administration forcefully called on companies to adopt stronger policies to protect user information: "We must do more to uphold Americans' high expectations that their right to privacy will be

(continued next page)

Box 7.5 (*continued*)

protected online."[9] On 1 May, President Clinton announced new legislative proposals to protect financial privacy.[10] Reflecting growing consumer concerns and citing technological advances that outpace measures to protect privacy online, the initiative would require companies to give customers a choice of whether or not firms can share sensitive information such as medical and financial data with third parties. While still endorsing industry self-regulatory efforts and not embracing the FTC recommendation, the administration has called for additional legal protections for certain sensitive information, warning that it would promote stronger legislation if industry's self-regulatory initiatives fail.

Taken together with other developments, including the proliferation of tough state privacy laws, these actions portend a move in the United States away from a self-regulatory approach toward increased government intervention. Even advocates of self-regulation recognize the shift in attitudes and are softening their opposition to greater federal oversight. In fact, concern for the proliferation of tough state privacy laws could actually encourage industry support for preemptive national privacy legislation.

While it is unlikely that Congress will enact the FTC proposal in 2000 due to the short legislative session and opposition from Republican lawmakers, it could lend support for strengthening the FTC's ability to fight fraud on the Internet.[11] Privacy concerns are registering high in political polls and focus groups, making it clear that policymakers will be forced to address the issue. With the growing consensus in the United States that industry self-regulation is inadequate, increasing government legislation is increasingly likely. But, at what cost?

---

1. Bob Tedeschi, "Electronic Commerce Report," *New York Times*, 6 March 2000, and Chet Dembeck, "Internet Self-regulation Dead on Arrival," *E-Commerce Times*, 31 March 2000.

2. See H.R. 4049 at http://thomas.loc.gov/cgi-bin/bdquery/z?d106:h.r.04049:

3. See Glenn Simpson, "Electronic Commerce Firms Start to Rethink Opposition to Privacy Regulation as Abuses, Anger Rise," *Wall Street Journal*, 6 January 2000. The article cited a late 1999 *Wall Street Journal*/NBC News Poll in which Americans were given a list of eight concerns that might face them in the new century and were asked to rank them; 29 percent of respondents ranked the loss of personal privacy at the top.

4. *Ibid.*

5. See http://www.ftc.gov.

6. John Schwartz, "FTC to Propose New Online Privacy Rules," *Washington Post*, 20 May 2000, E1, and Paul A. Greenberg & Chet Dembeck, "FTC Seeking Net Privacy Regulation," *E-Commerce Times*, 22 May 2000.

7. FTC (2000). *Privacy Online: Fair Information Practices in the Electronic Marketplace* (2000 Report) (May). http://www.ftc.gov/reports/privacy2000/privacy2000.pdf.

8. *Ibid.*

9. Remarks by President Clinton to the Forum on Communications and Society on the Information Age Agenda, Meeting of the Aspen Institute, 3 March 2000.

10. "The Clinton-Gore Plan to Enhance Consumers' Financial Privacy: Protecting Core Values in the Information Age," White House, 1 May 2000.

11. John Schwartz, "Republicans Oppose Online Privacy Plans," *Washington Post*, 21 May 2000.

(95/46/EC), which required EU member states to enact laws prohibiting the transfer of personal data to nonmember states that fail to ensure "adequate" privacy protection.[31] The directive gives European consumers unprecedented control over the data collected about them and requires companies to get explicit permission from consumers before using personal data (Swire and Litan 1998). European countries are still passing laws to implement the directive, and questions about its enforceability persist.

What happens when the government-mandate approach to privacy protection butts up against the economic realities of the global marketplace? When the European Union passed the directive, it clearly implied a substantial economic effect from embargoing personal data from Europe to the United States if the European Union determined that US firms following the US approach did not provide adequate privacy protection (Dennis, *E-Commerce Times*, 6 April 2000). To prevent this outcome, the United States and European Union promptly began negotiations on how to bridge their different approaches.

The United States argued that US companies adhering to voluntary privacy guidelines should be given a "safe harbor" from legal challenge under the directive. Agreement was finally reached in March 2000 which assures the European Union that information sent by firms to the United States will be protected. The regulatory safe harbor arrangement includes principles, the effect of which is to allow American firms receiving personal data from the European Union to subscribe to self-regulatory organizations such as BBB*Online*, provide reports to a European data protection authority, and be subject to legal action by the US FTC if they do not adhere to the rules (Mitchener and Wessel, *Wall Street Journal*, 24 February 2000). The data privacy accord also allows Europeans to inspect and change data that is collected about them, and to veto any transfer to third parties (Simpson, *Wall Street Journal*, 15 March 2000). The 15 EU member states approved the agreement in May, and after European Parliament consideration in the summer, the agreement is expected to be formally adopted in fall 2000.

Despite the accord, the issue is not fully resolved. Key questions concerning compliance, enforceability, and the effect on firms outside the United States must still be addressed. The compromise has been criticized by both consumer and industry groups—for lessening protections Europeans are guaranteed by law, and for importing EU privacy standards into the United States. A new group, the National Business Coalition for E-Commerce and Privacy, has raised questions of national sovereignty and characterized the agreement as a kind of nontariff barrier (Dennis, *E-Commerce Times* 6 April 2000). The issue is likely to be revisited as part

---

31. See http://europa.eu.int/eur-lex/en/lif/dat/1995/en_395L0046.html.

of further negotiations with the European Union to address data privacy for the financial services sector.[32]

Nevertheless, the accord represents the start toward an interoperable approach to the problem of conflicting legal and regulatory systems. The workout leaves European privacy standards in place, but allows for private-sector trustmark assurance and enforcement under US laws and policies. Some analysts have predicted that the proposal may develop into rules of privacy that could be applied internationally (Burgess, *Washington Post*, 24 February 2000). The accord, something of a hybrid between the market and mandated approaches, possibly portends a merging of the two approaches in future treatment of e-commerce issues.

Market vs. Mandate: Is There a "Right Way"?

Privacy protection represents one of the most contentious policy issues facing governments as they seek to balance the objective of promoting electronic commerce with citizens' desire for privacy. The problems will only get worse, as even more products—phones, TVs, cars—are connected to the Internet and the technology that enables data mining and profiling evolves.

How should governments balance these conflicting objectives? Does the comprehensive mandate model better protect privacy online? Or is the market approach combining laws and self-regulation preferable, since it preserves incentives for the private sector to continue to innovate for technologically superior solutions to satisfy government and consumer needs?

There is no right answer. Privacy involves sensitive individual values and, more broadly, how different societies perceive themselves. As discussed in chapter 2, privacy as an e-commerce issue is also marked by the difference in market power between those collecting information (industry) and those using the Internet (individuals), and perhaps also by an unsolvable divergence between social values and industry values. These market imperfections may mean an enhanced governmental role in setting privacy rules and either balancing interests or protecting Internet users.

Will a solution mandated by a government be worse economically than a solution that depends on market incentives? The economic "theory of the second best" shows that market and mandated solutions cannot be ranked by which comes closer to achieving the greatest economic well-being for a country as a whole. However, increased government intervention likely will mean less innovation by industry, and thus an Internet

---

32. US negotiators have argued that financial services should not be subject to the data privacy accord because specific legislation, the Financial Services Act, provides adequate protection. EU officials have not agreed. See *Inside US Trade*, 31 March 2000.

that might not satisfy user values as much as if government intervention was avoided.

On the other hand, increased government intervention may respond to important societal demands and there will be political pressure for intervention—although the cost to a country's development and engagement in electronic commerce should be fully acknowledged, as well as the potential for Balkanization of the Internet, which reduces network benefits for all. The key public policy question is less about the costs and benefits of different approaches than about how the threat to electronic commerce of government intervention can be managed and, hopefully, minimized.

The Role of Technology

Technology is both the cause of the problem and an important way to ameliorate it. Without question, the increasingly sophisticated means of collecting personal data exacerbates privacy issues. Yet technology also empowers individuals to make their own choices about how much privacy they demand.

When finalized this year, P3P, a specification being developed by W3C, will translate privacy statements on Web sites into machine-readable form. Users will then be able to specify the types of information they are willing to divulge, as well as whether the information can be shared with third parties. When a user visits a site that fails to meet the user's criteria, notice is given that allows users to block access. Thus privacy protections are being built into the on-line experience. Microsoft's announcement that it would include P3P in free Internet tools to be released in 2000 may go a long way in promoting its widespread use. Other approaches include W3C's Open Profiling Standard that allows users to determine what kind of information to reveal to Web sites. Widely available and inexpensive software programs like Guard Dog, Internet Junkbuster, Anonymizer, and others let users block sites from sending cookies.

Technology is not "the" answer to the privacy dilemma, but it is part of an effective industry response. It is a tool that allows individuals to make decisions based on their own preferences. "P3P is not a panacea for privacy, but it does represent an important opportunity to make progress in building greater privacy protections in the Web experience" (Center for Democracy and Technology 1999). Will governments accept technology as a sufficient solution, or will they argue that individuals need a champion?

A key component of the answer is education. Consumers need to understand the elements of their choices—in terms of both the technology available and industry self-regulation—in order to exercise their right to choose the protection they want. More information and public education, as well as an expansion of self-regulatory practices like BBB*Online* and TRUSTe should be promoted.

There is obviously no one-size-fits-all policy appropriate for all governments. Countries adopt policies that reflect their own legal traditions, political culture, and economic status, especially as it relates to access to technology. At the same time, governments seeking to improve the environment for electronic commerce would be wise to limit their intervention by pursuing an approach that combines instruments, including legislation, government-private sector partnerships, industry self-regulation (with monitoring and enforcement), and the promotion of privacy-enhancing technology. The challenge for government is to get the mix right for both national traditions and technological realities. Intensified international efforts to promote interoperable approaches to privacy would be useful.

Consumer Protection

The Internet offers consumers unparalleled opportunities of choice and access and, with more than 304 million users expected to be online in 2000, the potential for new business is extraordinary.[33] However, in the borderless, anonymous world of the Internet, buyers and sellers interact across national borders, making fraud and deception even more challenging. For the promise of electronic commerce to be realized, buyers and sellers need to have confidence that products they buy and the firms they deal with are fairly represented, they will get what they pay for and be paid for what they sell, and that legal recourse is available if they do not.

Government has encouraged consumer confidence through laws and regulations to protect consumers against fraud in the physical world; adapting policies to the electronic world has become an increasingly important priority. Protection for consumers online to date has been an extension of national laws and regulations. New laws specifically directed to electronic commerce do not seem needed, and until they are, policymakers should resist the temptation to legislate e-commerce-specific solutions.

But with cross-border electronic commerce, consumers and businesses face the differing laws of numerous countries. While B2B transactions often choose the law that applies through contractual terms, using the country of origin's laws as the default, this is not likely to be satisfactory for consumer transactions. The disputes that arise from on-line consumer purchases are likely to be of relatively small dollar value, making it difficult and expensive to pursue legal action. Consumers need affordable and simple ways to resolve disputes.

---

33. US Department of Commerce, Digital Economy 2000. June 2000 at: http://www.esa.doc.gov/.

A fundamental problem faced by consumers in electronic transactions is the absence of clear information. On-line contracts need to state the basics: seller's identity and location, total price, payment and shipping arrangements, any conditions on purchases, including warranties and return/refund arrangements, and mechanisms for addressing complaints.

The electronic medium also makes fraud and deception (in contrast to honest mistakes) easier. Marketing messages that entice consumers into impulse buying, get-rich-quick schemes, and copycat (fake) Web sites make it difficult for consumers to differentiate between scam, fraud, and the real thing.

Overall, policymakers must decide how to provide simple and interoperable approaches to consumer protections without emasculating enforcement of national protections against fraud and deception. The first step is to acknowledge what common approaches already have been embraced, since these are the foundations for any necessary multilateral enforcement efforts. The next step is to determine whether differing approaches represent fundamental disagreement on societal values and how best to bridge such differences.

As with privacy protection, the OECD has been the primary international forum to discuss consumer protection issues. In December 1999, the OECD adopted the Guidelines for Consumer Protection in the Context of Electronic Commerce to ensure that consumers are no less protected when shopping online than when they buy in the physical world. Intended to help governments formulate and implement consumer protection policies, as well as to provide guidance to businesses and consumers on fair business practices, the guidelines represent an international consensus on core principles to govern the relationship between buyers and sellers in the electronic world.[34] Although nonbinding, they help guide governments to provide consumers with basic protections. The goal is to eliminate uncertainties for both consumers and businesses in trading online and to help clarify their rights and responsibilities. Work within the OECD is now directed at getting the guidelines implemented, and educating consumers and business of their rights and responsibilities, and on alternative dispute resolution mechanisms.

As discussed in the privacy section, the United States employs a market-oriented approach to consumer protection online—primarily by applying

---

34. OECD Guidelines for Consumer Protection in the Context of Electronic Commerce is at http://www.oecd.org/dsti/sti/it/consumer/prod/guidelines.htm. The guidelines reflect existing consumer protections. They also encourage private-sector initiatives that include consumer representatives and emphasize the need for cooperation among governments, businesses, and consumers. They address a broad range of issues, including advertising and marketing practices, information about an online business's identity, contracting terms and conditions, secure payment mechanisms, consumer redress and dispute resolution, privacy protection, and consumer and business education.

and enforcing existing laws, and by promoting self-regulatory initiatives. To back up the market, the FTC has devoted substantial new resources to consumer protection on the Internet, setting up a new office to oversee Internet transactions, electronic commerce, and advertising. Educating business and consumers in the "rules of the road" for electronic commerce has been a priority; the FTC has generated extensive information about on-line practices, such as pyramid schemes, lottery scams, Internet auctions, and medical billing schemes, as well as safe shopping guidance.[35] The FTC is also exploring the use of alternative dispute resolution mechanisms for consumer transactions online.

The FTC's main tool is the aggressive enforcement of existing consumer protection laws. In 1999, nearly 18,000 Internet consumer fraud complaints were submitted to the FTC. Since 1994, the FTC has brought over 100 Internet-related cases, stopping the illegal conduct in every case (FTC 1999). Enforcement has centered on technology-based scams such as spam, hijacking, and "web cramming," as well as traditional scams—credit scams, and fraudulent auctions, business and investment opportunities, and health claims. In response to increasing allegations of internationally based Internet fraud, the FTC initiated an ambitious international project, in cooperation with law enforcement, governments, and consumer protection groups in 28 countries. As a result of a recent sweep of Web sites offering get-rich-quick schemes, the FTC put 1,600 sites on notice for alleged fraud (Clausing, *New York Times*, 13 March 2000). The action included participation by both public and private entities around the world. The Justice Department has also stepped up efforts to address Internet crime, launching the Internet Fraud Complaint Center in May 2000 (*E-Commerce Times*, 9 May 2000). The center will give consumers a place to lodge complaints and provide a centralized database to assist local, state, and federal law enforcement officials.

To address consumer protection issues, the European Union has released a Directive on Information Society Services, which includes electronic commerce, and clarifies the regulatory framework and safeguards the rights of consumers. The directive harmonizes rules to ensure that industry and citizens can supply and receive electronic commerce throughout the European Union. It builds on existing European Union rules for consumer protection, which cover contracts, electronic transactions, unfair terms in consumer contracts, misleading advertising, and consumer credit (European Union 29 February 2000).

Beyond governments, businesses, and consumers there are other "players." For example, consumer advocates from Europe and the United States, through the Transatlantic Consumer Dialogue, have recommended standards to give protection in the on-line world that matches protection

---

35. See http://www.ftc.gov/bcp/menu-Internet.htm.

in the off-line world. These standards include simplified contracts, limits on consumer liability, recourse to laws and courts in home countries, and cooperation among governments in support of legal redress (Transatlantic Consumer Dialogue 1999).

Regulatory bodies in most countries appear to have adequate authority to address fraudulent and deceptive practices online; enforcement of those laws for Internet-related issues will go a long way to reassuring consumers that protections do exist in the electronic world. Moreover, greater efforts by businesses to develop and adhere to self-regulatory guidelines and codes will also help address consumer concerns.

To the extent that self-regulatory approaches to consumer protection are deemed inadequate, however, governments will come under pressure to adopt new policies to fill the perceived regulatory void. Consumers must believe that they are afforded an equivalent level of protection as is available in traditional forms of commerce. Striking the appropriate balance between governmental intervention and self-regulation will remain a challenge for governments. Enhanced education of consumers, as well as development of new processes for alternative dispute resolution for on-line consumer transactions can help create an environment of greater confidence for consumers.

Content

While most governments support the free flow of information across national borders, the growth of electronic commerce has forced them to examine issues related to Internet content. Along with the many benefits of the Internet come the potential for it to carry unlawful and offensive activity. Child pornography, fraud, gambling, and material fomenting racism, hate crimes, violence, or other illegal activities are examples of the harmful or offensive content now readily accessible. Governments are increasingly challenged to try to strike a balance between limiting the use of the Internet for purposes contrary to societal values and security on the one hand, and freedom of expression on the other. Moreover, how or whether to mesh policy approaches across borders is an issue.

For most countries, existing laws that ban fraud or child pornography or those that regulate gambling, firearms, alcohol, or intellectual property seem sufficient. The US Justice Department in its new report, *The Electronic Frontier: The Challenge of Unlawful Conduct Involving the Use of the Internet*, found that, for the most part, existing laws are adequate to address unlawful activity on the Internet (US Department of Justice 2000). (See box 7.6.)

The European Union has an ambitious action plan to promote safer use of the Internet by combating illegal and harmful content (European Parliament 1999). The objectives of the four-year plan are to encourage industry and users to put in place systems of self-regulation, create filter-

Box 7.6 Legislating safe surfing for children: The US approach

The United States has made two attempts to legislate an approach to content objectionable to children.[1] The Children's Online Privacy Protection Act (COPPA), which took effect 21 April 2000, authorizes the FTC to set rules regulating data collection on Web sites targeted at children under the age of 13. Web-sites must notify parents of the site's information practices, obtain verifiable parental consent before collecting personal information on children, and give parents a choice as to whether their child's information will be disclosed to third parties.[2]

Not only does COPPA run the risk of court cases based on free speech, it also has direct economic implications. It is estimated that COPPA requirements will cost firms between $60,000 to $100,000 a year, leading a number of Internet companies to eliminate services to children under 13 rather than risk lawsuits (*Wall Street Journal*, 24 April 2000).

In addition to legislation, the United States has promoted a self-regulatory, local approach to content by empowering parents and teachers with the tools to protect children in a manner consistent with their values. The United States embraced this approach as the most effective and most compatible with the First Amendment; government and businesses have worked closely to give parents resources to promote safe online experiences for children.[3]

For example, the primary way citizens, especially parents, have addressed the content problem is through software that blocks or filters content deemed offensive or inappropriate. Software programs such as CYBERsitter and Net Nanny block access to Web sites based on certain words or phrases; filtering software, available through many ISPs, block sites containing certain keywords or sites with a particular label or rating. In addition, there are services like SafeSurf and RSACi that allow publishers to self-label, thereby allowing Web sites to be blocked based on their own ratings.

---

1. The Communications Decency Act to limit obscene material on the Internet was struck down by the Supreme Court in 1997 as infringing on free speech, and therefore, ruled unconstitutional. *Reno v. ACLU.*

2. See http://www.ftc.gov/kidsprivacy.

3. See http://www.GetNetWise.org.

---

ing and rating systems, promote awareness, and encourage coordination and compatibility between European and other approaches. European firms have formed the coalition INCORE, the Internet Content Rating for Europe, to promote self-regulation and create a rating and filtering system to meet the needs of European users.[36]

The OECD addressed the issue in 1998 through a Forum on Internet Content Self-Regulation, jointly sponsored with the Business and Industry Advisory Committee to the OECD, as well as in an inventory of national approaches to content on the Internet. In addition, W3C has set specifica-

---

36. See http://www.incore.org/what/what.htm.

tions for an Internet rating system known as Platform for Internet Content Selection (PICS), providing both self-labeling (by author or publisher) and third-party labeling, as well as accommodating a range of rating systems available to different countries and cultures.[37]

Industry has embraced technological solutions empowering users to control their own access to content as a way to forestall government regulation. In late 1999, the Bertelsmann Foundation, a nonprofit group associated with the German media conglomerate Bertelsmann A.G., unveiled recommendations for a global system that would include codes of conducts and rating systems that, among other purposes, parents can use with filtering software to protect children from harmful material online.[38]

The plan and the growing support for rating and filtering systems generally have raised serious concerns among civil libertarians and others that content filtering will lead to censorship. Groups like the American Civil Liberties Union and the Electronic Privacy Information Center fear that such systems threaten free expression on the Internet more effectively than national laws could. In some countries (including the UK and Australia), governments are already trying to mandate the use of PICS-facilitated systems, with penalties for companies that rate themselves incorrectly.

The same technologies that allow parents to filter information also allow government officials to embargo sensitive or subversive information. The Chinese government screens for politically sensitive words and has implemented regulations to control citizens' access to the Internet. New rules issued in January 2000 and designed to prevent the spread of "state secrets" via the Internet, are seen as a clear attempt to censor on-line content (Dembeck 2000). Moreover, ISPs operating in China can be held accountable for illicit material on the Internet, which is something that has happened in other countries as well.[39]

In Syria, before becoming president, Bashar Assad had been promoting Syria's advancement into the electronic world but said that local traditions may require "guidelines" for deciding if there should be controls on Internet access (Schneider 2000). Vietnam has announced its intention to control the Internet for security and cultural reasons, and the country's

---

37. See http://www.w3.org/PICS/Activity.

38. "Memorandum on Self-Regulation of the Internet" located at: http://www.stiftung.bertelsmann.de/Internetcontent/english/frameset_nojs.htm.

39. China is not the only country to hold ISPs liable for content on their servers. Liability concerns among ISPs have been growing, as some countries (UK) have sought to prosecute ISPs for distributing harmful content, with the end-result being closer cooperation with law enforcement, and adoption of self-regulatory plans. Germany, too, threatened to hold an AOL executive responsible for material in AOL chat room.

Ministry of Culture and Information plans to monitor on-line content.[40] In Malaysia, while ISPs are not required to monitor the Internet, they must limit public access to 100 high-impact pornographic sites identified by the government, as a statement of societal values.[41] And in March 2000, Zimbabwean President Robert Mugabe got a special bill through Parliament allowing government access to and control over e-mail content (Internet News South Africa, 24 March 2000).

Content on the Internet raises many of the same issues as the protection of privacy rights. Both entail individual and societal values. As with privacy, technology provides part of an effective government response and empowers individuals to make choices. Notwithstanding censorship concerns, governments and businesses worldwide will continue to embrace the use of technology as a large part of the answer to the problem of sexually explicit material on the Internet. Unlike with privacy, however, it appears that the content issue currently is being successfully managed at the national level, though with the potential that differing national approaches will lead to conflicts, possibly even trade barriers. Greater discussion and cooperation in national approaches to content are helpful in preventing differences from becoming significant barriers to electronic commerce.

---

40. The Internet Law and Policy Forum Working Group on Content Blocking at http://www.ilpf.org/work/content/htm.

41. See the Web site of the Singapore Government, Frequently Asked Questions for E-Commerce Business Policy, at http://www.ec.gov.sg/13081999/helpdesk_faq.html.

8

Government in the International Arena

As jurisdictions increasingly overlap, electronic commerce changes the relationships among governments, businesses, and citizens of different countries. The global reach of the Internet makes it virtually impossible for governments to effectively control policies and activities within national borders.

Thus, the public policy challenges posed by electronic commerce defy unilateral approaches. Even if a national consensus can be reached, the policies that result are likely to be, at best, ineffective without multilateral understandings, and at worst, conflict with other countries. Moreover, conflicting national approaches can undermine benefits of electronic commerce by Balkanizing the Internet. Multilateral approaches, therefore, are critical—and widely seen as such by most countries, with a few exceptions.

While no single international body has addressed the full range of electronic commerce issues, many organizations have devoted considerable effort to defining the challenges, crafting solutions, and working cooperatively on specific issues (see table 8.1) As national governments work through existing international bodies, nongovernmental organizations (NGOs) and other groups are also addressing the international issues raised by electronic commerce. At the heart of this effort is the increasingly important and growing role being played by the private sector, especially the work of businesses to ensure technical interoperability. Businesses are also assuming functions that traditionally belonged to governments.

Multilateral efforts to deal with electronic commerce, involving both the public and the private sectors, are taking place in three organizationally distinct ways:

Table 8.1 International organizations addressing e-commerce issues

	Aid	Trade	Tax	Electronic signatures	IPR	Standards	Security	Privacy	Consumer protection	Content	Education
WTO		▪									
ITU						▪	▪				
UNCITRAL				▪							▪
UNCTAD											▪
UNESCO							▪		▪		▪
World Bank	▪										
WIPO					▪						
OECD			▪	▪			▪	▪	▪		▪
APEC				▪							▪
FTAA				▪		▪					▪
EU					▪	▪	▪	▪	▪	▪	▪
ICANN								▪			
W3C										▪	
IETF						▪					

- International organizations, or functional institutions such as the WTO, ITU, UNCITRAL, and WIPO seek to adapt existing policies to the electronic world.

- Regional organizations and international coordinating bodies—the OECD, UNCTAD, European Union, Asia-Pacific Economic Cooperation (APEC), and Free Trade Area of the Americas (FTAA)—address various e-commerce issues.

- New groups that are collaborative partnerships of government, companies, and nonprofit organizations. Among these are GBDe, ICANN, and W3C.

Some of these groups have parallel concerns that have resulted in converging views and possible approaches, despite the lack of formal coordination. This is especially true of many issues associated with a trusted environment and a legal framework. Other issues have not been so fortuitously handled, among them privacy and the protection of personal data, in part because these bring to the fore differences in societal values and governmental approaches to policymaking.

Is the international framework for addressing e-commerce issues too fragmented and ad hoc, dispersed across too many national and international, formal and informal, and official and private bodies? Or is this fluid, evolving approach appropriate to the pace of change of the Internet and electronic commerce? In particular, for issues that do not yet enjoy international consensus, will the current international discussions help formulate interoperable yet national approaches, and thereby forestall the potential that national conflicts will limit the full realization of network benefits?

Functional Institutions

The first group of specialized institutions are working to adapt existing rules and policies to the electronic world. It includes, among others, the ITU, UNCITRAL, and WIPO (see boxes 8.1 and 8.2). Since most legal and commercial codes governing how businesses interact with each other and consumers were established before the Internet, these frameworks may need to be adjusted to meet the new realities. The objective of these institutions is to ensure that rules that apply to the digital world are, if not the same as, at least equivalent to those of the physical world. For the most part, existing principles and disciplines remain valid.

On the other hand, as in the case of tax regimes, there can be tensions over whether the economic and social benefits of the Internet and electronic commerce are maximized using the existing frameworks. One organization where this tension is particularly clear is the WTO.

Box 8.1 United Nations-related organizations dealing with electronic commerce

International Telecommunications Union (http://www.itu.org)

As the international organization within which governments and the private sector coordinate global telecommunications networks and services, the International Telecommunications Union (ITU) has led in setting standards on the overall architecture of the global information infrastructure, including integration of public switched telephone networks and Internet Protocol (IP) networks. The ITU has emphasized development of standards for electronic commerce and communication system security for multimedia terminals; standards for electronic commerce related to infrastructure and security; educational materials to raise the awareness of the role of telecom reform and regulation in electronic commerce; and technical assistance to facilitate electronic commerce infrastructure and service in developing countries.

UNCITRAL (http://www.uncitral.org)

One of the first international organizations to undertake work on electronic commerce was the United Nations Commission on International Trade Law (UNCITRAL). In 1996, UNCITRAL adopted a Model Law on Electronic Commerce to assist states in devising domestic legislation to govern the use of alternatives to paper-based methods of communication and storage of information.[1] The model law has had a significant influence on national laws; it generally provides a framework to minimize legal obstacles and establish a more secure legal environment for electronic commerce. Numerous countries, including the United States in the Millennium Digital Commerce Act passed by Congress in 1999, have adopted or incorporated principles from the UNCITRAL Model Law to domestic legislation.[2]

In addition, UNCITRAL's Working Group on Electronic Commerce is addressing the issue of electronic signatures and certification authorities. Draft Uniform Rules on Electronic Signatures are being drafted to promote the use of electronic signatures through a set of standards on the basis of which digital signatures and other electronic signatures may be legally recognized.[3] The draft rules also address standards to be met by certification authorities in issuing certificates for legal recognition, and the need for mutual recognition of "trusted" certificates on a global basis.

UNCTAD (http://www.unctad.org)

As the principal United Nations agency concerned with trade and development, the UN Conference on Trade and Development (UNCTAD) has concentrated its efforts on stimulating interest and awareness of the economic and social benefits of electronic commerce in developing countries. Through a series of "E-Commerce and Development" workshops and regional meetings in 1998 and 1999, UNCTAD has promoted both the exchange of experiences among entities involved in electronic commerce and cooperation among governments and business to encourage infrastructure development. Ongoing activities include dissemination of electronic commerce-related information to developing countries, training activities, and analytical studies on the economic, social, and legal implications of electronic commerce for developing nations.[4]

(continued next page)

World Trade Organization (WTO)

The WTO[1] has done a substantial amount of work on electronic commerce, both directly on its trade-related aspects and more generally on the infrastructures necessary to the development of global as well as domestic electronic commerce (see Mann and Knight 2000, WTO 1998).

   However, the cross-cutting and rapidly evolving environment of electronic commerce challenges both the organizing structure of the WTO (GATT and GATS, and the role of subcommittees) and how its members operate (request-offer negotiations and negative vs. positive commitments). As the body that addresses global trade issues, the WTO is ideal for the exchange of information and insights on how countries approach both domestic and cross-border aspects of electronic commerce. But to the extent that the WTO is a negotiating body, which balances requests and offers as the way to implement trade liberalization, it may need to change its strategy to get superior outcomes, both global and local.

What Governments Have Accomplished in the WTO

Because electronic commerce was evolving so quickly, the 1998 Geneva Ministerial agreement imposed a temporary moratorium on customs duties for all products delivered over the Internet. It also commenced a

---

1. See Catherine L. Mann and Sarah Cleeland Knight, "Electronic Commerce in the World Trade Organization" in *The WTO after Seattle*, edited by Jeffrey Schott, Institute for International Economics, July 2000.

Box 8.2   Other functional institutions

World Intellectual Property Organization

The World Intellectual Property Organization (WIPO)[1] has been the forum for the negotiation of treaties requiring adequate and effective protection of copyrighted works and sound recordings, including the communication, reproduction, and distribution of electronically transmitted data in cyberspace. (See chapter 7 for a more detailed discussion of intellectual property protection on the Internet.)

Bringing existing treaties into force has been a priority for WIPO, and a significant effort has been aimed at developing countries. A series of regional meetings were held in 1999, out of which grew WIPO's Digital Agenda, to promote the adjustment of the international framework to facilitate electronic commerce through ratification of the WCT and WPPT; extension of principles to audiovisual performances, broadcasters rights, and a possible international instrument on the protection of databases; and establishment of rules to govern disputes between the domain names system and intellectual property rights. WIPONET, an information network to promote the greater use and exchange of information technologies among member states and to create a global process of patent examination and grants activities, will provide greater access to developing countries to use IP assets in electronic commerce.

The World Bank

The World Bank has focused on opportunities represented by the Internet and information age for developing countries and economies in transition.[2] Specifically, the World Bank Group supports the efforts of governments to develop information-based activities and the required information infrastructure by providing resources and expertise, primarily from the private sector for information (especially telecommunications) infrastructure, and helping to provide access to information and communications to those living in poor and rural areas.

The Information for Development Program (*Info*Dev) of the World Bank provides grants and loans to assist countries in taking advantage of economic development opportunities provided by electronic commerce. The World Bank provides extensive technical assistance, training, and funding to countries for the development of communications and information networks and on the use of the Internet. Conference and workshops have focused on legal and regulatory reforms, including best practices regarding liberalization of markets, global connectivity, and convergence, to promote the growth of electronic commerce. Programs are intended to help establish the ground rules for the digital marketplace in developing countries. For further discussion of World Bank programs, see Chapter 9.

---

1. See http://www.wipo.org.

2. See http://www.worldbank.org/infodev/projects/faq.htm.

---

comprehensive work program to examine the trade-related aspects of electronic commerce. Four separate working groups—the Goods Council, the Services Council, the TRIPs Council, and the Trade and Development Committee—were coordinated by the General Council.

A key motivation for the moratorium was the difficulty of distinguishing between physical and electronic delivery of products bought over the

Internet and the blurring of the traditional distinction between goods and services. Existing WTO rules on trade in goods would seem to apply to products bought electronically but distributed physically (like vitamins from drugstore.com that arrive via DHL). On the other hand, an architectural blueprint delivered electronically would likely be a kind of service. But what about music downloaded from the Internet but not on a hard medium like a CD). Is this a good or a service? Should these products fall under the purview of GATS, GATT, or neither?

The General Council's work program on electronic commerce highlighted a number of issues that warranted further review. The November 1999 Seattle Ministerial failed to launch a new round of trade talks, leaving unresolved an agenda on a range of trade issues, including electronic commerce. At that time, there was a general convergence of views that WTO members should not impose new barriers to electronic commerce. A new round would likely have continued the moratorium on duties, reinforcing the principle of forbearance regarding electronic commerce as well as showing a commitment to the main tenant of the WTO—liberalization.

More broadly, the WTO has helped to liberalize or at least address the service-sector infrastructures that are a prerequisite for growth of electronic commerce. Tariffs and restrictions on computers and other IT products were set at zero under Information Technology Agreement (ITA) I, and the range of products is likely to be broadened in ITA II. The Basic Telecommunications Agreement covers commitments for telecommunications liberalization. Financial services are addressed in the Financial Services Agreement. Distribution systems may be discussed under Trade-Related Measures (TRIMs) and delivery services will be considered in GATS2000. Electronic commerce depends on the synergies among service sectors for maximum economic benefit.

In the absence of agreement to launch a new round of trade negotiations, it is not clear how the WTO will address e-commerce issues. Though it is unclear whether the moratorium has expired, the important point is that no country has acted yet to impose new duties.[2]

What Future Negotiations Should Accomplish

Because of the economic and social importance and the global reach of electronic commerce and the infrastructures on which it depends, it is essential that WTO members commit to the maximum possible liberalization of electronic commerce. WTO members should agree to continue the electronic commerce work program in their mandate for new negotiations

---

2. The US has taken the position that the moratorium is still in effect since the Ministerial did not end, but was suspended; the European Union and others believe that the moratorium was in effect only until Seattle, and there has been no agreement to extend the moratorium.

so as to continue the process of education and shared experiences. This approach can pave the way for a comprehensive treatment of electronic commerce—and its infrastructures—which will encourage growth and benefit all WTO members.

1. *Reaffirm that existing WTO principles and disciplines apply to electronic commerce.*

While the electronic world poses certain challenges to the current trade policy framework, traditional WTO principles of nondiscrimination, transparency, and market openness remain valid for electronic commerce. New rules are not necessary if the principle of liberalization fundamental to the WTO is honored.

With electronic commerce still in its infancy, it is too early to determine how digitized products delivered over the Internet should be classified. Premature classification could have a profound impact on the future growth of electronic commerce, given the differences in how GATT and GATS approach liberalization. Moreover, given the pace of change, extensive resources and efforts are probably misguided toward this activity.

Where the application of these agreements to electronic commerce is not clear, the most liberalizing approach should prevail. This might mean that electronic delivery of goods and services would be treated more favorably than other forms of delivery. For example, insurance products could be sold over the Internet even though the physical presence of foreign insurance firms had not yet been scheduled for liberalization under GATS. The bias toward liberalization engendered by electronic commerce can stimulate the further development of electronic commerce, as well as encourage liberalization and deregulation throughout the economy.

2. *Extend the moratorium on customs duties on electronic transmissions.*

Ideally, WTO members will make permanent and binding the practice of not imposing customs duties on digitized products. The longer countries keep electronic commerce duty-free, the more these activities will flourish and clarify the benefits of a more liberal domestic and international trade environment. If WTO members allow the moratorium to expire, they will encourage fragmentation by different taxes and tariff types and rates. Businesses will waste time and energy "forum-shopping," which will discourage technological growth in countries where seamless markets are most important.

3. *Negotiating methods need greater creativity and leadership.*

The debate on whether to classify electronic transactions as GATT or GATS reveals how country delegations approach negotiating methodology. The US proposal on services in mid-summer 1999 argued for the "use of all appropriate negotiating modalities, including request-offer, horizontal, and sectoral approaches."[3]

In the *horizontal* approach, negotiators seek to apply liberalizing measures like transparency and good governance in regulations, as well as consistency of ownership across sectors to a broad range of services. They might seek to eliminate any discrimination across a particular mode of delivery (like electronic commerce or rights of establishment) or a range of services (like financial services and small package delivery) (Esserman 1999).

Horizontal negotiations recognize that service sectors are interconnected and that for maximum economic benefits liberalization must proceed on several fronts at once. Otherwise the benefits from liberalizing one sector (say, lower telecommunications costs) are simply absorbed into a protected sector (such as higher air cargo costs). The horizontal approach to liberalization is particularly valuable for electronic commerce, where the synergies between services sectors are especially apparent.

That said, request-offer negotiations will likely still be important, and will require industrial countries to have clearer vision. Specifically, industrial and developing countries need to negotiate across manufacturing and services sectors. Businesses and workers in the high-tech and services sectors in industrial countries stand to benefit from the liberalization of electronic commerce and its infrastructures. Developing countries stand to benefit through the new opportunities created by electronic commerce, as well as through the increased efficiencies of electronic commerce in traditional sectors. This is a clear win-win proposition.

The overall benefits could be reduced, however, if markets are not open for those more efficiently produced goods and services. Developing countries, for example, face barriers in textiles and apparel and some elements of data processing, communications, and software programming—precisely those areas in which electronic commerce can enhance the competitiveness of developing-country producers.

Trade negotiations often have political as well as economic aspects. Regardless of the benefits of unilateral liberalization or horizontal negotiations, if negotiators in industrial countries fail to acknowledge the need to lower barriers to products from developing countries, those countries may limit their commitments to liberalize electronic commerce. This would reduce benefits for all countries. Trading off an extension of the moratorium for reduced barriers in other sectors, while politically difficult, would nonetheless be the most liberalizing and beneficial outcome of future negotiations.

---

3. Preparations for the 1999 Ministerial conference; communication from the United States, Further Negotiations As Mandated by the General Agreement on Trade in Services (GATS), as replicated in *Inside U.S. Trade*, 30 July 1999.

4. *Extend the electronic commerce work program, but avoid linkages to technical assistance.*

WTO members must foster an environment that allows consideration of how electronic commerce issues are unique, even while falling under the WTO principle of liberalization. The current WTO work program has provided only a shallow understanding of how electronic commerce is changing the global economy. For example, should the Basic Telecom Agreement be expanded to embrace broadband infrastructure and services, or should technology products for the Internet qualify for tariff reduction under ITA II? Should interoperability, standards, and universal access be addressed? Such questions could be addressed through the WTO work program, with special attention to developing-country concerns.

A future WTO work program on electronic commerce should have the following two features:

1. The work program should be subject to the General Council rather than fragmented throughout the WTO, or put under the Services Council.[4] While input from councils and committees is important, the cross-cutting nature of electronic commerce means that the General Council must lead. Close coordination of the work program under the General Council will also help developing countries with their smaller negotiating staff participate more fully. Certainly, too, this work program should be a non-negotiating forum.

2. The private sector is leading the way in setting global technological standards for electronic commerce; it can also help resolve policymaking concerns such as tax administration and privacy protection. Private-sector participation has been the hallmark of all the regional trade forums' discussions of electronic commerce (including those proceeding under APEC and FTAA). The contribution the sector can make to the WTO work program is vital.

Several developing countries are concerned about how any WTO e-commerce commitments will affect them. Their concerns include infrastructure, equitable access, and technological and human capacity for e-commerce growth. A few of these countries, including the Southern African nations, have gone so far as to propose that an extension of the moratorium be tied to "technical assistance for the building of telecommunication infrastructure" for developing countries (see Southern African Development Community 1999).

While WTO negotiators should be prepared to negotiate across industrial and services sectors, they need to be wary of responding to such

---

4. This was suggested by the European Union, in keeping with the view that all electronic commerce transactions should be classified as services.

developing-country demands. The WTO has neither the people nor the funds to meet them. Other organizations—perhaps UNCTAD, World Bank, and the ITU—are better suited to provide technical training, and the World Bank and regional development banks can offer funding for infrastructure investment as can the private sector. These organizations can help ensure that the benefits from electronic commerce accrue equitably among countries at different stages of development.

Conclusion

To establish a predictable environment in which electronic commerce can thrive, the WTO must ensure that the benefits of this new form of international trade will be realized by consumers in all countries. To do so, the WTO must make sure that electronic commerce remains free from international trade barriers and continues to drive domestic and global growth.

The stakes are enormous. In the United States, where electronic commerce has its strongest hold, the IT sector contributes approximately 8 percent of the economy. The remarkable growth in IT-related industries, especially those directly linked to electronic commerce, has helped to create the longest period of peacetime economic growth (with low inflation) in US history. Over the last four years, IT-related industries have contributed to more than one-third of the growth of real output for the US economy (US Department of Commerce 1999).

Such gains are available to all countries, not just first-users like the United States and Europe; liberalization via electronic commerce is not a zero-sum game. Indeed, the importance of network benefits means that second movers can gain more faster. Electronic commerce offers particular promise to developing countries. Market innovations and improved market efficiencies gained through electronic commerce and its prerequisite infrastructures will most affect those sectors and countries where coordination and transactions costs are highest.

For all countries, failure to acknowledge how electronic commerce fully integrates both services and goods sectors, to treat it as a separate sector, or to tax it as a service will undermine the WTO objective of liberalization. It will impede the exploration into new processes, products, and markets and squander the opportunity to leap forward to the next stage of economic development.

Coordinating and Regional Institutions

The second category of international activity has been among multilateral and regional entities attempting to coordinate separate aspects of electronic commerce. This category includes the OECD, UNCTAD, APEC, FTAA, and the European Union.

Box 8.3 OECD research and activities

In the area of privacy and security, the Directorate for Science, Technology, and Industry developed the 1980 OECD Guidelines on the Protection of Privacy and Transborder Flows of Personal Data, 1992 OECD Guidelines for the Security of Information Systems, 1997 OECD Guidelines on Cryptography Policy, 1998 Inventory of Approaches to Authentication and Certification in a Global Networked Society, and 1999 Inventory of Controls on Cryptography Technologies. In addition, the OECD Committee on Fiscal Affairs addressed the issue of electronic commerce and taxation in the 1997 OECD Tax Framework Conditions. In 1999, the OECD Council approved Guidelines for Consumer Protection in the Context of Electronic Commerce. In addition, the OECD has conducted statistical work on Internet and electronic commerce indicators, as well as reports on the economic and social impact of electronic commerce.[1]

The conferences sponsored by the OECD — The Forum on Electronic Commerce (Paris, October 1999); the Ministerial Conference—A Borderless World: Realizing the Potential of Global Electronic Commerce (Ottawa, October 1998); and Dismantling the Barriers to Global Electronic Commerce (Turku, Finland, November 1997) have resulted in a comprehensive set of measures to promote electronic commerce on a global basis. The OECD's stated objective is to carry out its work in a manner cooperative, and complementary with efforts underway in other international organizations.[2]

---

1. See http://www.oecd.org/dsti/sti/it/ec/index.htm for OECD reports and policy analysis documents.

2. See http://www.oecd.org/dsti/sti/it/ec/act/paris ec/paris-ec about.htm for a description of the purpose of the OECD Forum on Electronic Commerce, held in Paris, 12-13 October, 1999.

These coordinating and regional forums have been useful in helping members find common ground and share experiences. They have helped countries find a common voice and increased their ability to participate in higher-level multilateral forums like the WTO. The need for this will only increase. Members need, and should demand more of, their coordinating and regional institutions.

Organization for Economic Cooperation and Development

The OECD has been at the forefront in examining how electronic commerce affects business activity and public policy, conducting extensive research and analysis on a broad range of issues.[5] Moreover, through major international meetings and conferences, the OECD has established itself as a forum for dialogue among stakeholders—national governments, international organizations, the private sector, and representatives of civil society—on aspects of electronic commerce (see box 8.3). While the OECD

---

5. See http://www.oecd.org/dsti/sti/it/ec/index.htm/.

does not make laws, it has established useful baseline principles to guide work in areas where it has clear competency, among them privacy and authentication, taxation, and consumer protection.

In 1998, the OECD adopted the *Action Plan for Electronic Commerce,* which was further updated at the 1999 Forum.[6] It outlines activities and recommendations responding to four themes: (a) building trust for users and consumers; (b) establishing ground rules for the digital marketplace; (c) enhancing the information infrastructure for electronic commerce; and (d) maximizing the benefit of electronic commerce.

Private-sector groups have played a significant role in the OECD's work on electronic commerce. Under the umbrella of the Alliance for Global Business, a broad range of businesses constructed a framework for e-commerce policymaking with detailed recommendations in *A Global Action Plan for Electronic Commerce prepared by Business with Recommendations to Governments.*[7] The OECD has thus facilitated an active role for the private sector in addressing e-commerce issues. Supplementing this dialogue with labor and business organizations, the 1999 Forum included for the first time, a "public voice" meeting to address the societal dimensions of electronic commerce. This was cosponsored by the Electronic Privacy Information Center and Imaginons un Réseau Internet Solidaire (IRIS). Moreover, the OECD has now identified outreach to and dialogue with nonmember countries as a new objective.

While the OECD is often viewed as addressing only the needs of rich nations, it has taken the lead on several issues for which it has competence and which will affect all countries—primarily taxation, privacy, and consumer protection. In each of these areas, the OECD has established itself as the principal international organization addressing the subject, served as a productive forum for discussion and consensus building, and published guidelines that have become internationally accepted principles.

Recognizing the risk for duplication of effort, the OECD has generally concentrated on issues that are not being addressed by functional institutions or for which there is no appropriate international body. At times, however, some members have been critical of OECD involvement in especially sensitive issues, such as encryption.

The OECD has been useful in analyzing and making available information on e-commerce issues. This type of information is especially helpful to smaller, nonmember countries trying to keep abreast of the flood of e-commerce initiatives.[8]

---

6. See http://www.oecd.org/dsti/sti/it/ec/act/paris_ec/pdf/forum_report.pdf.

7. *See* http://www.oecd.org/dsti/sti/it/ec/act/paris_ec/pdf/bizac_e.pdf.

8. The OECD has prepared a particularly helpful document, the Report on International and Regional Bodies: Activities and Initiatives in Electronic Commerce, produced for the 1998 Ottawa Ministerial Conference. The report is organized by issue and is kept current. It can be found at http://www.oecd.org/dsti/sti/it/ec/act/paris_ec/pdf/intbod_e.pdf.

Some observers have suggested that given its past work on e-commerce issues and its considerable resources, the OECD could do more to help coordinate national policies and international forums addressing e-commerce questions. In particular, because its members include the major players in electronic commerce, the OECD could help bridge the gap between differing country approaches to issues like privacy—should members be willing.

Can the OECD broaden its role? First, several issues must be addressed:

- OECD is limited by its membership to industrialized countries. Effective international discussion and coordination requires broader participation of developing countries. While the OECD has outreach programs, a more comprehensive and regularized way for developing countries to contribute would be necessary. A more active role for the Development Center is one avenue.

- Because OECD decisions are not binding, they are useful only to the extent members reach consensus. Still, to the extent that these discussion yield principles, they do help guide national decision-makers.

- OECD members generally do not view it as a forum for resolution or negotiation of disputes.

European Union

The European Union[9] has responded to a broad range of electronic commerce concerns, including privacy, electronic signatures, and consumer protection. It also sponsors research and technology programs.

In 1997, the European Union released a comprehensive set of proposals for advancing electronic commerce. *A European Initiative in Electronic Commerce* (COM[97]0157) addressed three areas—access to the global marketplace, legal and regulatory issues, and a favorable business environment. Building on this framework, in December 1999, the European Commission launched the *eEurope Initiative: An Information Society for All*, which proposes ambitious targets for all Europeans to realize the benefits of the Information Society. This political initiative is intended to bring every citizen, school, and business into the digital age, create a digitally literate Europe, and accelerate the growth of electronic commerce especially for small- and medium-sized enterprises.[10]

Beyond providing information and coordinating electronic commerce activities among its 15 members, the European Union has adopted a series of directives (some already mentioned) that in effect govern how European

---

9. See http://www.ispo.cec.be/Ecommerce/.

10. See http://europa.eu.int/comm/information_society/index_en.htm.

countries address issues like data privacy, electronic signatures, and consumer protection. But business has criticized the EU regulatory approach as "an unclear mix of overlapping, contradictory, and ill-suited laws that stall e-commerce initiatives" (Lewell 1999).

In 1998, the European Union called for greater worldwide coordination of policies affecting electronic commerce. The Communication on Globalization and the Information Society: The Need for Strengthened International Coordination advocated an international enabling framework for the emerging global electronic marketplace. Noting that development of the Internet depends partly on the extent to which international rules are consistent, the commission discussed shortcomings of the current ad hoc system of international initiatives, specifying the lack of general oversight and of a predictable way to address issues, lack of coordination between groups addressing similar issues, and no systematic involvement by user and consumer groups.[11]

Commissioner Martin Bangemann proposed an Internet Charter that would establish "a set of internationally agreed, legally nonbinding objectives and principles encouraging a simplified regulatory governance of the Internet, consistent with *inter alia* security, safety and soundness, privacy, jurisdiction, liability, taxation, copyright and data protection considerations, pursuing the greatest interoperability across borders" (European Parliament 1998). The proposal never advanced due, in part to the negative reaction from the business community.

Asia-Pacific Economic Cooperation

Through the Telecommunications Working Group, APEC members have worked over the past five years to liberalize and expand the telecommunications and information sectors—the basic infrastructure for electronic commerce.[12] In the final declaration of their November 1997 meeting, APEC leaders stressed the importance of electronic commerce and directed ministers to undertake a work program in the region. They declared, "This initiative should recognize the leading role of the business sector and promote a predictable and consistent legal and regulatory environment that enables all APEC economies to reap the benefits of electronic commerce."

In 1998, APEC ministers endorsed the Blueprint for Electronic Commerce and its principles for promoting the use of electronic commerce in the region, and promulgated an APEC-wide electronic commerce work program. The Electronic Commerce Steering Group was established in

---

11 Introductory Note from the Committee of Permanent Representatives to the Telecommunications Council, dated 13 May 1998.

12. See http://www.ecommerce.gov/apec/.

1999 to implement the blueprint and coordinate electronic commerce activities within APEC. It has already produced a study of the legal foundations for electronic commerce, a legal guide for online contracting, and an e-commerce readiness assessment tool to help countries gauge their openness to electronic commerce and identify areas where reforms are necessary. Current goals include paperless trading by 2005, a virtual multimedia resource center, and initiatives to ensure consumer protection.

Free Trade Area of the Americas

Another regional body that is primarily a coordinating group is the Free Trade Area of the Americas (FTAA).[13] In 1997, the Second Summit of the Americas Plan of Action called for (a) strengthening the capacity of countries in the hemisphere to benefit from the knowledge-based global economy and (b) promoting the growth of the communications and information industries as part of national and regional integration. In 1998 the ministers established the FTAA Joint Government-Private Sector Committee of Experts on Electronic Commerce, a non-negotiating group of public officials and private-sector experts, to make recommendations on ways to broaden the benefits of electronic commerce in the region.

A detailed report with recommendations for strengthening the infrastructure, increasing participation, clarifying the rules of the market, increasing consumer confidence, and dealing with electronic commerce in FTAA negotiations was submitted to the ministers in September 1999.[14]

New Collaborative Groups

New bodies have formed to deal with challenges specific to the Internet. These are private sector groups concerned primarily with standards development and fostering interoperable e-commerce policies. The private sector is thus leading the way in setting global technology standards for the Internet. In one case, government helped establish a new international entity, but most were initiated by the private sector. Despite their informality, these entities nonetheless constitute a new type of international coordination to address technical, and in some cases, policy issues.

Internet Corporation for Assigned Names and Numbers

The Internet Corporation for Assigned Names and Numbers (ICANN)[15] is an example of the private sector assuming responsibilities previously

---

13. See http://www.ftaa-alca.org/.

14. See http://www.ecommerce.gov/.

15. See http://www.icann.org/.

handled by government. For more than 25 years, the US government, mostly through contractors like the Internet Assigned Numbers Authority (IANA) and Network Solutions Inc. (NSI), managed informally many of the technical aspects of the Internet, including the maintenance of the list of assigned Internet numbers and names.[16] The explosive growth of the Internet in recent years, however, necessitated the creation of a more formal technical management and policy body. In its June 1998 Statement of Policy on the Management of Internet Names and Addresses (the White Paper), the US government called on the Internet community to create a new not-for-profit organization of stakeholders to administer the Internet domain name and address system.[17]

Formed in October 1998, ICANN is a nonprofit corporation created by a global coalition of Internet businesses and technical and academic communities. The US government designated ICANN as the coordinator of four Internet functions: management of the domain name systems, allocation of Internet Protocol (IP) address space, assignment of protocol parameters, and management of the root server system.

ICANN's board is composed of 19 volunteer directors, including the president, who on an interim basis is Esther Dyson, the renowned publisher of the Internet newsletter *Release 1.0*. Nine interim members were appointed in October 1998, and an additional nine were elected in fall 1999 by ICANN's three supporting organizations.[18] The original nine members are due to be replaced in 2000-01 by new directors elected at large by the Internet community. The process of transitioning responsibilities from the US government is scheduled to be completed in September 2000.

ICANN's charter is *not* to "run the Internet" but rather to facilitate coordination and management of key technical tasks (referred to by Dyson as "managing the Internet's plumbing" [1999]). It is an unprecedented effort to build a global private governing body representative of Internet users. Nonetheless, the potential scope of ICANN's charter, as well as its

---

16. Domain names are the common names (e.g., http://www.iie.com—the system of suffixes such as .com, .org, .edu associated with email or Web site addresses) that correspond to unique Internet Protocol (IP) numbers that serve as addresses on the Internet for the routing of information.

17. The White Paper can be found at http://www.ntia.doc.gov/ntiahome/domainname/6_5_98dns.htm.

18. ICANN's bylaws provide for three supporting organizations to provide substantive policy recommendations and serve as formal institutional forums for business, technical and noncommercial communities to participate in ICANN. The Address Supporting Organization reviews the system of IP addresses; the Domain Name Supporting Organization is concerned with the domain name system; and the Protocol Supporting Organization addresses technical standards that allow computers to communicate over the Internet. Each names three directors to the ICANN board. See http://www.icann.org/support-orgs.htm for more information on the role of the supporting organizations.

recent activities, have been criticized by governments and groups the world over.

Challenges Facing ICANN

It is not surprising that ICANN has been surrounded by controversy almost since its creation. Notwithstanding ICANN's mandate to oversee technical functions of the Internet, these functions often cannot be isolated from broader policy issues (Clausing 2000c), so questions arise about the scope of ICANN's authority. The process of trying to forge consensus among both the current and the *potential* Internet community worldwide is made even more difficult by the fact that the organization is trying to get itself up and running as it also transitions the domain name registry system from a monopoly to a competitive environment—a messy task under any circumstances (Clausing 2000c).

The major criticisms of ICANN fall into three categories—lack of transparency and accountability in decision-making, including selection of board members; the breadth of ICANN's authority, and the potential it offers for both undue influence of special interests wanting to "regulate" the Internet and under-representation of current non-users; and the aim of introducing competition into domain name registration.

Initially ICANN meetings were not open to the public, fueling the fears of some critics that ICANN was a conspiracy of big business to control the Internet. In response, the board opened meetings and now posts agendas in advance, making inputs and outputs of its decision-making process more transparent.

The major challenge, however, is how ICANN can fairly represent the diverse interests of the global Internet community.[19] This question has arisen most markedly with regard to the process for selecting the At-Large members of the board. ICANN's original plan allowed any Internet user over the age of 16 with e-mail and postal addresses to become a member and therefore eligible to participate in the international elections.[20] The plan, however, generated significant opposition from public interest groups.

---

19. The issue of Internet governance is one that has been actively promoted by the Markle Foundation, which announced its plan to dedicate $100 million over five years to ensure that the public's needs are served, The foundation provided $200,000 to ICANN to increase public accountability, which enabled ICANN to begin outreach and education and to build its at-large membership so Internet users worldwide can vote. See http://www.markle.org/program/pit/index.html.

20. Originally ICANN's plan required a quorum of at least 5,000 registered members, and permitted members to vote electronically using PIN numbers received in the mail. The indirect election would vote on an 18-person At-Large Council, which would in turn elect nine At-Large Board Members. The election was to have been completed by 30 September 2000.

The Center for Democracy and Technology (CDT) and Common Cause released a report in March 2000 criticizing ICANN's proposal for at-large elections (Common Cause nd). The report concluded that the plan was flawed, in part because the millions of Internet users worldwide have little understanding of ICANN and its mission, and therefore cannot knowledgeably select technically capable board members. The groups urged changes to more broadly engage the Internet community so as to minimize the opportunity for organized minorities to capture the election; permit direct elections of the nine board members; and establish a clear nominating process and election rules. Although not reflected in the report, others were concerned about the under-representation of developing countries and regions, especially Asia and Africa, in ICANN's structure.

Under pressure to complete the election by the September 2000 transition deadline, during a rancorous March 2000 meeting in Cairo ICANN's board resisted the recommendation to postpone elections and revamp the process. But ultimately, the board agreed to revise the plan and hold direct elections for five new members by 1 November 2000, while studying the at-large membership process to determine how the final four board members should be chosen. Under the new process, each new director will represent a geographic region: Africa, Asia/Pacific, Europe, Latin America/Caribbean, and North America. ICANN also launched at-large membership and educational programs, as well as designed new election procedures and named a nominating committee.[21] While public interest representatives heralded ICANN's decision to change the process as a defining moment for the Internet, a truly representative election process is far from assured. Engaging the millions of Internet users worldwide, let alone assuring their participation in elections, is an unprecedented experiment in global democracy.

Other critics have expressed concern about the scope of ICANN's authority, fearing that its mission is too broad and that limitations on its authority have not been stated clearly. This has led to repeated calls for ICANN to assure the Internet community, even via contractual provisions with registrars, that it will restrict its policy activities to those spelled out in the charter agreements with the US government. ICANN believes its authority is sufficiently delimited by its bylaws and the terms of the White Paper, but has been willing to adopt the desired language.

A significant issue is that ICANN does not have a stable source of funding. When the US Government devolved its responsibilities to ICANN, it did not provide funding. Until recently, ICANN relied on voluntary donations, including contributions from some Internet-related

---

21. For more details, see http://www.icann.org/nomcom/call.htm, and the site maintained by ICANN Watch, a watchdog group assembling information on ICANN's activities, at http://www.icannwatch.org.

corporations. This raised questions of inappropriate influence by special interests. In order to finance its operations on a sustainable basis, ICANN suggested a permanent cost-recovery structure of a $1 annual fee on registered addresses. Characterized by opponents as a "domain name tax" (Dyson 1999) the fee was deferred while a task force studied funding options and recommended ways to cover ICANN's costs (Hillebrand 1999c).[22]

In the meantime, the current agreement to collect dues from the more than 200 country-specific Internet registries has run into problems (Bridis 2000). Generic-top-level domain registries (.com, .org, .net) already account for most of ICANN's income, but country-code-top-level domain operators (.uk, .fr, etc.) agreed last winter to pay 35 percent of ICANN's annual operating expenses (or about $1.5 million). Fees based on the number of addresses registered in each domain, ranging from $500,000 for Germany to $500 for Zimbabwe were assessed but have been challenged. ICANN officials have denied that failure to collect the fees jeopardizes ICANN, but it is clear that secure funding is critically important to the long-term viability of the organization (King 2000).

The third significant challenge for ICANN is how to manage the process of introducing competition into the domain name registration system. While there is broad support for privatization of the function generally, the method has been attacked. In accordance with its charter to facilitate fair and open competition, ICANN has established a system to accredit new registrars and create operational guidelines. Unfortunately, ICANN's authority was bitterly contested by NSI, which had held the government-authorized monopoly on domain name registrations. This resulted in protracted negotiations and a complicated process for new registrars.

The parties finally agreed in November 1999 on many outstanding issues, but other questions, such as the administration and delegation of top level domain names, remain (Hillebrand 1999b). More than 70 new domain name registrars have been accredited worldwide to provide competitive services for registration of .com, .net, and .org domains. In addition, ICANN has endorsed the recommendation of an advisory group to create more top-level domains (such as .law, .med, etc.) although who will run the registry and whether or not trademark holders will receive preferred treatment for widely recognized marks have not been settled.[23]

A new procedure adopted by ICANN for arbitrating domain name disputes—the Uniform Dispute Resolution Policy (UDRP)—represents

---

22. Some in Congress have been critical of the fact that the Clinton administration even established ICANN, as suggested by the title of a 1999 oversight hearing: "Is ICANN Out of Control?"

23. Proposals for ICANN to expand Internet addresses have been criticized by several companies as exacerbating problems with cybersquatting. See USA Today, 6 March 2000.

Box 8.4 What's in a name? Cybersquatting and intellectual property protection for domain names

Amazon.com filed a suit in US federal court and in Greece against Amazon.gr, in part because the Greek company was using the Amazon name, and in part because the Greek owner was "willing" to sell the name for $1.6 million. The Greek company was cybersquatting, but to what extent is a company's domain name intellectual property, protected by trademark law?

The WIPO began in 1998 a consultation process on the links between protection of IP and Internet domain names and submitted the final report to ICANN in April 1999.[1] ICANN adopted in October the Uniform Domain Name Dispute Resolution Policy, which took effect on January 1, 2000. WIPO has created a online dispute resolution site, and has established a "domain name resolution service" to handle cybersquatting. In less than 2 months, 89 cases have been filed and several have been resolved.[2] In the United States, several pieces of legislation have also addressed cybersquatting, including the 1999 Anti-cybersquatting Consumer Protection Act, which extends the Lanham Act to the Internet, in which federal court is the avenue for remedy.[3]

But, when domestic and international jurisdictions overlap, where is the "high-ground"? In Taiwan, for example, registering a domain names is quick, easy, and cheap. But, if the company wants trademark protection, it must apply a different registry with a longer wait and higher price.

Moreover, surprisingly, numerous internationally active business have not trade-marked their domain names, and have not even registered the names in many of the domestic markets in which they operate. Is this because the geography of the Internet is not bounded by the domestic moniker that is represented by .fr or .uk? Or do these firms figure that they can get any future disputes resolved through ICANN?

Finally, how extensive should trademark protection of domain names be? In some sense, this is a question similar to the patent protection of business-method software. Can the obvious be trademarked around the world?

---

1. Available at WIPO, Pub. No 439, 30 April 1999. See http://www.wipo2.wipo.int.

2. David McQuire, "WIPO, ICANN Happy with Cybersquatting Decision," *Newsbytes,* 28 February 2000. See www.emarketer.com/enews/022800 cybersquat.html.

3. For more details, see Gilbert, Robert D., "Cybersquatters Beware: There Are Two Ways To Get You," *New York Law Journal*, 24 January 2000.

---

the first globally enforceable anti-cybersquatting remedy. It designates WIPO as the body to handle violation of trademark rights for registers of generic top-level domain names that require arbitration before registration. The UDRP is the Internet's first mandatory deliberation mechanism to help decide complicated questions of when owning a domain name is legitimate and when it constitutes "cybersquatting" (see box 8.4).

Assessment

Predictably, the privatization of the domain name system has run into some difficulties; as the organization evolves, problems associated with the transition to private management and open consensus-based governance are likely to continue. Important progress has been made, however, in part due to ICANN's willingness to respond to concerns raised by the Internet community. It is not a perfect organization—nor can it be expected to be so with its challenging and unprecedented mandate and numerous stakeholders—but critics have unfairly maligned ICANN, without offering viable alternatives (Miller 1999).

If ICANN were to fail, as some critics predict, options would include creation of a new organization or return to governmental administration—both near-impossible at this point. It is not likely that any new organization would stand a better chance of succeeding, as ICANN opponents contest any central control of the Internet. And the time is past when the US government can or should perform ICANN's functions.

ICANN is a truly novel experiment in a private-sector-led approach to electronic commerce. The Internet community generally, and private industry in particular, have a tremendous stake in seeing that the experiment thrives. ICANN needs time to continue to evolve in a transparent manner. Elections in 2000 will be an important test of whether ICANN can institute representative procedures, and gain the confidence of Internet users and governments alike.

Secure funding that does not raise conflict-of-interest concerns is essential. The magnitude of ICANN's tasks seems overwhelming. The board has done a reasonable job against great odds in getting the organization up and running, but more dialogue with the Internet community and governments will help build the consensus it needs.

Expanding Role of the Private Sector

A clear trend, discernible in all international efforts, is the increase of private-sector participation in e-commerce policy issues. Multilateral bodies, once the sole domain of government, now routinely include private-sector representatives in deliberations. Businesses have risen to the challenge, taking on new responsibilities in establishing and enforcing "rules of the road" for electronic commerce (US Government Working Group on Electronic Commerce 1999).

The increase in private-sector leadership is both appropriate and necessary, given the pace of change and how little governments know about e-commerce developments. If the principle of private sector leadership is to have meaning, business must thus be encouraged to establish its own rules and enforcement system to deal with privacy protection, objectionable content, and other challenges.

New formal and informal international advisory groups have formed to advise governments and international institutions, including the GBDe

Box 8.5 Global Business Dialogue on Electronic Commerce (GBDe)

One example of a private sector group that formed specifically to address the policy challenges presented by the online economy is the Global Business Dialogue on Electronic Commerce (GBDe). The group originated from a 1998 meeting of the Business Roundtable with European Commissioner Martin Bangemann, to discuss the need for strengthened international coordination of Internet-related issues. Faced with conflicting policies, rules, and regional regulations that pose obstacles to the emerging online economy, business CEOs formed the GBDe to provide input to governments and international organizations concerning the regulation of electronic commerce. It represents an unprecedented collaboration of senior business leaders from more than 60 companies from countries as diverse as South Africa, Venezuela, and South Korea, along with the US, Europe, and Japan.[1] Its credo is to improve business coordination at the global level, suggest ways to avoid conflicting policies and patchwork legislation and, where regulation cannot be avoided, work with governments develop business-led, self-regulatory systems.[2]

GBDe's first major meeting took place in September 1999, where consensus recommendations were presented for a future policy framework for electronic commerce. Fundamental to the group is the belief that inconsistent local, national and international regulatory constraints will result in the failure of many economic benefits to be realized by consumers and businesses to be realized. Accordingly, GBDe developed principles and recommendations to address critical issues of authentication and security, consumer confidence, content, information infrastructure, intellectual property rights, jurisdiction, liability, protection of personal data and tax/tariffs. After establishing itself as an influential voice for industry in discussing e-commerce issues with governments during its first year, GBDe's 2000 workplan includes additional work on privacy, dispute resolution, and trust-marks, as well as enhancing its advocacy and educational efforts.

In a short time, GBDe has become an influential and effective vehicle to communicate industry perspectives, as well as to promote public-private sector cooperation and dialogue on regulatory issues that could impede the dynamic growth of electronic commerce.

---

1. The companies comprising GBDe represent some of the most influential information technology companies from around the world. See http://www.gbde.org/structure/bsc/global.html.

2. See http://www.gbde.org/.

(see box 8.5 on GBDe),[24] the Alliance for Global Business (1999), and the Internet Alliance.[25]

Traditional industry advocacy groups have also engaged in e-commerce issues. The Transatlantic Business Dialogue and the International Chamber of Commerce are two examples of business groups adopting new

---

24. See http://www.gbde.org for the Workplan of the Global Business Dialogue on Electronic Commerce.

25. The Internet Alliance is an association of policy professionals representing the online industry on the state, federal, and international levels. See http://www.Internetalliance.org.

initiatives to address e-commerce issues.[26] Private-sector groups, especially in the United States, have also actively engaged in efforts to develop self-regulatory mechanisms.

There has been a significant increase in the number of private-sector non profit groups addressing aspects of electronic commerce as well. The Internet Society, a professional membership society with more than 150 organizational and 6,000 individual members in over 100 countries, is concerned with the growth and evolution of the Internet.[27] It is the organizational home for groups responsible for Internet infrastructure standards, including the IETF (see box 8.6).

With over 500 members worldwide, CommerceNet operates as a virtual organization whose members fight efforts that inhibit the growth of electronic commerce.[28] The International Law and Policy Forum (ILPF) was started by a group of Americans concerned about keeping legal and technical standards up to speed with Internet developments. The ILPF has matured into an international group of legal and policy experts dealing with cross-border aspects of the electronic medium.[29]

There are countless other interest groups concerned with specific Internet issues. The Transatlantic Consumers Dialogue and Consumers International advocates on behalf of consumers; the Center for Democracy and Technology, Privacy International, and the American Civil Liberties Union address privacy protection and individual rights; and the Children's Partnership and other groups engage on issues of content.

Improving the International Environment for Electronic Commerce

Are current ad hoc multilateral efforts to deal with e-commerce issues adequate? How can national policies be made more interoperable? If coordination must be enhanced to achieve policy interoperability, what form should it take? Is there a need for principles and policies to help guide governments and international entities that deal with electronic commerce?

To date there have actually been few major conflicts among the countries and international bodies addressing e-commerce issues. A convergence

---

26. The International Chamber of Commerce (ICC) has concentrated on trust, publishing a draft Uniform International Authentication and Certification Practices and issued General Usage in International Digitally Ensured Commerce (GUIDEC) to ensure trustworthy digital transactions the Internet.

27. See http://www.isoc.org.

28. See http://www.commerce.net.

29. See http://www.ilpf.org.

Box 8.6 Major standards and technology bodies

W3C (http://www.w3.org/)

An example of the formation of an industry group to deal with specific Internet-related issues is World Wide Web Consortium (W3C). Founded in 1994 and led by Tim Berners-Lee, creator of the World Wide Web, W3C develops common protocols to ensure interoperability of the Internet. It is an international industry consortium jointly hosted by the Massachusetts Institute of Technology Laboratory for Computer Science (MIT/LCS) in the United States; the Institut National de Recherche en Informatique et en Automatique (NRIA) in Europe; and the Keio University Shonan Fujisawa Campus in Japan. Services provided by the Consortium include: a repository of information about the World Wide Web for developers and users; reference code implementations to embody and promote standards; and various prototype and sample applications to demonstrate use of new technology. For example, Platform for Internet Content Selection (PICS) was developed by W3C to deal with the issue of content on the Internet. Another specification, P3P, will translate privacy statements on Web sites into machine readable form, allowing individuals to decide how much personal information to divulge to Web sites. Specifications and reference software are made freely available throughout the world.

IETF (http://www.ietf.org/)

Another technical body formed to deal with specialized aspects of EC such as standards is the Internet Engineering Task Force (IETF). IETF is one of a number of loosely organized international groups of network designers, operators, vendors, and researchers concerned with the evolution of the Internet architecture and the smooth operation of the Internet. IETF is the principle body engaged in development of new Internet standards specifications. IETF's mission includes identifying and proposing solutions to pressing operational and technical problems in the Internet; specifying the development or usage of protocols and the near-term architecture to solve technical problems; making recommendations regarding the standardization of protocols and protocol usage in the Internet; and providing a forum for the exchange of information within the Internet community between vendors, users, researchers, agency contractors and network managers. While it is not a traditional standards organization, many of the specifications produced become de facto standards.

has emerged on many e-commerce policy principles, including legal codes and intellectual property.

Electronic commerce is just getting started. As it grows, will the challenges for policymakers grow with it? Or have we already glimpsed the most fundamental of them? Already there are serious philosophical differences in approaches, as evidenced by the United States and the Europeans, with the United States generally favoring market-oriented self-regulatory solutions, and the European Union preferring more comprehensive mandated approaches.

On the one hand, the private sector is concerned that electronic commerce may be stifled by conflicting national approaches to policy issues, with the potential for overlapping and contradictory approaches likely to increase as electronic commerce takes hold.[30] On the other hand, as electronic commerce grows, domestic political opponents of globalization and liberalization are likely to pressure their own governments in ways that undermine electronic commerce.

At a minimum, therefore, national, regional, and international approaches must be coordinated, especially on such complex cross-border issues as Internet taxation, payment systems, electronic authentication, and security. On other issues, such as privacy, content, and consumer protection, national approaches will differ, and coordinated international approaches are unlikely. Interoperable policy solutions *are* possible; they need to be pursued promptly before differences in national approaches become barriers to the growth of electronic commerce.

How can governments best promote interoperable e-commerce policies? Multilateral efforts to date have resulted in consensus on some important aspects of electronic commerce, including:

- agreement by a number of countries and international organizations on general principles, such as that the private sector should lead;

- broad acceptance of certain rules and agreements, such as the WIPO's treaties on intellectual property rights, the ITU's technical standards, the WTO moratorium on duties, and the ICANN mandate on domain names;

- consultation, in numerous forms and forums, among them the WTO, OECD, APEC, and FTAA; and

- information sharing, through the UNCITRAL model law, APEC's efforts to help countries gauge their openness to electronic commerce and identify areas where reforms are necessary, the OECD's forums on a broad range of e-commerce issues, and UNCTAD's roundtables of shared experiences.[31]

---

30. See box 8.5 and the statement of the Global Business Policy Dialogue, http://www. gbde.org.

31. The current ad hoc framework of international entities—formal and informal, official and non-governmental—addressing aspects of electronic commerce, in essence, constitutes a regime. International regimes are "sets of implicit or explicit principles, norms, rules and decision-making procedures around which actors' expectations converge on a given issue area" (Krasner 1983, 2). International regimes are usually, but not always, characterized by the presence of international organizations. For example, while there is an international environmental regime in the form of agreements and protocols, there is no formal international organization embodying the regime.

According to Joseph S. Nye, one of the founders of modernist international relations theory, a regime can: (1) facilitate diplomacy, coordination of national policies, and identification of shared interests; (2) provide information; (3) promote greater discipline by states and other participants toward compliance with the rules, principles and expectations; and (4) facilitate burden-sharing when necessary (Nye 1990, 255-57).

Among the options to promote multilateral policy interoperability are:

- creating an international institution to develop, coordinate, and enforce policies,
- formalizing and broadening consensus through a treaty or convention,
- promoting universal acceptance of principles and policies, and
- enhance discussion and information sharing.

Creating a formal international organization for electronic commerce is neither necessary nor desirable. On the one hand, electronic commerce pervades so many broad issue areas—taxation, privacy, security, and others—that it is impractical for a single international body to address the vast range.[32] On the other hand, e-commerce-specific issues, such as standards and intellectual property, can best be dealt with by existing international organizations. Thus, the creation of a new overarching international institution "to handle" e-commerce issues, even if it were politically possible, would likely create more problems than it would solve. There cannot nor should there be a global Internet government.

For the same reasons, a formal Internet treaty or convention would be too complicated an effort for the likely minimal practical benefit. In fact, the widespread perception of serious risks associated with greater structural formalization—the tendency toward regulatory and institutional creep—appear (appropriately) to have doomed proposals for an Internet Charter to address the future organization and management of the Internet.[33]

More modest steps to promote an international environment conducive to the growth of electronic commerce are warranted. Universal acceptance of common principles and policies to underpin national and international actions would be helpful. An international framework of principles could help reduce the potential for conflicting approaches and shape national policies before barriers are erected, inform the work of international bodies, and encourage greater dialogue on complex issues. Put in other terms, widespread agreement on basic principles could aid coordination and promote international policy interoperability. It would also help govern-

---

32. The only existing international organization that could potentially do that is the OECD, which has already addressed numerous electronic commerce-related issues. With membership limited to 29 industrialized countries, even with inclusion of observer countries including some developing nations, the OECD would appear to be too narrow for global discussions.

33. See *Communication to the Council from the Commission,* 28 February 1998 at http://www.ispo.cec.be/eif/policy/governance.html, and the Report on the Communication from the Commission on Globalisation and the Information Society: The Need for Strengthened International Coordination (COM[98]0050—C4-0153/98).

Box 8.7   Government-endorsed principles to support electronic commerce

Since 1997, Australia, Canada, Chile, China, Columbia, Egypt, the European Union, France, Ireland, Korea, Japan, the Netherlands, the United Kingdom, and the United States have signed bilateral statements, endorsing a shared vision and policy principles to foster the growth of global electronic commerce. In addition, international groups such as APEC, FTAA, and WTO have also adopted statements endorsing various e-commerce principles.

The joint statements include fundamental principles and policies that governments agree should guide the development of electronic commerce. General principles include:

- the private sector should lead;
- governments should avoid unnecessary restrictions on electronic commerce and foster its development through a clear, consistent, and predictable legal framework;
- industry self regulation should be encouraged through codes of conduct, guidelines, and technological solutions to met public interest goals; and
- international cooperation is important in promoting the development of electronic commerce.

Beyond these principles, some statements outline an agenda of ongoing cooperation and dialogue in key areas. Among these are:[1]

- continuation of the duty-free status of the Internet;
- ratification of the WIPO Copyright Treaty and Performances and Phonograms Treaty;
- clear, consistent, neutral and non-discriminatory taxation of electronic commerce;
- removal of barriers to electronic transactions, including support for interoperable and technologically neutral global approaches to authentication;
- support for effective means of protecting privacy;
- support for effective protection of consumers online;
- access to encryption technology that meet business, consumer, and government needs;
- commitment to extend the benefits of electronic commerce to all parts of society (overcome the digital divide); and
- the right and ability of individuals to control access to content sent over the Internet through filtering and other technologies.

---

1. Statements vary, with some being more specific and others only addressing some of the policies noted.

ments fend off domestic political opponents of the liberalization needed to support domestic electronic commerce.

Some countries have already articulated principles and signed agreements endorsing a shared vision to foster the growth of electronic commerce; these represent a good starting point (see box 8.7). To multilateralize the process begun by Australia, the UK, the United States, and others would help solidify what appears to be a fairly strong global consensus on certain policies to guide electronic commerce. The effort could also promote discussion of issues on which there is not yet international consensus, such as privacy, consumer protection, and security. Securing widespread acceptance of common principles could be accomplished in a number of ways: through bilateral or regional initiatives, existing international bodies, or a targeted multilateral initiative.

Going beyond principles, actions to promote greater information access and sharing could also help to facilitate policy interoperability. By its nature, the speed of e-commerce developments is hard to keep up with, even for larger countries with ample resources. For example, even the United States, with its significant government resources devoted to electronic commerce fails to maintain a comprehensive, up-to-date official government Web site on the subject.[34] Links to other governments' e-commerce Web sites are not current, nor is there systematic tracking of developments internationally. Developing countries, with fewer human and financial resources to devote to e-commerce policy issues in international forums, have an even more difficult time keeping pace.

Greater information sharing could take several forms. Regional groups like APEC, FTAA, and the European Union and the coordinating bodies of the OECD and UNCTAD already provide some information to members, but these secretariats should be more active. Greater links among international bodies as well as information about developments in individual countries would be helpful. Countries could learn of new technologies for electronic authentication; multilateral bodies or companies could track World Bank grants or loans for specific projects; and developing countries, in particular, could share best practices and solutions to common concerns.

A web of dynamic sources of information about publications and activities worldwide, including links to the international bodies that address aspects of electronic commerce, would be of significant assistance. The Internet is perfectly set up to do this. Multilateral, regional, and functional bodies must now recognize that they do not have the corner on knowledge or information, and that when members get information from or about other groups it is an indication of the strength and value of their home organization, not evidence of its weakness. Organizations need to see the value of network benefits.

Adopting common principles and sharing more information should result in greater coordination among countries, and less conflict of national policies. Where national approaches differ, enhanced dialogue can help promote interoperable policies. Such efforts would benefit countries and other stakeholders interested in maximizing the network benefits of electronic commerce. Moreover, multilateral commitments to the principles

---

34. See http://www.ecommerce.gov.

and policies of the e-commerce regime would help governments resist political opponents of globalization when they zero in on electronic commerce.

The public policy challenges posed by electronic commerce defy unilateral approaches. It is not enough, however, to take a multilateral approach. Effective coordination and policy interoperability are needed. The current international environment for electronic commerce can and should be improved.

9

Government and Development: Closing the Digital Divides

Despite the rapid growth of the Internet, many governments, businesses, and individuals still remain unconnected to its benefits. Among the least-developed countries—where the requisite technological infrastructure, the economic means, and the training may be lacking—only a few are using the Internet for e-mail, let alone for information-gathering or electronic commerce. Even in countries with relatively high Internet penetration, including the United States and those in Western Europe, people with less income and education (among other factors) are without access. There is a growing concern among policymakers that the digital divide between developed and developing countries—as well as within countries—represents a market imperfection, and that the Internet is worsening traditional socioeconomic imbalances.

Once firmly in place, however, the Internet holds the potential to help developing countries and disenfranchised communities leapfrog stages in their economic development, and reach the point where growth is derived more from knowledge and skills and less from resource endowments or manufacturing ability. Traditional barriers to the global marketplace, such as physical remoteness, can be reduced with Internet access. Electronic commerce allows businesses to tailor goods and services to fit the needs of smaller, less affluent consumer bases such as those in developing countries. And technological developments permit governments to forgo expensive investments in infrastructure like copper telecommunications lines for more advanced (and in some cases cheaper) alternatives like third-generation wireless communications.

Hence there are two driving motivations for governments to bridge the digital divide: the risk of exclusion and the potential for inclusion (Braga

1998). Governments are getting involved, often in partnership with the private sector and international agencies like the World Bank. The strategies vary, but typically include building Internet access capabilities (technological as well as financial), and training individuals and businesses to use the Internet and electronic commerce. Some countries, including Malaysia and the United Arab Emirates, are going further by dedicating substantial public funds to finance business incubators and construct technology investment parks.

Can governments succeed in bringing the Internet to those areas where the private sector has not? Should governments intervene beyond streamlining regulations and stimulating private incentive? The majority of current government initiatives to bridge the digital divide are too new for anyone to perform a formal cost-benefit analysis, but some conclusions can be made about their success. One thing is clear, widespread diffusion of the Internet is not possible unless governments create a facilitative policy environment, including general liberalization of the infrastructures that make the Internet and electronic commerce possible.

No government intervention can substitute for these important reforms. Nonetheless, in certain limited cases, particularly education, government can play a more active role. The development of human capital is especially important to ensure that all groups have the skills necessary to keep pace with the rest of the world, and advance. Other, more capital-intensive, interventions like wholesale, publicly-funded business incubators and building extensive technology parks, however, are much less likely to succeed, given that government decision-making proceeds much more slowly than technological innovation.

The Digital Divide: Rapid, but Uneven, Spread of the Internet

The Internet has spread to more people in more places more quickly than any other communications tool in history, including the telephone, the radio, the PC, and the TV. Today, traffic on the Internet (as measured by the number of Web sites visited by each host) doubles at least every 100 days (ITU 1999, 18).

This remarkable growth, however, has been anything but even. Two kinds of digital divide have emerged: one that separates developing from developed countries, and one that creates disenfranchised groups within countries.

Developing countries tend to lag behind developed countries in levels of Internet penetration. And in every country, regardless of development level, those with less wealth and education (among other characteristics, including greater age) are much less likely to be using the Internet. Indeed, across the globe, today's typical Internet user is male, under 35, college-

Table 9.1 Distribution of Internet users as a percentage of regional population

	Regional population (as a percentage of the world's population)	Internet users (as a percentage of regional population)
United States	4.7	26.3
OECD (excluding the United States)	14.1	6.9
Latin America and the Caribbean	6.8	.8
Southeast Asia and the Pacific	8.6	.5
East Asia	22.2	.4
Eastern Europe and the CIS	5.8	.4
Arab States	4.5	.2
Sub-Saharan Africa	9.7	.1
South Asia	23.5	.04
World	**100**	**2.4**

Source: UNDP, *Human Development Report 1999*, p. 63.

educated, highly paid, urban-based, and English-speaking (UNDP 1999, 63).

The first digital divide separates developed from developing countries, as Internet penetration is correlated with GDP per capita as well as household income. (See figure 1.5.) Although almost all countries now have some Internet connectivity, and the total number of Internet users is growing at breakneck speed, there are still significant disparities in penetration levels. As of mid-1999, there were more Internet hosts in Finland than in all of Latin America and the Caribbean, and more hosts in New York than in all of Africa (ITU 1999, 21). The United States, which has less than 5 percent of the world's population, is home to over 25 percent of all Internet users; South Asia, with almost 24 percent of the world's population, is home to 0.04 percent (table 9.1).

Disparities in Internet access necessarily translate into differences in the use of electronic commerce. Currently, the United States dominates with approximately 85 percent of the world's electronic commerce, with Western Europe and Asia making up almost all of the rest.[1] Although the US share is expected to decline in the near term as electronic commerce takes off in Europe and East Asia, many other parts of the world, including much of Africa and parts of South Asia and Latin America, are growing more slowly.

---

1. OECD, (1999b, 29). Some sources attribute between 1 and 3 percent to other areas of the world, principally Latin America.

Figure 9.1   The distribution of language, 1999

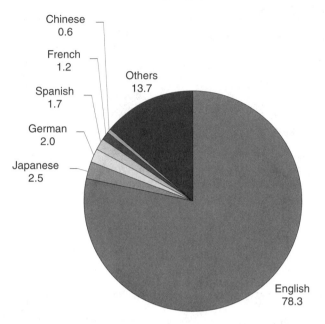

Chinese
0.6

French
1.2

Spanish
1.7

German
2.0

Japanese
2.5

Others
13.7

English
78.3

Source: The Economist (11 March 2000): 55. Using OECD data.

These disparities are shaping the evolution of the Internet and electronic commerce. Around 80 percent of all Web sites are in English, and much of the information as well as the products offered over the Internet are tailored to US and Western European consumers (ITU 1999, 36) (see figure 9.1). A November 1999 survey by UNESCO and Woyaa, an African Internet portal, found that except for South Africa, there are remarkably few African-based Web sites on the Internet. Moreover, hardly any African businesses have expertise in Web site design or content creation, and many are unaware of the benefits of using the Internet and electronic commerce.[2]

As the UNESCO/Woyaa survey suggests, income is just one determinant of Internet penetration. Other factors, including education and cultural acceptance of the Internet, are perhaps even more important. For example, in a survey in Western Europe, 53 percent of respondents in Sweden had used the Internet in the two weeks before the survey, but only 33 percent in countries of comparable or even higher GDP per capita, including the UK, the Netherlands, Switzerland, and Austria.[3] A similar

2. See the report at http://www.woyaa.com/topWeb/top50report.html.

3. See "Digital Divide Still Apparent in Europe," 12 April 2000, at http://www.nua.ie/ surveys/?f = VS&art_id = 905355714&rel = true.

contrast exists in six Middle Eastern countries at roughly the same level of human development (a measurement including life expectancy, educational level, and per capita GDP): Lebanon and Jordan have much higher Internet penetration than Saudi Arabia, Tunisia, Algeria, or Syria (ITU 1999, 22-23).

The second digital divide occurs within individual countries, in that income and education, as well as other factors like age and gender, tend to be correlated with Internet access. Though the United States has one of the highest levels of Internet penetration in the world, the US Department of Commerce has documented a growing digital divide since 1995. By examining Census Bureau data on home and work access to telephones, computers, and the Internet, the Department of Commerce has found that, while access is increasing among all demographic groups and geographic locations, a technological disparity is widening along racial, income, age, and geographic lines. According to its most recent report, *Falling through the Net III*, released in July 1999:

- those households with incomes at or greater than $75,000 are more than 20 times more likely to have Internet access than those at the lowest income levels, and more than nine times more likely to have a computer at home;

- regardless of income, whites are more likely to have access to the Internet from home than blacks or Hispanics have from any location. For households with less than $75,000 in income, the gaps between white and black households and white and Hispanic households have increased approximately 5 percentage points since 1997;

- regardless of income, those in rural areas are lagging behind in Internet access. Even at the lowest income levels, those in urban areas are more than twice as likely to have Internet access than those earning the same income in rural areas;

- educated households are far more likely to be connected to the Internet. The divide in access between those at the highest and lowest education levels has increased 25 percent.[4]

Research by other governments and groups like the UN, the ITU, the International Data Corporation, and other private researchers shows that in countries as diverse as the UK and Bangladesh, an internal digital divide has emerged along income, education, gender, and age lines. For example:

---

4. Taken from the Executive Summary of *Falling through the Net III*. These reports are available free on the NTIA Web site at http://www.ntia.doc.gov/ntiahome/digitaldivide/. Additional research by Donna Hoffman and Thomas Novak at Vanderbilt University, which uses data from the CommerceNet/Nielsen Internet Demographic Study, echoes the NTIA's findings.

- In South Africa, the typical Internet user had an income seven times the national average, and 90 percent of Latin American Internet users came from upper-income households. Buying a computer costs the average Bangladeshi more than eight years' income.

- Nearly one-third of the world's Internet users have at least one university degree—in the UK it is 50 percent, in China almost 60 percent, in Mexico 67 percent, and in Ireland almost 70 percent.

- Women account for only 25 percent of Internet users in Brazil, 17 percent in Japan and South Africa, 16 percent in Russia, 7 percent in China, and 4 percent in the Arab States.

- The average Internet user in the United States is 36, and in China and the UK, under 30 (UNDP 1999, 62).

Is Government Intervention Needed?

Since the Internet and electronic commerce are so new, it is only logical that those with first access have greater education and wealth. Certainly, there is a time lag between when early adopters begin to use the Internet and when the new technologies diffuse broadly. Rapidly declining prices for IT products—in particular, computer hardware—will go far to help those of lower income to become Internet users. Yet even as income becomes a less important determinant of Internet penetration, other factors, including a lack of the requisite skills or even interest, could exclude many businesses, individuals, and even governments from the benefits of the Internet and electronic commerce.

Moreover, there is the question of time: How long is it reasonable for countries or groups to wait for access? Indeed, should they wait at all, particularly given the promise of the Internet and electronic commerce to enable countries and groups to leapfrog stages of development, in part by allowing their more active participation in global competition and commerce? If *access* is not the issue, what role can or should governments play in promoting *usage?*

Not only policymakers but importantly also the private sector have a responsibility to work toward closing the international and domestic digital divides. Given network effects, the costs of connecting an additional individual or business or country to the Internet are relatively small compared to the benefits of having more and more participants.

Examples of how businesses in smaller countries and disadvantaged communities can quickly benefit from Internet access and electronic commerce abound. Here are a few:

- A women's weaving cooperative in an isolated village in Guyana is selling its principal product, hammocks, over the Internet for $1,000 each (*New York Times*, 28 March 2000).

- In Peru, indigenous Ashaninkas use public Internet booths to sell their crafts over the Web (*Business Week*, 1 November 1999).

- A man in New York has created an Internet company through which immigrants from Ghana can buy goats for their families and villages back home (Braga 2000).

- Firms in Africa can now access and bid on procurement contracts tendered by General Electric.

- In many developing countries, small businesses (with help from private Web firms, trade associations, chambers of commerce, as well as government agencies sometimes), are forming electronic malls that can attract many more potential customers than the storefront on main street.

As these examples suggest, the Internet can expose poorer and more remote businesses to a much larger and wealthier set of buyers. In this way the Internet enables competition on a more equal footing. More governments are responding to the risk of exclusion and the potential for inclusion, increasing public assistance to bridge the digital divide. The differences in these approaches necessitate continuing analysis of the relative success of each strategy. Government assistance—typically in the form of pilot projects and partnerships with the private sector—can, for instance, be aimed at individuals communities or businesses. The projects can promote use of the Internet through diffused points of public access, such as schools, libraries, and business centers, or through a more centralized location, such as a state-run technology park.

Most pilot projects focus on enhancing the technological and financial ability to access the Internet. An equal if not greater requirement is educating businesses and individuals about the benefits of using the Internet to trade in goods and services, as well as learn and communicate.

The following sections provide examples of how governments are intervening to bridge the international and domestic divides between those with access and those without. The examples are a starting point for sharing experiences and analyzing the success of government interventions. What they show is that the least intrusive projects typically have the greatest potential for success, as do those that collaborate with the private sector. Projects that are more capital intensive, such as exclusive government funding of business incubators or building of extensive technology parks, are more likely to compete against rather than support the private sector.

Building Capabilities

Access

Using the Internet requires a number of different technologies, processes, and protocols, but the most basic requirement—and the one in which many governments are investing—is access. Access requires a technological method of connecting to the Internet (usually by dialing in over fixed local telephone lines) and the financial capability to pay for Internet connections.

Direct Funding of Access

The most direct government strategy is therefore to increase the number of fixed telephone lines, which, as discussed in Chapter 3, is usually an outcome of liberalization of the communications sector. Some countries have leapfrogged this technology and are investing in advanced access infrastructure like cable and other broadband systems, as well as wireless, fiber optics, and satellites. What, therefore, has been the experience with direct funding of access?

For example, South Korea's Cyber Korea 21 Project will create a country-wide high-speed network by 2001 so that "anyone, anywhere, at any time" can receive multimedia services (Kim Dae-jung 1999). In Taipei, the Easy City Project aims to bring low-cost broadband access to every city resident. Most of the cable rewiring for this project will be paid for by private-sector TV operators (*Asia Internetnews,* 12 January 2000).

Underway for more than four years is the SingaporeONE ("One Network for Everyone") program in which the government has invested some $300 million to build a countrywide broadband infrastructure. The government's National Science and Technology Board and the National Computer Board contracted with the state-controlled telephone and cable companies, SingTel and Singapore Cable Vision, to give every individual and business in the country high-speed broadband access. As part of a general government strategy to increase computer and Internet use, SingaporeONE was supposed to help transform Singapore into an "intelligent island, where IT is exploited to the fullest to enhance the quality of life of the population at home, work and play."[5]

While the SingaporeONE program was launched in mid-1998 with great fanfare, it was met with only a tepid response from the public. The government had projected 100,000 users would be accessing the broadband network by the end of 1999, but only 25,000 of Singapore's over 700,000 Internet users had signed up by that date. As the chief executive for multimedia at SingTel, Paul Chong, admits, "The (takeup rate) has been a bit slower than we had wanted it to be (*Business Week Online,* 10 January 2000)."

The problems that have caused SingaporeONE to fall short of its goals should warn other governments about the pitfalls of intervening in the rapidly-changing Internet marketplace. First, in its vision to connect the entire country in a broadband network, the government did not anticipate

---

5. From the SingaporeONE Web site, http://www.s-one.gov.sg/.

the rapidity with which regular telephone prices in Singapore would decline. Though the cheapest package for broadband is $20 for 10 hours of monthly use, fixed telephone line access through Pacific Internet and StarHub is practically free (*Business Week Online*, 10 January 2000).

Second, in an effort to protect SingTel from international competition, the government forbade foreign telecom companies from connecting undersea cables to Singapore's broadband network. Thus, though broadband users enjoy very fast Internet access within Singapore itself, the connection slows considerably when a user goes to a site outside of the country (*Business Week Online*, 10 January 2000). Singapore's government may now open up the SingaporeONE network to foreign competition, a move that should decrease prices, improve service, and bring more users onto the network.

In some areas with little funding and where the private sector has not yet shown much interest, international nonprofit organizations and aid agencies are engaged in getting access off the ground. USAID's Leland Initiative is a $15-million program to use satellites to establish an Internet gateway and dedicated access for local ISPs throughout Africa.[6] The initiative has worked in 21 sub-Saharan African countries, including Benin, Eritrea, Kenya, Tanzania, and Zimbabwe. It has become clear that access alone does not promote electronic commerce or development. Consequently, as an important precursor to receiving assistance from the Leland Initiative, governments must agree to allow Internet services delivered by private-sector ISPs, and free and open access to information on the Internet, information that will help businesses communicate and develop and encourage governments to share best practice and experience.

Financial Incentives to Promote Access

Many governments and aid agencies are helping build the technological capacity for widespread access to the Internet. But a lower-cost, and potentially more successful, strategy is to use financial incentives to encourage access to an existing or even a developing infrastructure. As the number of users increases, policymakers can persuade the private sector to invest its own monies in creating a state-of-the-art Internet backbone, since the potential payoff is larger for every additional connected individual.

The US E-Rate Program, for example, requires the nation's telecommunications companies to give schools and libraries reduced rates for Internet connections and equipment, including networking hardware, hubs, routers, network servers, and cable. Despite initial protests by the telecom companies, the program has been very successful in getting US children

---

6. See the Leland Initiative Web site at http://www.info.usaid.gov/regions/afr/leland/project.htm.

connected to the Internet (over 90 percent now have some kind of access), and it has overwhelming public approval (Kennard 1999).

It is not just governments that can use financial incentives to encourage access. The Ford Motor Company and Delta Airlines have recently announced programs to provide their employees around the world with home computers and Internet access for as little as $5 per month. The companies are encouraging employees and their families to use the computers and connections as well. In the United States, 3Com has donated $1 million in networking equipment and consulting services to cities around the country to help minorities and low-income families access the Internet (*E-Commerce Times*, 6 April 2000). And in Latin America, Telefónica is hooking up public schools to the Internet for free. The programs make good business sense for Telefónica if schoolchildren grow up to become active users of the Internet and electronic commerce (*Business Week*, 1 November 1999).

Making Access Accessible

Access must be accessible—that is, the Internet needs to be where people are, not the other way around. So, a number of countries are looking to encourage Internet use by providing points of public access, like Internet cafes, public telephone offices, or even post offices. El Salvador's Infocenters Program, for instance, seeks to establish places throughout the country where individuals can access high-speed, high-quality Internet connections at low cost. Administered by the country's Ministry of Economy, the Infocenters will be licensed to private-sector companies, which will be responsible for day-to-day operations. These licensees could form the nucleus of a new generation of Internet entrepreneurs to serve the El Salvadoran community.

In other countries, the private sector is taking the lead. The Argentine company NetKiosk manufactures and distributes standalone units that allow users to connect to the Internet. The company generates revenue solely through selling advertising on the units, which are typically located in areas like hotel lobbies (*New York Times*, 16 December 1999).

These examples suggest that governments can play a role in access, but the private sector often plays a very important initial role. It will continue to play a role in finding creative ways to promote greater Internet use. The private sector gains because the value of each user to the network is greater than just one. It is critical that governments design their programs so as to complement rather than compete against the private sector.

Education

Policymakers in most countries play a central role in education funding—both in the narrow sense of schooling and in the broader sense of training.

It is no surprise that many are increasing funding to educate individuals and businesses not only on how to use the Internet for schooling, information-gathering, and electronic commerce, but also the value of doing so. Many of these programs are offered through schools, universities, or technical-training centers. However, experience shows that the most successful programs go beyond donating or subsidizing computer or networking equipment, to training and instruction on how to use the equipment and the connections to make them relevant in daily life.

Internet in the Classroom

Integrating the Internet into the classroom is one type of involvement. Most educational programs such as the US E-Rate program provide primary and secondary schools with computer equipment and Internet connections. The government of South Korea plans to wire all classrooms and make sure that all 480,000 school teachers have laptop computers (*Associated Press*, 24 January 2000). In Morocco, too, providing schools with computers and networking hardware has been a major thrust of government and international aid programs—yet that hardware sits in its original packaging because training in how to use it was not part of the original funding package.[7] Similarly, new computers in US schools are often idle because there are no trained employees to handle software or networking glitches (*New York Times on the Web*, 26 April 2000).

Training educators on how best to use Internet technologies as part of their teaching method remains the biggest challenge, especially at the primary and secondary levels.[8] Policymakers are responding with increased funding for teacher training in Internet and IT, and computers and networking generally. Among the priorities for Spain's $2.5 billion "InfoXXI: The Information Society for Everyone" program is the government-funded training of 125,000 new teachers of information technology (King 1999).

One approach that works well is for educators to share their experiences through the Internet. Mark LaFleur, teacher and principal of the James Faulkner Elementary School in rural Stoddard, New Hampshire in the United States, shows how educators can gradually integrate safe, effective, and enthusiastic use of the Internet into schools and classrooms (LaFleur 2000). There are many other educator sites where teachers can "compare notes" and find teaching materials, including one on the World Bank's *Info*Dev Web site and another on Discovery.com.

At the university level, government involvement appears less necessary, as both public and private universities are already embracing the Internet and distance learning. Regional universities are expanding into Internet-

---

7. Field research by Catherine L. Mann and Sarah Cleeland Knight, September 1999.

8. This is confirmed by the more extensive analysis presented in ITU (1999,91).

linked universities like the Instituto Tecnológico y de Estudios Superiors de Monterrey in Mexico. Many standalone universities offer world class education because they have access to much larger, more up-to-date, and cheaper online libraries. This is of key importance when funds are tight and knowledge is expanding so rapidly. University researchers are also forming networks to which researchers from developing countries have equal access.

There is a critical need to train adults outside of the university system, especially as Internet penetration is highly concentrated among younger people. The Taipei city government now offers every city resident three hours of free Internet training. As the city's mayor, Ma Ting-jeou, explained, "I want everyone to wake up and read an electronic paper, then use the Internet to check traffic conditions and see which parking garages still have empty spaces" (*Asia InternetNews*, 12 January 2000). In addition, the city is offering free e-mail accounts; 70,000 city residents have taken advantage of this service.

Training People in Information Technologies

Three hours of Internet training may not seem long enough to introduce newcomers to the benefits of the Internet, but for many developing countries even the Taipei program would overtax budgets. Moreover, in addition to integrating the Internet into the classroom, it is an important platform for training workers in information technologies. These workers can be the foundation for more rapid growth and development; yet the least-developed countries often cannot afford such training, thus increasing the chances of being left further behind. For the least-developed countries, international donor agencies like the World Bank are stepping in. These agencies use distance education to teach individuals about computers and information technology—they become the trainers who can then teach the educators, as well as build the foundation for deeper integration of the Internet and electronic commerce into business, government, and society. The African Virtual Network broadcasts interactive instruction by satellite in English and French to over 9,000 students in 22 African countries. The network will soon offer degrees in computer science, computer engineering, and electrical engineering.[9]

Technical training in developing countries is also supported by groups like the Internet Society (http://www.isoc.org), an international association of Internet professionals. And the private sector is now active: The partnership between Cisco Systems and UNDP (The Asia Pacific Development Information Program) will set up 10 Cisco Networking Academies

---

9. See the African Virtual Network's Web site at http://www.avu.org. The World Bank has contributed approximately $6.5 million and the communications company Intelsat is donating free satellite time for the project.

in developing countries in the Asia Pacific Region. These academies will train students in skills specific to building and maintaining network technologies. The pilot program is in Kuala Lumpur, where the master teachers will be educated who will then teach at centers in Bangladesh, Bhutan, Cambodia, Fiji, India, Malaysia, Nepal, Papua New Guinea, and Sri Lanka (asia.Internet.com, 27 August 1999).

Computer and Internet literacy can be an extremely attractive asset for developing countries in bidding for international high-tech investment. In India, the government began stressing education in computers and engineering through its Institutes of Technology in the 1950s and 1960s. Now more than 600 companies export software services from India, employing almost 300,000 computer engineers (*New York Times*, 16 December 1999). Many of these companies are located in Bangalore, which offers tax incentives for software exporters. In Singapore there is a computer for every two students, and the country boasts some of the world's highest science and math test scores (*Red Herring*, January 2000). The importance of such training will only increase over time, as companies integrate computers and the Internet more and more into their production processes and service offerings.

Incubators

High-tech success seems to come when many firms can cluster together, anchored by scientists, educational institutions, and financial and managerial capital: Route 128 in Massachusetts, Silicon Valley in California, Bangalore in India. Is there a recipe for success, or is the process more organic? Since the evidence is mixed, some governments are actively dedicating public funds to create high-technology business incubators, including direct finance of start-up businesses. However, probably the most important features of business incubators—spirited entrepreneurship and management expertise—can only be created by the private sector. Governments need to be very careful to avoid undercutting the development of the local Internet marketplace in an effort to create it.

The United States is unique in its devotion of private, early-stage capital toward new companies in the IT sector in general, and Internet start-ups in particular. Even in the world's most developed markets, innovative ideas for Internet start-ups can be stillborn for lack of capital. Although the United States and the European Union dedicate similar amounts to early-stage capital (about $9.4 billion per year), in the United States, 50 percent of that is dedicated to the IT sector compared to 7 percent in Europe (*Financial Times*, 23 December 1999).

Governments are trying to counteract this trend through direct financial assistance, which can include loans or loan guarantees, grants, or tax relief. In South Korea, the government is planning to spend one trillion won this year to help create 5,000 computer-oriented venture companies. These companies are expected to generate more than 100,000 jobs (*South China Morning Post Technology*, 4 January 2000). An important question is can government-directed funding create the right environment of market discipline, managerial focus, and entrepreneurship?

An alternative strategy is more or less government support for business incubators that offer new businesses a range of legal, accounting, and managerial services. These can be important in helping entrepreneurs make contacts and secure vital seed funding. Independent studies in the United States have found that companies participating in incubator programs typically experience healthy growth and higher-than-average survival rates. They also have a large community benefit, in that they create jobs both directly and indirectly.[10]

Enterprise Ireland (http://www.enterprise-ireland.com) is a combination of both financial support as well as business incubator. It is a government agency with an annual budget of over $300 million that promotes Irish start-ups in a variety of sectors, including information technology. In exchange for an equity stake in a new business, Enterprise Ireland assists with business plans, financial and legal contacts, financial support, technical expertise, and market research. It sponsors trade development activities and its trade missions for Irish high-tech start-ups to Silicon Valley have resulted in two sizeable strategic alliances.

Unlike in education, in financing business incubators governments run the risk of competing against the private sector. Many private venture capitalists already offer portfolio companies incubator-like services, including management expertise. And the emergence of formal private incubators has become prevalent. One well-known example is CMGI (now a NASDAQ-100 company), which finances new companies while at the same time supplies what it calls "intellectual capital," including infrastructure support, mentoring, and partnerships.[11] GeoCities and Lycos are two of the many successful Internet companies CMGI has helped to create. SpeedVentures is a European incubator that provides financing, strategic services, as well as office space and support services through "speedhouses" ("Natural Born Winner," TIME, June 19,2000 Special Report e-Europe). Japanese Softbank is best known for its financial depth. Chambers of commerce or other trade associations can offer incubator services, if not financing. The US Chamber of Commerce, for example, is introducing a new ebiz program, which will offer online incubator services to start-up companies in any industry.[12]

---

10. This study was performed in 1997 by the University of Michigan. See http://www.nbia.org/facts.html.

11. See http://www.cmgi.com.

12. See http://www.uschamber.com.

Technology Parks

Technology parks are supercharged business incubators: They offer a mix of services (technological and financial assistance, as well as training), but at a centralized location. They often offer investment incentives like reduced tax rates, an up-to-date physical infrastructure (office buildings, roads, etc), and simplified government regulations, which make them quite like the more traditional export processing zone. Technology parks also encourage the transfer and commercialization of technology and often have a strong research link with a university.[13] These parks are a big investment.

Many of the newest technology parks seek to attract investment specifically from Internet and IT firms. One example of such a park is Malaysia's Multimedia Super Corridor (MSC).[14] The $10-20 billion project near the capital city of Kuala Lumpur began in 1999 and will comprise an area slightly larger than Singapore. According to Prime Minister Mahatir, the MSC is intended to be "a centrally located incubator for high-tech companies looking to penetrate the Pacific Rim and Asian markets" (*Newsbytes News Network*, 12 February 1998). Scheduled for completion in 2005, the MSC will offer high-tech investors high-speed computer connections, Internet and intranet software and applications, and advanced construction techniques for buildings, homes, and public transportation. Called by *Business Week* "one of the most ambitious government projects ever conceived in Asia," the MSC has investment pledges from high-tech giants like Microsoft and Oracle (*Business Week*, 29 March 1999).

While it is far too early to assess the success or failure of the MSC, some observations can be made about its potential to capture investment from the world's largest high-tech companies. Even with high employment and significant technology transfer from multinational high-tech companies to indigenous businesses (an expectation that may not prove realistic), the government would be hard-pressed to recoup its initial investment.

Also, pledges of investment from high-tech firms are susceptible to a range of influences, including macroeconomic performance and government policies toward investment and the Internet. When Prime Minister Mahatir Mohammad blamed the Asian financial crisis on multinational conspirators, and the government moved to restrict content on the Internet, many investors scaled back their initial investment pledges and others backed away altogether. Said one member of the MSC advisory panel, "The essence of Silicon Valley is not in fiber optic cables, it is the creative, innovative drive, with large numbers of people racing to create

---

13. Theodore Moran, work in progress.

14. See the Multimedia Super Corridor's Web site at http://www.mdc.com.my/.

new ideas. That's hard to sustain in an atmosphere tinged with political repression" (*Business Week*, 29 March 1999). This is a reminder that the overall policy environment is the most important factor in diffusing the Internet and electronic commerce into unconnected areas.

One approach to evaluating the potential of these technology parks, is to look to the experience many countries have had with a more traditional model for public investment: export processing zones (EPZs). Research suggests that EPZs create a sizeable financial burden on a country, without any guarantee of return (Alter 1991, Madani 1999). While some EPZs have raised employment, especially among women, their overall success is more strongly correlated with a country's general policy of liberalization and its macroeconomic performance. Furthermore, EPZs can engage each other in a downward cycle of competition, in which each is trying to outdo the others in terms of investment incentives.[15]

Conclusion

Experience with EPZs should temper government's rush to expend huge sums of public monies for capital-intensive technology parks. The Internet is a particularly inappropriate sector for this kind of government intervention, given that the lightning-speed of change in information technologies makes it extremely difficult to predetermine outcomes.

But government and the private sector together do need to encourage the uptake of the Internet and electronic commerce, especially among individuals and businesses in disadvantaged communities. Network effects mean that the greater the number of Internet users, and the more diverse they are, the greater the value of the Internet marketplace. Programs like the US E-Rate program can persuade the private sector to make additional investments in infrastructure. Education, not only on how to use the Internet and its requisite technologies, but also on why they are important to individuals and businesses, is another area for government action, as Ireland and South Korea demonstrate.

Such actions, however, cannot substitute for a facilitative policy environment that encourages competition in communications, financial services, and distribution and delivery. Governments should also be wary of programs that compete with rather than complement the private sector, including the provision of grants or tax breaks to Internet companies.

In the end, policymakers will need to tailor pilot projects to encourage Internet access to the unique needs of the businesses and individuals in each country. The balance between government action and private-sector leadership is delicate. It should be evaluated not just for immediate impact but for how it will affect the Internet in years to come.

---

15. Alter (1991).

10

Conclusions and Recommendations

Prerequisites

Electronic commerce depends on synergies among infrastructures.

Electronic commerce depends on different service-sector infrastructures, namely communications systems, financial payment systems, and distribution and delivery. The synergies among these infrastructures are critical.

Generally, a liberalizing environment that includes privatization, competition, and independent regulation will ensure that Internet access is cheap and of high quality, that online payments take place in a secure and real-time environment, and that products bought online move from seller to buyer quickly and reliably. Removing barriers in only one or two of these infrastructures is not sufficient for electronic commerce to grow and flourish. Governments need to embrace across-the-board reforms.

Electronic commerce depends on the public-private partnership.

With a diminished role for government in the Internet marketplace, the private sector is ultimately responsible for growing electronic commerce. Arms-length governance generally will ensure that the current dynamism continues and that maximum benefits accrue to the greatest number of users. At the same time, government policymaking does affect the speed and direction of electronic commerce development, whether by the removal of existing barriers or the facilitation of correct incentives.

189

One area where governments and the private sector should work together is the evolution and interoperability of technical and process standards. Governments that prematurely set standards run the risk of being rendered obsolete by technological developments and of constraining innovation by the private sector. Government standard-setting bodies and international groups should therefore work closely with industry groups to set voluntary and flexible standards for electronic commerce.

Government support of key legal reforms will foster electronic commerce.

Beyond removing barriers, there are areas where government intervention is appropriate and can have a positive effect on electronic commerce with minimum intrusion on the private sector. A clear and predictable legal framework will increase certainty and trust in electronic commerce. Governments should work to achieve international interoperability of domestic rules, regulations, standards, and protocols as they apply to electronic commerce so as to encourage the growth of the Internet marketplace. In addition, government can help ensure that people know their rights and responsibilities under the laws.

Human capital and entrepreneurship are more critical than ever.

While the market creates compelling incentives for businesses and individuals to become active in electronic commerce, some people are unfamiliar with the benefits of the Internet, and some businesses do not know how to apply the Internet to their activities. Governments can help. Education in general and in technical areas like computer software and Web development will ensure that individuals have the skills and the interest necessary to participate in the Internet marketplace. Encouraging flexibility and supporting entrepreneurship will enable people to take advantage of the dynamic environment. Sponsoring education, trade fairs, and Web site competitions and the like, jointly with the private sector can also encourage the use of electronic commerce, and help close the divide between those with Internet access and those without.

Policymaking in an Environment of Rapid Technological Change

Define objectives, not technological solutions.

In the electronic world, the only certainty is change. Given that no one can predict how the technology will evolve, it is important to avoid absolute rules that crowd out potential solutions. Governments can define objectives to govern behavior in the Internet marketplace, but they should refrain from choosing among technological solutions. The watchword is flexibility.

For example, policymakers should be wary of mandating particular digital signature, certification, or encryption technologies; private-sector innovation in the marketplace will stay ahead of whatever governments demand. The benefits of network effects will encourage interoperable approaches by the private sector. Mandating a particular solution could lock in a suboptimal choice, reducing private-sector incentives and possibly limiting network benefits.

Use technology to meet local needs and applications.

The technologies that make up the Internet marketplace are global. Cross-border trade of finished products, as well as the fragmentation of the value-added chain to locations around the world, are now the norm rather than the exception. Thus it is possible to access research, commercial effort, and management expertise online.

Network effects in the Internet marketplace mean that the benefits of joining are immediate and large, while the costs are relatively low. The individual participant does not bear the costs to set up the network, just the costs to link in. When global technologies are exploited by local talent to meet local needs and fill local interests, the costs of Internet access will be lower and the benefits to the country greater. Overall, the Internet marketplace becomes more diverse and therefore more valuable to all users. It therefore makes sense for many countries and firms to "draft in" behind global technology leaders rather than start from scratch.

Technology is a solution for policymakers, but it is not the sole solution.

The Internet and electronic commerce, as part of the IT sector, is both a source of macroeconomic growth and can underpin solutions to public policy challenges. In the United States, the IT sector has been largely responsible for the decade-long economic boom with low inflation. Similar economic effects are beginning to be felt in other parts of the world, including Europe.

The Internet improves how governments and businesses perform their core functions and allows policies to be customized to fit local preferences and priorities. Information on best practices can be more easily compiled, disseminated, and taught so that smaller countries and underserved groups can leapfrog stages of economic development. Programs that cultivate human capital with little monetary investment have a high probability of success.

But technology cannot solve all problems of development, big and small, and blindly promoting technology is a mistake. Interventionist programs like publicly financed technology parks carry high sunk costs and are less flexible; they often compete against private efforts. Governments should beware of "build it and they will come."

Policymakers should embrace the liberalizing force of electronic commerce.

Policymakers need to make choices about how to treat electronic commerce, whether to allow its liberalizing forces to shine through or to limit them. Although the objective of technological neutrality—treating transactions via the Internet no more or less favorably than transactions via other means—seems reasonable, it actually does not make sense in today's world where no field is "level." In the WTO, e-commerce transactions can be a force for deeper liberalization of international trade and faster domestic growth if members embrace the original liberalizing principles behind the WTO.

Policymaking in the Global Environment of Overlapping Jurisdictions

With electronic commerce, policy must be interoperable, though not "one size fits all."

There is no one "right" answer regarding the role of government in the electronic world, because resources as well as societal values and priorities differ. Privacy, consumer protection, and content on the Internet are issues where governments are coming to very different conclusions as to what combination of self-regulation and governmental intervention is best for their constituents. To garner the maximum network benefits of the Internet, it is critical that decisions by governments, businesses, and individuals be interoperable.

Intervention to meet society's needs must maintain private incentives.

In certain areas, including privacy, conflicting incentives may argue for an enhanced governmental role. The economic theory of the second best demonstrates that self-regulation (or the market approach) and intervention (or the mandated approach) cannot be ranked as to which achieves the highest welfare. In neither case will the needs of all individuals be met. Nor can we be sure that society's needs are met. However, the market-oriented approach preserves the incentives for the private sector to innovate to find superior solutions; innovation is a critical need in this dynamic environment.

Global, regional, and sectoral forums should promote deeper interchange.

The Internet changes government's role in the international arena. Standards, laws, taxes, and policies implemented by national jurisdictions will be hard to enforce over cross-border transactions. Governments working with common principles and deeper understanding of different implementations are more likely to find approaches that are interoperable across international boundaries.

Because the Internet marketplace affects so many policy areas, countries should rely more on their regional groups for representation at multilateral bodies and as clearinghouses of information, expertise, and best practices within the region and around the world.

Private-sector participation and dialogue with society's advocates should be welcomed by all these forums and incorporated into any recommendations and action plans.

Policymakers need to be proactive in how they perform their core functions.

The new marketplace of the Internet and electronic commerce is changing the relationships between government, business, and consumers. Governments need to be forward looking in determining how to best perform core functions, especially procurement and taxation.

In particular, certain characteristics of the Internet marketplace—global, information-rich, diversity in products, fragmented production—strain existing tax and tariff regimes. Indirect taxes like VAT and direct taxes that are allocated internationally on the basis of permanent establishment will be undermined and will become increasingly administratively burdensome, or simply will not make sense. Policymakers should consider now a plan to redesign a regime to more efficiently and effectively raise revenues including a focus on labor income, not transactions.

As policy issues converge and policy choices are not independent.

Increasingly, the choices that policymakers make on one set of policy concerns impinge on their policy choices on other issues.

For example, the classification of all cross-border electronic transactions as services has implications for the choice of tax regime. Maintaining the current tax regime and supporting it by using the technology of trusted third parties has implications for privacy. Pursuing privacy protection through a mandated approach has implications for cross-border trade.

Consequently, policymakers need to pursue a consistent strategy. An "e-commerce czar" or minister-without-portfolio with the mandate to look across agencies at the cross-cutting aspects of electronic commerce will help maintain momentum for reforms as well as help encourage consistency of approach. This person should embody the guiding principles of interoperable and heterogeneous policies that preserve private incentives.

References

Alliance for Global Business. 1999. *Global Action Plan for Electronic Commerce—Prepared By Business With Recommendations for Governments*, 2nd ed. http://www.oecd.org/dsti/sti/it/ec/act/paris_ec/pdf/bizac_e.pdf (October).

Alter, Rolf. 1991. Lessons from the Export Processing Zone in Mauritius. *Finance and Development* 28 No. 4 (December): 7-11.

@plan. 2000. *@plan Internet Poll™ Reveals Privacy as Most Important Internet Issue Among Online Users*. http://biz.yahoo.com/prnews/000306/ct_plan_ne_2.html (6 March).

Arzano, Franco. 1997. Main Results and Key Issues. Conference on Building the Global Information for the 21st Century: New Applications and Business Opportunities—Coherent Standards and Regulations. Hosted by the European Commission Directorate General III, Brussels. http://www.ispo.cec.be/standards/conf97/report5.html (1-3 October).

Asia Internetnews. 2000. *Taipei Authorities Offer Free Internet Training*. http://www.asia.internet.com/2000/1/1203-taiwan.html (12 January).

Bank for International Settlements (BIS) Committee on Payroll and Settlement Systems. 2000. *Survey of Electronic Money Development*. Publication No. 38. Basle: Bank for International Settlements (May).

Basu, Rajiv, and Therese Visser. 1999. India. *International Tax Review* (September): 57-60.

BBBOnline. 2000a. *BBBOnline Reliability Program Reaches 5,000 Businesses*. Press release. http://www.bbbonline.org/about/press/051600.html (26 May).

BBBOnline. 2000b. *New Online Privacy Protection Tool to Transcend Borders*. Press release. http://www.bbbonline.org/about/press/051800.html (18 May).

Beck, Thorsten, Ross Levine, and Norman Loayza. 1999. *Finance and the Sources of Growth*. Policy Research Working Paper 2057. Washington: World Bank.

Bertelsmann Foundation. 1999. *Memorandum on Self-regulation of the Internet*. http://www.stiftung.bertelsmann.de/english/internetcontent/.

Braga, Carlos A. Primo. 1998. *Inclusion or Exclusion?* http://www.unesco.org/courier/1998_12/uk/dossier/txt21.htm.

Braga, Carlos A. Primo. 2000. Comments. Globalization of Cyberspace Conference. Washington: Johns Hopkins University School of Advanced International Studies (16 March).

Brookes, Martin, and Zaki Wahhaj. 2000. *The Shocking Economic Effect of B2B.* Goldman Sachs Global Economics Paper No. 37. Global Economics Week (3 February).

Center for Democracy and Technology. 1999. *Behind the Numbers: Privacy Practices on the Web.* http://www.cdt.org/privacy/990727privacy.pdf (4 August).

Center for Democracy and Technology. 2000. *P3P and Privacy: An Update for the Privacy Community.* http://www.cdt.org/privacy/pet/p3pprivacy.shtml (28 March).

Center for Democracy and Technology. 2000. *ICANN's Global Elections: on the Internet, for the Internet.* http://www.cdt.org/dns/icann/study (March).

Choi, Soon-Yong, Dale O. Stahl, and Andrew B. Whinston. 1997. *The Economics of Electronic Commerce: The Essential Economics of Doing Business in the Electronic Marketplace.* Indianapolis: Macmillan Technical Publishing.

Claessens, Stijn, Asli Demirgüç-Kunt, and Harry Huizinga. 1998. *How Does Foreign Entry Affect the Domestic Banking Market?* Research Working paper 1918. Washington: World Bank.

Clarke, George R. G., et al. 1999. *The Effect of Foreign Entry and Argentina's Domestic Banking Sector.* Research Working Paper 2158. Washington: World Bank.

Clinton, William J., President. 2000. Remarks to the Forum on Communications and Society on the Information Age Agenda. Meeting of the Aspen Institute. http://www.whitehouse.gov/WH/Work/030300_1.html (3 March).

Commission on Globalisation and the Information Society. 1998. *The Need for Strengthened International Coordination.* COM(98)0050—C4-0153/98. http://www.ispo.cec.be/eif/com9850.html.

Commission on Globalisation and the Information Society. 1998. *Communication to the Council from the Commission.* http://www.ispo.cec.be/eif/policy/governance.html (28 February).

Daley, William. 2000. *Commerce Announces Streamlined Encryption Export Regulations.* Department of Commerce press release (12 January).

Demirgüç-Kunt, Asli, and Ross Levine. 1999. *Bank-based and Market-based Financial Systems: Cross-country Comparisons.* Policy Research Working Paper 2143. Washington: World Bank.

Denizer, Cevdet. 1997. *The Effects of Financial Liberation and New Bank Entry on Market Structure and Competition in Turkey.* Research Working Paper 1839. Washington: World Bank.

Dyson, Esther. 1999. Prepared testimony of the Interim Chairman of the board of directors, Internet Corporation for Assigned Names and Numbers, before the House Committee on Commerce, Subcommittee on Oversight and Investigations (22 July).

Economic Report of the President. 2000. Transmitted to the Congress together with the Annual Report of the Council of Economic Advisers. Washington: US Printing Office.

Electronic Privacy Information Center. 2000. *Privacy and Human Rights 1999: An International Survey of Privacy Laws and Developments.* http://www.privacyinternational.org/surveys/summary.html.

Esserman, Susan. 1999. Approaching the New Round: American Goals in Services Trade. Testimony before the Senate Finance Subcommittee on Trade (21 October).

European Parliament and Council. 1999. *Action Plan on Promoting Safer Use of the Internet. Decision No. 276/1999/EC.* http://www2.echo.lu/legal/en/internet/actplan.html (25 January).

European Parliament. 1998. *The Need for Strengthened International Coordination, Report of the Commission on Globalization and the Information Society.* COM998(0050-C4-0153/98). Committee on Economic and Monetary Affairs and Industrial Policy (14 October).

European Union (EU). 1998. *Introductory Note from the Committee of Permanent Representatives to the Telecommunications Council.* http://europa.eu.int/ (13 May).

European Union (EU). 1995. *Directive on the Protection of Personal Information.* http://europa.eu.int/eur-lex/en/lif/dat/1995/en_395L0046.html.

European Union (EU). 2000. *Directive on Certain Legal Aspects of Information Society Services, In Particular Electronic Commerce, in the Internal Market [Directive on electronic commerce],* SEC(2000) 386. http://www.ispo.cec.be/ecommerce/legal/legal.html (29 February).

Federal Trade Commission. 1999. *The FTC's First Five Years: Protecting Consumers Online.* http://www.ftc.gov/os/1999/9912/fiveyearreport.pdf (December).

Federal Trade Commission. 1998. *Privacy Online: A Report to Congress.* http://www.ftc.gov/reports/privacy3/toc.htm (June).

Fernald, John. 1997. *Roads to Prosperity? Assessing the Link Between Public Capital and Productivity.* Board of Governors of the Federal Reserve System International Finance Discussion Paper No. 592.

Fried, Lisa I. 2000. Can Feds Keep Up With E-patents? *New York Law Journal.* __http://www.lawnewsnetwork.com/stories/A19493-2000Mar23.html (24 March).

Fusco, Patricia. 2000. *Taxing Commission Approves Report to Congress.* http://www.internetnews.com/ec-news/article/0,2171,4__331801,00.html (31 March).

General Accounting Office (GAO). 1999. *Electronic Banking: Enhancing Federal Oversight of Internet Banking Activities.* GAO/GGD-99-91 (July).

Gilbert, Robert D. 2000. Cybersquatters Beware: There are Two Ways to Get You. *New York Law Journal.* http://www.nylj.com/tech/012400t4.html (24 January).

Global Business Dialogue. 1999. *Workplan.* http://www.gbde.org/media/papers/workplan.html.

Goolsbee, Austan. 2000. In a World Without Borders: The Impact of Taxes on Internet Commerce. *Quarterly Journal of Economics* (forthcoming).

Goolsbee, Austan, and Jonathan. 1999. Evaluating the Costs and Benefits of Taxing Electronic Commerce. *National Tax Journal,* 52(3) (September): 413-28.

Groff, Bradley K. 2000. Patent Protection for Business Methods: E-commerce and Beyond. *Georgia Bar Journal,* http://www.gabar.org/ga__bar/febcov3.htm (February).

Group of 10. 1997. *Electronic Money: Consumer Protection, Law Enforcement, Supervisory, and Cross Border Issues.* Report of the working party on electronic money. Basle: Bank for International Settlements (April).

Gwilliam, Ken. 2000. *Introductory Lecture.* World Bank EDI Regulation Course. http://www.worldbank.org/html/fpd/transport/pol__econ/forms.htm.

Haltiwanger, John, and Ron Jarmin. 1999. Measuring the Digital Economy. Paper presented at Understanding the Digital Economy: Data, Tools, and Research: Department of Commerce Conference (25-26 May).

Horvath, Katherine. 1999. *Patents Protect Your Business Methods.* Cincinnati: Frost and Jacobs LLP. http://www.frojac.com/pubs/Patents__Protect__Business__Methods.html.

United Nations Development Program (UNDP). 1999. *Human Development Rep rt, 1999.* New 1ork: Oxford University Press.

Information Technology Association. 2000. *Denial of Service Survey Finds Concerns Prevalent; Leadership Lacking.* Press release. http://www.itaa.org/news/pr/PressRelease.cfm?ReleaseID=951846486 (29 February).

International Chamber of Commerce. 2000. *Uniform International Authentication and Certification Practices . . . Guidelines for Ensuring Trustworthy Digital Transactions over the Internet.* http://www.iccwbo.org/home/guidec/guidec.asp.

International Telecommunications Union (ITU). 1999. *Challenges to the Network: Internet for Development.* Geneva: International Telecommunications Union.

Internet Law and Policy Forum. 2000a. *Survey of State Electronic & Digital Signature Legislative Initiatives.* http://www.ilpf.org/digsig/update.htm.

Internet Law and Policy Forum. 2000b. *Content Blocking Working Group.* http://www.ilpf.org/work/content.htm.

Krasner, Stephen D. 1983. Structural Causes and Regime Consequences: Regimes as Intervening Variable. In *International Regimes,* ed. by Stephen D. Krasner. Ithaca, NY: Cornell University.

LaFleur, Mark. 2000. Presentation at Emerging Electronic Communities: Commerce, Education, and Public Policy sponsored by Kanagawa Foundation for Academic and Cultural Exchange and Tokyo American Center, American Embassy, Hayama Japan.

Leavitt, Michael. 2000. Presentation at the Forum on Technology and Innovation, Washington, DC. An Initiative of the Council on Competitiveness (8 March).

Lewell, John. 1999. *Forrester Slams internet Regulations in Europe*. http://www.internet-news.com/intl-news/article/0,2171,6_70291,00.html (19 February).

Lessig, Lawrence. 1999. *Code and Other Laws of Cyberspace*. New York: Basic Books.

Levine, Ross, Norman Loayza, and Thorsten Beck. 1999. *Financial Intermediation and Growth: Causality and Causes*. Research Working Paper No. 2059. Washington: World Bank.

Lukas, Aaron. 1999. *Tax Bytes: A Primer on the Taxation of Electronic Commerce*. Washington: Cato Institute.

Madani, Dorsati. 1999. *A Review of the Role and Impact of Export Processing Zones*. Working Paper. Washington: The World Bank.

Mann, Catherine L., 1999. *Is the U.S. Trade Deficit Sustainable?* Washington: Institute for International Economics.

Mann, Catherine L., and Sarah Cleeland Knight. 2000. Electronic Commerce in the World Trade Organization. In *The WTO after Seattle* ed. by Jeffrey J. Schott. Washington: Institute for International Economics.

Maskus, Keith. 2000. *Intellectual Property Rights in the Global Economy*. Washington: Institute for International Economics (forthcoming).

Matrix Information and Software Directory Services, Inc. (MIDS). 1999. *The State of the Internet*. http://www.mids.org/mmq/index.html (July).

Mattoo, Aaditga, and Ludger Schuknecht. 2000. Trade Policies for Electronic Commerce. World Bank mimeo (20 April).

McBeth, John. 1999. internet for All. *Far Eastern Economic Review* 51 (18 November).

Miller, Harris. 1999. *ICANN—Seeing Eye to Eye*. http://www.itaa.org/news/view/vp19990810.htm (10 August).

National Research Council Computer Science and Telecommunications Board. 1996. *Cryptography's Role in Securing the Information Society*. Washington: NRC Computer Science and Telecommunications Board.

National Telecommunications and Information Administration (NTIA). 1999. *Falling Through the Net III: Defining the Digital Divide*. http://www.ntia.doc.gov/ntiahome/digitaldivide/ (July).

Nua internet Surveys. Various. http://www.nua.ie/surveys/how_many_online/index.html.

Nua Internet Surveys. 2000. *Digital Divide Still Apparent in Europe*. http://www.nua.ie/surveys/?f = VS&art_id = 905355714&rel = true (12 April).

Nye, Joseph. 1990. *Bound to Lead: The Changing Nature of American Power*. New York: Basic Books.

Olender, Kurt. 2000. *Sealing Contracts with Digital Signatures*. http://www.ecommercetimes.com/news/special_reports/olendera.shtml.

Oliner, Stephen D., and Daniel E. Sichel. 2000. *The Resurgence of Growth in the Late 1990s: Is Information Technology the Story?* Federal Reserve Board Working Paper. Washington: Federal Reserve Board.

Olson, Macur. 2000. *Power and Prosperity*. New York: Basic Books.

Organization for Economic Cooperation and Development (OECD). 2000a. *Guidelines for Consumer Protection in the Context of Electronic Commerce*. http://www.oecd.org/dsti/sti/it/consumer/prod/guidelines.htm.

OECD. 2000b. *Model Tax Convention*. http://www.oecd.org//daf/fa/treaties/treaty.htm and http://www.oecd.org//daf/fa/material/mat_07.htm#material_Model.

OECD. 1999a. *Progress Report on the OECD Action Plan for Electronic Commerce*. http://www.oecd.org/dsti/sti/it/ec/act/paris_ec/pdf/progrep_e.pdf (23 September).

OECD. 1999b. *The Economic and Social Impact of Electronic Commerce.* Paris: OECD.

OECD Working Party on Information Security and Privacy. 1999c. *Inventory of Instruments and Mechanisms Contributing to the Implementation and Enforcement of the OECD Privacy Guidelines on Global Networks.* DSTI/ICP/ICCP/REG(98)12/FINAL. Paris: OECD (11 May).

OECD. 1998. *Report on International and Regional Bodies: Activities and Initiatives in Electronic Commerce.* http://www.oecd.org/dsti/sti/it/ec/act/paris_ec/pdf/intbod_e.pdf.

OECD. 1997a. *The Communications Revolution and Global Commerce: Implications for Tax Policy and Administration.* Paris: OECD Committee on Fiscal Affairs.

OECD. 1997b. *Electronic Commerce: The Challenges to Tax Authorities and Taxpayers.* Round table discussion between business and government, Turku, Finland (18 November).

Petrazzini, Ben. 1996. *Global Telecom Talks: A Trillion Dollar Deal.* Policy Analysis 44. Washington: Institute for International Economics.

Pincus, Andrew J. 1999a. The Role of Standards in Growth of Global Electronic Commerce. Statement before the Committee on Commerce, Science and Technology, Subcommittee on Science, Technology, and Space, United States Senate. http://www.ogc.doc.gov/ogc/legreg/testimon/106f/pincus1028.htm (28 October).

Pincus, Andrew J. 1999b. H.R. 1714, Electronic Signatures in Global and National Commerce Act. Statement of the general counsel of the U.S. Department of Commerce before the House Judiciary Committee, Subcommittee on Courts and Intellectual Property. http://www.ogc.doc.gov/ogc/legreg/testimon/106f/pincus0930.htm (30 September).

President's Working Group on Unlawful Conduct on the Internet. 2000. *The Electronic Frontier: The Challenge of Unlawful Conduct Involving the Use of the Internet.* http://www.usdoj.gov/criminal/cybercrime/unlawful.htm (March).

Privacy International. 2000. *Privacy and Human Rights 1999: An International Survey of Privacy Laws and Developments.* http://privacyinternational.org/survey/summary.html.

Rogers, Neil. 1999. *Recent Trends in Private Participation in Infrastructure.* Public Policy for the Private Sector No. 196. Washington: World Bank.

Rolph, Brad, and Jay Niederhoffer. 1999. Transfer Pricing and E-commerce. *International Tax Review* (September): 34-9.

Sandburg, Brenda. 2000. *PTO Ups the Ante.* http://www.law.com/ (5 April).

Shapiro, Carl, and Hal R. Varian. 1999. *Information Rules: A Strategic Guide to the Network Economy.* Boston: Harvard Business School Press.

Sher, Judd A. 1999. A Band-Aid or Surgery: It is Time to Evaluate the Health of the Permanent Establishment Concept. *Tax Management Journal* (9 July): 415-26.

Singapore Government. 2000. *Frequently Asked Questions for E-commerce Business Policy.* http://www.ec.gov.sg/13081999/helpdesk_faq.html (March).

Singh, Simon. 1999. *The Code Book: The Evolution of Secrecy from Mary Queen of Scots to Quantum Cryptography.* New York: Doubleday.

South African Development Community. 1999. *SADC Ministers' Agreed Negotiating Objectives for the Third WTO Ministerial Conference.* http://www.wto.org/wto/ddf/ep/public.html (1 October).

Swire, Peter P., and Robert E. Litan. 1998. *None of Your Business. World Data Flows, Electronic Commerce, and the EU Privacy Directive.* Washington: Brookings Institution Press.

Tanzi, Vito. 1999. Does the World Need a World Tax Organization? In *The Economics of Globalization,* ed. Razin, Assaf, and Efrim Sadka. London: Cambridge University Press, 173-86.

Tech Law Journal. 1998. *Disbursement of E-rate Funds Begins.* http://www.techlawjournal.com/educ/19981125.htm (25 November).

Transatlantic Consumer Dialogue (TACD). 1999. *Recommendations on Food, Electronic Commerce, and Trade.* http://www.tacd.org/documents.html (23-24 April).

United Nations. *Cisco Delivers internet Education to Asia Pacific.* 1999. http://www.asia.internet.com/ (27 August).

United Nations Conference on Trade and Development. 2000. *Building Confidence: Electronic Commerce and Development.* UNCTAD/SDTE/MISC.11.

United Nations Development Programme. 1999. *Human Development Report.* New York: Oxford University Press.

United Nations Educational, Scientific and Cultural Organization (UNESCO)/Woyaa.com. 1999. *Survey of African-based Web sites.* http://www.woyaa.com/topweb/top50report.html (November).

United States. 1999. Preparations for the 1999 Ministerial Conference: Communication from the United States: Further Negotiations as Mandated by the General Agreement on Trade in Services (GATS). *Inside Trade* (30 July).

United States. 1998a. *Privacy and Electronic Commerce.* http://www.doc.gov/ecommerce/privacy.htm (June).

United States. 1998b. *Statement of Policy on the Management of internet Names and Addresses [the White Paper].* http://www.ntia.doc.gov/ntiahome/domainname/6__5__98dns.htm (June).

US Agency for International Development. 2000. *USAID Leland Initiative: Africa Global Information Infrastructure Project.* http://www.info.usaid.gov/regions/afr/leland/project.htm (27 June).

US Department of Commerce. 1999. *The Emerging Digital Economy II.* http://www.ecommerce.gov (June).

US Department of Commerce. 2000. *Digital Economy 2000.* http://www.ecommerce.gov (June).

US Department of the Treasury. 1996. *Selected Tax Policy Implications of Global Electronic Commerce.* http://www.ustreas.gov/taxpolicy/internet.html (November).

US Government Working Group on Electronic Commerce. 1999. *Towards Digital eQuality, Second Annual Report.* http://www.ecommerce.gov/annrpt.htm (17 December).

University of Michigan. 1997. *Business Incubation Works: Results from the Impact of Incubator Investments Study.* http://www.nbia.org/facts.html.

Wallsten, Scott J. 1999. *An Empirical Analysis of Competition, Privatization, and Regulation in Africa and Latin America.* Working Paper 2136. Washington: World Bank.

Wellenius, Bjorn. 1997. *Extending Telecommunications Service to Rural Areas—the Chilean Experience: Awarding Subsidies through Competitive Bidding.* Public Policy for the Private Sector No. 105. Washington: World Bank.

Wellenius, Bjorn, et al. 1992. *Telecommunications: World Bank Experience and Strategy.* Discussion Paper 192. Washington: World Bank.

White House. 2000. *The Clinton-Gore Plan to Enhance Consumers' Financial Privacy Protecting Core Values in the Information Age.* Washington: White House (1 May).

White House. 1997. *A Framework for Global Electronic Commerce.* Washington: White House. http://www.ecommerce.gov/framewrk.htm (July).

World Bank. 2000. *Why Is the Transport Sector Important?* http://www.worldbank.org/html/fpd/transport/whytsimp.htm (June).

World Trade Organization (WTO). 1998. *Electronic Commerce and the WTO.* Switzerland: World Trade Organization.

WTO. 1999. *Communication from the European Communities and Their Member States on the WTO Work Programme on Electronic Commerce.* http://www.wto.org/wto/ddf/ep/public.html (9 August).

Index

Asia-Pacific Economic Cooperation
  (APEC), 157-58
asymmetric market power, 37, 38, 39
AT&T, 53
Australia
  access fees, 48
  government's use of information, 126n
authentication issues
  certification and, 111-15
  concept of, 111n
  credit cards, 64
  digital delivery, 75
  purpose, 107

B2B. *See* business-to-business electronic
  commerce
Banco 1 (Brazil), 11, 59
Bangladesh, 34, 178
banking, electronic banking, 59-61
BarnesandNoble.com, 89
Basic Telecommunications Agreement,
  52, 149, 152
BBB*Online*, 128, 129b
Bertelsmann Foundation, 139-40
bill-paying services, 42, 61
binding conventions, on electronic
  transactions, 112-13
bots, 36
Brazil
  access, 34
  digital divide, 178
  distribution and delivery, 74
  on-line banking, 59
  taxes online, 97
BTG, Inc., 30
Bulgaria, 63
  government Web site, 96-97
bundling, 30-32
  banking services, 59
business incubators, 185-86
business-method software, 119-20
business-to-business electronic commerce
  (B2B), 22-23
  cost savings, 23, 24t
business-to-consumer electronic
  commerce (B2C), 23
buyers
  bundling, 31
  data mining companies, 38
  preferences, 30

CA. *See* certification authorities
Canada
  export sales in e-commerce, 16

government's use of information, 126n
  privacy issues, 124b
capital, for Internet start-ups, 185-86
Caribbean
  Internet hosts, 175
  Internet users as percentage of
    regional population, 175t
  transport development, 74
CDMS (code division multiple access), 55
cell phones, 34
Center for Democracy and Technology
  (CDT), 161, 166
central banks, 65, 67
certainty and trust
  content issues, 138-41
  government's role, 79
  intellectual property, 75, 117-21
  legal framework, 104-15
  standards, 115-16
  trusted environment, 121-38
certification authorities (CA), 112
change, 1, 191
charge-back liability, 64
Chief Counselor for Privacy (US), 128
children
  child pornography, 138
  content issues, 138, 139b
  interest groups, 166
Children's Online Privacy Protection Act
  (COPPA), 139b
Chile
  procurement, 99
  telecommunications rates, 51
China
  access, 48
  ChinaTradeWorld.com, 99-100
  communications, 101
  content censorship, 140
  credit cards, 52
  digital divide, 178
  interfaces, 54
  Internet training, 184
  Internet use, 15
China.com, 15
ChinaTradeWorld.com, 99-100
Cisco Systems, 11, 53, 71-72, 184-85
classroom, Internet in, 183-84
clickstream behavior, 38, 48
Clipper Chip, 110b
CMGI, 186
co-regulation, 126
collection limitation principle, 125b
Colombia, 74

commercial code, 105-06
Common Cause, 161
Commons, Tragedy of the, 37-38
"Communication on Globalization and
     the Information Society: The Need
     for Strengthened International
     Coordination" (EU), 157
communications
  of governments, 100-102
  infrastructure, 47-55
competition, financial sector, 58
competition policy, 35-37
computable-general-equilibrium model
     (GTAP model), 25
consumer protection, 3
  Consumers International, 166
  fraud and deception, 135-38
  interest groups, 166
  intellectual property and, 120-21
  OECD, 155
  Transatlantic Consumers Dialogue, 166
content issues, 138-41
contracts, 105-06
convergence, 52-55
  Internet telephony, 53-54
cookies, 38, 124b
coordinating forums, 153-58
Copyright ˜reaty, 118, 118n
copyrights. See intellectual property
     protection laws
cost reductions, tax administration, 82
cost savings
  B2B electroni˛ commerce, 23
  models for measuring, 23, 25-26
credit cards, 61-62
  charge-back liability, 64
  China, 52
  El Salvador, 62
  international surcharge, 53
  security, 106, 107n
cross-border transactions, 40
  GATT or GATS classification, 87
  as norm, 191
  services, 90
  services classification, 194
  VAT issues, 90
customs duties, 150
CYBERsitter, 139b
cybersquatting, 163, 163b
Cybertrader, 29

A Declaration on Authentication for
     Electronic Commerce, 113

Declaration on Protection of Privacy on
     Global Networks (OECD), 125
Dell Computer, 31, 72
Delta Airlines, 182
Deutsche Post, 74
developing countries
  access, 34
  barriers, 151
  benefits from electronic commerce
     (model), 25
  digital divide, 174-75
  distribution and delivery, 73
  emerging markets, 5-6
  ICANN under-representation, 161
  international transactions, 66
  Internet adoption, 33
  Internet telephony, 54
  language issues, 29
  local entrepreneurs, 36
  negotiations, 151
  online banking, 59
  SIDSnet (Small Islands Development
     States Network), 102
  technical training, 184-85
  telecommunications infrastructure, 48
  transport protection, 74
  WTO commitments, 152
digital cash, 66-67
digital delivery, 75
digital divide, 4 , 173-88
  growth, 174
  within countries, 177
digital signatures. See electronic
     signatures
digitized products
  classifying, 150
  customs duties, 150
  VAT, 89
direct taxation, 82, 86-88, 90-92
  royalty income, 91-92n
  transfer pricing, 91-92n
  undermined, 194
Directive on a Community Framework
     for Electronic Signatures, 114
Directive on Electronic Commerce (EU),
     105-06
Directive on Information Society Services
     (EU), 137
distance education, 184
distribution and delivery, 2, 69-75
  digital delivery, 75
  liberalizing, problems, 74
  outsourcing, 71-73

Morocco, 74-75
Federal Trade Commission (FTC) (US)
  consumer protection, 136-37
  privacy issues, 130-31b
  scams and fraud, 137
  self-regulatory commitments, 128
fiat money, 67
financial sector
  competition, 58
  transaction costs, 59
financial services, electronic banking, 59-
    61
Financial Services Agreement, 149
financial structure, effects on, 55
financial systems, 57
  components, 57-58
  economic development and, 58-59
  liberalization, 67
financial transactions, 10
Finland, Internet hosts, 175
first movers, 35
Ford Motor Company, 29, 30, 182
foreign exchange, 65-66
Forum on Internet Content Self-
    regulation (OECD), 138
forum-shopping, 67, 82, 150
fragmentation, 31
fraud and deception, 135-38
Free Trade Area of the Americas
    (FTAA), 158
freedom of expression, 139b, 140
Freeserve, 48
freight transport market, Internet
    applications, 72f, 73f
frictionless markets, 32
frictions. See economic frictions
FTAA Joint Government-Private Sector
    Committee of Experts on Electronic
    Commerce, 158
functional institutions, 145-53
  other functional institutions, 148b
  United-Nations related, 146-47b
  what future negotiations should
    accomplish, 149-53
  WTO, 147-49
    what governments have
      accomplished, 147-49

Gateway Computer, 31
GATS
  cross-border transactions, 87
  electronic "soft goods," 84-86
GATT
  cross-border transactions, 87

GBDe. See Global Business Dialogue on
    Electronic Commerce
GDP
  benefits from e-commerce, 25
  cost savings of B2B electronic
    commerce, 23
  value added by transport, 70
General Electric, 30
Geneva ministerial agreement, 147-49
GeoCities, 186
Ghana, 178
Gilmore Commission, 84, 85b, 88
  trusted third parties (TTP), 92
A Global Action Plan for Electronic
    Commerce Prepared by Business with
    Recommendations for Government
    (OECD), 155
Global Business Dialogue on Electronic
    Commerce (GBDe), 123, 164-65, 165b
global marketplace, government
    jurisdictions, 40
global reach, 82
goods and services tax (GST), 88b
governance issues, Internet, 160n
government assistance, to bridge digital
    divide, 178
government intervention
  diversity in approach, 40-41
  economics of network effects, 32-34
  legal framework, 190
  policy interoperability, 33-34
  privacy issues, 39
  private incentives and, 193
government operations
  alternative tax regimes, 94-96
  how governments should respond, 86-
    92
  shoring up existing tax systems, 92-93
  taxation and tariffs, 81-96
    how governments have responded,
      81-86
  trusted third parties, 92-93
government policymaking. See
    policymaking
government-endorsed principles, to
    support electronic commerce, 170-71,
    170b
governments
  administration, 96-98
  communication, 100-102
  e-commerce minister, 42
  efficiencies from new technologies, 79
  IT strike force, 98

motivations to bridge digital divide, 173-74
procurement, 98-100
  WTO agreement, 101b
redefining powers, 79
GovWorks.com, 99, 100
GPA. *See* Agreement on Government Procurement
Grameenphone, 34
growth, of Internet and electronic commerce, 2 , 11-13, 16-17
  compound annual growth, 13f
  factors contributing, 13-14
  number of Internet hosts, 14f
  United States, 16
  users by world region, 15f, 16
  years to reach 50 million users, 13f
GSM Global Roaming Forum, 55
GSM (global system for mobile communications), 55
GUIDEC (General Usage for Internationally Digitally Ensured Commerce), 112
Guidelines for Consumer Protection in the Context of Electronic Commerce (OECD), 136, 136n
Guidelines on Cryptography Policy (OECD), 109
Guidelines on the Protection of Privacy and Transborder Flows of Personal Data, 123, 126b
Guyana, 178

hacker attacks, 106
harmonizing up/down tax rates, 88
horizontal negotiations, 151
hosts, 13, 14f
human capital, 5, 190
Human Development Index, 17
human factor, 41
human rights and privacy issues, 123

IBM (International Business Machines)
  on-line and on-site stores, 90n
  procurement, 11
  Sri Lankan on-line debits, 63
ICANN (Internet Corporation for Assigned Names and Numbers), 115, 158-64
  assessment, 163-64
  challenges, 160-63
  described, 159060
  funding, 162
  supporting organizations, 159n

under-representation of developing countries, 161
IETF. *See* Internet Engineering Task Force (IETF)
income, financial sector related, 58
income per capita, Internet diffusion and, 17
income taxes
  business or royalty, 86, 88
  corporate, 90
  individual, 90
incomplete markets, 37, 38, 39
incubators, 185-86
India
  computer literacy, 185
  electronic signature, 114
  Internet telephony, 53
  Internet use, 14-15
  tax regimes, 86
  trusted third parties, 92-93
indirect taxation, 83, 86-88, 88b
individual participation principle, 126b
Indonesia, 29
*Info*Dev (Information for Development Program), described, 148b, 183, 184
information, 26
  market imperfections, 27
information aggregation, 35-36
information, market for
  imperfections, 37-41
    asymmetric, 37
    incomplete markets, 37
information sharing, 171
information technology (IT)
  global reach, 27
  labor productivity growth, 22t
  macroeconomic implications, 21-26, 24t
    economic growth and, 22
    US experience, 21-22
  measuring, 12b
  training people, 184
  US economic boom, 153, 191-92
innovation, 5
institutional factor, 41
insurance products, 150
intellectual property protection laws, 117-21
  business-method software, 119-20
  consumer protection, 120-21
  transmitted materials, 118-19
  why raise the issue, 117-18
intellectual property rights
  certainty and trust, 75

content issues, 138
credit-card liability, 62
Defense Logistics Agency, 99
digital divide, 177
E-Rate Program, 88, 181-82, 188
electronic signatures legislation, 113
encryption policy, 109, 110-11b
exports of "strong" encryption, 108, 108n, 109
interfaces, 54
Internet in classroom, 183
Internet users as percentage of regional population, 175f
legal issues, 104-06
National Business Coalition for E-Commerce and Privacy, 132
National Institute for Standards and Technology (NIST), 116
official Web site on electronic commerce, 171
patent rights, 119-20
personal data transfer, 93
post office innovations, 75
privacy issues, 39, 127, 128, 132-33, 132n
professional licensing online, 100
sales tax system, 88b, 89-90
standards and protocols, 116
tax regimes, 84
Gilmore Commission, 85b
taxes online, 97
wireless connections, 55
US Agency for International Development (USAID), 34, 181
US Chamber of Commerce, 186
US Patent Office (USPTO), 119, 120
use limitation principle, 126b
USTPO. *See* US Patent Office

value added from information, 82
VAT (value-added tax)
administering, 89
concept of, 88b
cross-border transactions, 87-88
European tax regimes, 84-86
service transactions, 89
undermined, 194
Venezuela, 74
Victoria's Secret, 41-42
Vietnam, 140
viruses, 106
voice-over Internet services, 53

W3C. *see* World Wide Web Consortium
Wal-Mart, 71

Wassenaar Arrangement, 109
Web crawlers, 36
Web sites
data flow, 91
language use, 15
WebTV, 34, 54
Western Europe
distribution and delivery, 74
Internet penetration, 176
Internet use, 14
telecommunications, 50
See also EU
WIPO (World Intellectual Property Organization)
Copyright Treaty, 118, 118n
created, 118
described, 148b
domain name use, 153
intellectual property protection, 117
Performances and Phonograms Treaty, 118, 118n
wireless connections, 55
women, 178
World Bank
Information for Development Program (*Info*Dev), 148b, 183, 184
information-based activities, 148b
telecommunications regulation, 52
World Intellectual Property Organization. *See* WIPO
World Tax Organization, proposed, 93
World Wide Web, 14
World Wide Web Consortium (W3C)
authentication and certification, 113
described, 167b
Open Profiling Standard, 134
Platform for Internet Content Selection (PICS), 138-39
Platform for Privacy Practices (P3P), 134
WTO (World Trade Organization)
Basic Telecommunications Agreement, 52
digitally delivered products, 75
electronic commerce as challenge, 87
electronic commerce, 147-49
GATS2000, 149
General Council, 148-49, 152
government procurement agreement, 100, 101b
Seattle Internet tax regimes, 85b
tax regimes, 83
TRIMS agreements, 149

TRIPS and intellectual property rights,
117, 120
what future negotiations should
accomplish, 149-53
what governments have accomplished,
147-49

Zimbabwe, 140

Other Publications from the Institute for International Economics

* = out of print

POLICY ANALYSES IN INTERNATIONAL ECONOMICS Series

The Lending Policies of the International Monetary Fund*   John Williamson
August 1982   ISBN 0-88132-000-5

"Reciprocity": A New Approach to World Trade Policy?*   William R. Cline
September 1982   ISBN 0-88132-001-3

Trade Policy in the 1980s*
C. Fred Bergsten and William R. Cline
November 1982   ISBN 0-88132-002-1

International Debt and the Stability of the World Economy*   William R. Cline
September 1983   ISBN 0-88132-010-2

The Exchange Rate System*, Second Edition
John Williamson
Sept. 1983, rev. June 1985 ISBN 0-88132-034-X

Economic Sanctions in Support of Foreign Policy Goals*
Gary Clyde Hufbauer and Jeffrey J. Schott
October 1983   ISBN 0-88132-014-5

A New SDR Allocation?*   John Williamson
March 1984   ISBN 0-88132-028-5

An International Standard for Monetary Stabilization*   Ronald L. McKinnon
March 1984   ISBN 0-88132-018-8

The YEN/Dollar Agreement: Liberalizing Japanese Capital Markets* Jeffrey A. Frankel
December 1984   ISBN 0-88132-035-8

10 Bank Lending to Developing Countries: The Policy Alternatives*   C. Fred Bergsten, William R. Cline, and John Williamson
April 1985   ISBN 0-88132-032-3

11 Trading for Growth: The Next Round of Trade Negotiations*
Gary Clyde Hufbauer and Jeffrey R. Schott
September 1985   ISBN 0-88132-033-1

12 Financial Intermediation Beyond the Debt Crisis*   Donald R. Lessard, John Williamson
September 1985   ISBN 0-88132-021-8

13 The United States-Japan Economic Problem*
C. Fred Bergsten and William R. Cline
October 1985, 2d ed. January 1987
          ISBN 0-88132-060-9

14 Deficits and the Dollar: The World Economy at Risk*   Stephen Marris
December 1985, 2d ed. November 1987
          ISBN 0-88132-067-6

15 Trade Policy for Troubled Industries*
Gary Clyde Hufbauer and Howard R. Rosen
March 1986   ISBN 0-88132-020-X

16 The United States and Canada: The Quest for Free Trade*   Paul Wonnacott, with an Appendix by John Williamson
March 1987   ISBN 0-88132-056-0

17 Adjusting to Success: Balance of Payments Policy in the East Asian NICs*
Bela Balassa and John Williamson
June 1987, rev. April 1990 ISBN 0-88132-101-X

18 Mobilizing Bank Lending to Debtor Countries*   William R. Cline
June 1987   ISBN 0-88132-062-5

19 Auction Quotas and United States Trade Policy*   C. Fred Bergsten, Kimberly Ann Elliott, Jeffrey J. Schott, and Wendy E. Takacs
September 1987   ISBN 0-88132-050-1

20 Agriculture and the GATT: Rewriting the Rules*   Dale E. Hathaway
September 1987   ISBN 0-88132-052-8

21 Anti-Protection: Changing Forces in United States Trade Politics*
I. M. Destler and John S. Odell
September 1987   ISBN 0-88132-043-9

22 Targets and Indicators: A Blueprint for the International Coordination of Economic Policy* John Williamson and Marcus H. Miller
September 1987   ISBN 0-88132-051-X

23 Capital Flight: The Problem and Policy Responses*   Donald R. Lessard and John Williamson
December 1987   ISBN 0-88132-059-5

24 United States-Canada Free Trade: An Evaluation of the Agreement*
Jeffrey J. Schott
April 1988   ISBN 0-88132-072-2

25 Voluntary Approaches to Debt Relief*
John Williamson
Sept.1988, rev. May 1989 ISBN 0-88132-098-6

26 American Trade Adjustment: The Global Impact*   William R. Cline
March 1989   ISBN 0-88132-095-1

27 More Free Trade Areas?* Jeffrey J. Schott
May 1989   ISBN 0-88132-085-4

28 The Progress of Policy Reform in Latin America*   John Williamson
January 1990   ISBN 0-88132-100-1

29 The Global Trade Negotiations: What Can Be Achieved?*   Jeffrey J. Schott
September 1990   ISBN 0-88132-137-0

30 Economic Policy Coordination: Requiem or Prologue?*   Wendy Dobson
April 1991   ISBN 0-88132-102-8

BOOKS

Toward Renewed Economic Growth in Latin America*   Bela Balassa, Gerardo M. Bueno, Pedro-Pablo Kuczynski, and Mario Henrique Simonsen
1986   ISBN 0-88132-045-5

Capital Flight and Third World Debt*
Donald R. Lessard and John Williamson, editors
1987   ISBN 0-88132-053-6

The Canada-United States Free Trade Agreement: The Global Impact*
Jeffrey J. Schott and Murray G. Smith, editors
1988   ISBN 0-88132-073-0

World Agricultural Trade: Building a Consensus*
William M. Miner and Dale E. Hathaway, editors
1988   ISBN 0-88132-071-3

Japan in the World Economy*
Bela Balassa and Marcus Noland
1988   ISBN 0-88132-041-2

America in the World Economy: A Strategy for the 1990s   C. Fred Bergsten
1988   ISBN 0-88132-089-7

Managing the Dollar: From the Plaza to the Louvre*   Yoichi Funabashi
1988, 2d ed. 1989   ISBN 0-88132-097-8

United States External Adjustment and the World Economy*   William R. Cline
May 1989   ISBN 0-88132-048-X

Free Trade Areas and U.S. Trade Policy*
Jeffrey J. Schott, editor
May 1989   ISBN 0-88132-094-3

Dollar Politics: Exchange Rate Policymaking in the United States*
I.M. Destler and C. Randall Henning
September 1989   ISBN 0-88132-079-X

Latin American Adjustment: How Much Has Happened?*   John Williamson, editor
April 1990   ISBN 0-88132-125-7

The Future of World Trade in Textiles and Apparel*   William R. Cline
1987, 2d ed. June 1990 ISBN 0-88132-110-9

Completing the Uruguay Round: A Results-Oriented Approach to the GATT Trade Negotiations*   Jeffrey J. Schott, editor
September 1990   ISBN 0-88132-130-3

Economic Sanctions Reconsidered (2 volumes)
Economic Sanctions Reconsidered: Supplemental Case Histories
Gary Clyde Hufbauer, Jeffrey J. Schott, and Kimberly Ann Elliott
1985, 2d ed. Dec. 1990 ISBN cloth 0-88132-115-X
                        ISBN paper 0-88132-105-2

Economic Sanctions Reconsidered: History and Current Policy
Gary Clyde Hufbauer, Jeffrey J. Schott, and Kimberly Ann Elliott
December 1990   ISBN cloth 0-88132-140-0
                        ISBN paper 0-88132-136-2

Pacific Basin Developing Countries: Prospects for the Future*   Marcus Noland
January 1991   ISBN cloth 0-88132-141-9
                        ISBN 0-88132-081-1

Currency Convertibility in Eastern Europe*
John Williamson, editor
October 1991   ISBN 0-88132-128-1

International Adjustment and Financing: The Lessons of 1985-1991*   C. Fred Bergsten, editor
January 1992   ISBN 0-88132-112-5

North American Free Trade: Issues and Recommendations
Gary Clyde Hufbauer and Jeffrey J. Schott
April 1992   ISBN 0-88132-120-6

Narrowing the U.S. Current Account Deficit*
Allen J. Lenz
June 1992   ISBN 0-88132-103-6

The Economics of Global Warming
William R. Cline/June 1992   ISBN 0-88132-132-X

U.S. Taxation of International Income: Blueprint for Reform*   Gary Clyde Hufbauer, assisted by Joanna M. van Rooij
October 1992   ISBN 0-88132-134-6

Who's Bashing Whom? Trade Conflict in High-Technology Industries   Laura D'Andrea Tyson
November 1992   ISBN 0-88132-106-0

Korea in the World Economy   Il SaKong
January 1993   ISBN 0-88132-183-4

Pacific Dynamism and the International Economic System*
C. Fred Bergsten and Marcus Noland, editors
May 1993   ISBN 0-88132-196-6

Economic Consequences of Soviet Disintegration*
John Williamson, editor
May 1993   ISBN 0-88132-190-7

Reconcilable Differences? United States-Japan Economic Conflict
C. Fred Bergsten and Marcus Noland
June 1993   ISBN 0-88132-129-X

Does Foreign Exchange Intervention Work?
Kathryn M. Dominguez and Jeffrey A. Frankel
September 1993   ISBN 0-88132-104-4

Sizing Up U.S. Export Disincentives*
J. David Richardson
September 1993   ISBN 0-88132-107-9

NAFTA: An Assessment
Gary Clyde Hufbauer and Jeffrey J. Schott/rev. ed.
October 1993   ISBN 0-88132-199-0

Adjusting to Volatile Energy Prices
Philip K. Verleger, Jr.
November 1993   ISBN 0-88132-069-2

The Political Economy of Policy Reform
John Williamson, editor
January 1994   ISBN 0-88132-195-8

WORKS IN PROGRESS

The Impact of Increased Trade on
Organized Labor in the United States
Robert E. Baldwin
New Regional Arrangements and the World
Economy
C. Fred Bergsten
The Globalization Backlash in Europe and
the United States
C. Fred Bergsten, Pierre Jacquet, and Karl
Kaiser
The U.S.-Japan Economic Relationship
C. Fred Bergsten, Marcus Noland, and
Takatoshi Ito
China's Entry to the World Economy
Richard N. Cooper
The ILO in the World Economy
Kimberly Ann Elliott
Reforming Economic Sanctions
Kimberly Ann Elliott, Gary C. Hufbauer, and
Jeffrey J. Schott
Free Trade in Labor Agency Services
Kimberly Ann Elliott and J. David Richardson
The *Chaebol* and Structural Problems in
Korea
Edward M. Graham
Fighting the Wrong Enemy: Antiglobal
Activists and Multinational Enterprises
Edward M. Graham
The Political Economy of the Asian Financial
Crisis
Stephan Haggard
Ex-Im Bank in the 21st Century
Gary Clyde Hufbauer and Rita Rodriquez, eds.
NAFTA: A Seven Year Appraisal of the Trade,
Environment, and Labor Agreements
Gary Clyde Hufbauer and Jeffrey J. Schott
Prospects for Western Hemisphere Free Trade
Gary Clyde Hufbauer and Jeffrey J. Schott
Price Integration in the World Economy
Gary Clyde Hufbauer, Erika Wada and
Tony Warren

Reforming the IMF
Peter Kenen
Imports, Exports, and American Industrial
Workers since 1979
Lori G. Kletzer
Reemployment Experiences of Trade-
Displaced Americans
Lori G. Kletzer
Transforming Foreign Aid: United States
Assistance in the 21st Century
Carol Lancaster
Globalization and Creative Destruction in the
US Textile and Apparel Industry
James Levinsohn
Intellectual Property Rights in the Global
Economy
Keith E. Maskus
Measuring the Costs of Protection in Europe
Patrick Messerlin
Dollarization, Currency Blocs, and U.S. Policy
Adams S. Posen
Germany in the World Economy after the
EMU
Adam S. Posen
Japan's Financial Crisis and Its Parallels to
U.S. Experience
Adam S. Posen and Ryoichi Mikitani, eds.
Sizing Up Globalization: The Globalization
Balance Sheet Capstone Volume
J. David Richardson
Why Global Integration Matters Most!
J. David Richardson and Howard Lewis
The WTO after Seattle
Jeffrey J. Schott, ed.
Worker Perceptions and Pressures in the
Global Economy
Matthew J. Slaughter
India in the World Economy
T. N. Srinivasan and Suresh D. Tendulka
Exchange-Rate Regimes for East Asia:
Reviving the Intermediate Option
John Williamson

Australia, New Zealand, and Papua New Guinea
D.A. INFORMATION SERVICES
648 Whitehorse Road
Mitcham, Victoria 3132, Australia
tel: 61-3-9210-7777
fax: 61-3-9210-7788
e-mail: service@dadirect.com.au
http://www.dadirect.com.au

Caribbean
SYSTEMATICS STUDIES LIMITED
St. Augustine Shopping Centre
Eastern Main Road, St. Augustine
Trinidad and Tobago, West Indies
tel: 868-645-8466
fax: 868-645-8467
e-mail: tobe@trinidad.net

United Kingdom and Europe (including Russia and Turkey)
The Eurospan Group
3 Henrietta Street, Covent Garden
London WC2E 8LU England
tel: 44-20-7240-0856
fax: 44-20-7379-0609
http://www.eurospan.co.uk

Northern Africa and the Middle East (Egypt, Algeria, Bahrain, Palestine, Jordan, Kuwait, Lebanon, Libya, Morocco, Oman, Qatar, Saudi Arabia, Syria, Tunisia, Yemen, and United Arab Emirates)
Middle East Readers Information Center (MERIC)
2 bahgat Aly Street
El-Masry Towers, Tower #D, Apt. #24, First Floor
Zamalek, Cairo EGYPT
tel: 202-341-3824/340 3818;
fax 202-341-9355
http://www.meric-co.com

Taiwan
Unifacmanu Trading Co., Ltd.
4F, No. 91, Ho-Ping East Rd, Sect. 1
Taipei 10609, Taiwan
tel: 886-2-23419646
fax: 886-2-23943103
e-mail: winjoin@ms12.hinet.net

Argentina
World Publications SA.
Av. Cordoba 1877
1120 Buenos Aires, Argentina
tel/fax: (54 11) 4815 8156
e-mail:
http://wpbooks@infovia.com.ar

People's Republic of China (including Hong Kong) **and Taiwan** (sales representatives):
Tom Cassidy
Cassidy & Associates
70 Battery Place, Ste 220
New York, NY 10280
tel: 212-706-2200   fax: 212-706-2254
e-mail: CHINACAS@Prodigy.net

India, Bangladesh, Nepal, and Sri Lanka
Viva Books Pvt.
Mr. Vinod Vasishtha
4325/3, Ansari Rd.
Daryaganj, New Delhi-110002
INDIA
tel: 91-11-327-9280
fax: 91-11-326-7224 ,
e-mail: vinod.viva@gndel.globalnet.
ems.vsnl.net.in

South Africa
Pat Bennink
Dryad Books
PO Box 11684
Vorna Valley 1686
South Africa
tel: +27 14 576 1332
fax: +27 82 899 9156
e-mail: dryad@hixnet.co.za

Thailand
Asia Books 5 Sukhumvit Rd. Soi 61
Bangkok 10110 Thailand
(phone 662-714-0740-2 Ext: 221, 222, 223
fax: (662) 391-2277)
e-mail: purchase@asiabooks.co.th
http://www.asiabooksonline.com

Canada
RENOUF BOOKSTORE
5369 Canotek Road, Unit 1,
Ottawa, Ontario K1J 9J3, Canada
tel: 613-745-2665
fax: 613-745-7660
http://www.renoufbooks.com

Colombia, Ecuador, and Peru
Infoenlace Ltda
Attn: Octavio Rojas
Calle 72 No. 13-23 Piso 3
Edificio Nueva Granada, Bogota, D.C.
Colombia
tel: (571) 255 8783 or 255 7969
fax: (571) 248 0808 or 217 6435

Japan and the Republic of Korea
United Publishers Services, Ltd.
Kenkyu-Sha Bldg.
9, Kanda Surugadai 2-Chome
Chiyoda-Ku, Tokyo 101
JAPAN
tel: 81-3-3291-4541;
fax: 81-3-3292-8610
e-mail: saito@ups.co.jp
**For trade accounts only.
Individuals will find IIE books in leading Tokyo bookstores.**

South America
Julio E. Emod
Publishers Marketing & Research Associates, c/o HARBRA
Rua Joaquim Tavora, 629
04015-001 Sao Paulo, Brasil
tel: (55) 11-571-1122;
fax: (55) 11-575-6876
e-mail: emod@harbra.com.br

**Visit our Web site at:
http://www.iie.com
E-mail orders to:
orders@iie.com**